Praise for *Creating Mindful Leader* from CEOs, HR, and L&D leaders

"Joe Burton demystifies mindfulness and makes it easy to take your first steps to being a happier, more effective, and balanced leader. We've never needed the help more than now. Corporate life is often chaotic and it's getting worse. I wish this book had infiltrated the media and advertising industry earlier!"

Charles Courtier, retired CEO, MEC

"This is a perfect and timely read for stressed-out professionals. Mindfulness and emotional intelligence skills are the keys to unlocking greater possibilities and living life with purpose for modern leaders. Joe Burton provides the deep insights and training tips to make mindfulness a part of every successful career."

Chip Wilson, Founder, Lululemon

"*Creating Mindful Leaders* explores one of the most pervasive challenges of our time: overwhelming busyness, accomplishment addiction, and the imbalances that come from being constantly 'on.' Speaking from his own experience and with plenty of humor, Joe shares an important message for leaders and simple practices for bringing sanity back into our workplaces and our lives. If only one person in every organization can read this book, may it be the leader!"

Elizabeth A. Stanley, PhD, associate professor at Georgetown University and creator of Mindfulness-based Mind Fitness Training (MMFT)

"I love how this book uses personal stories and research that everyone can relate to. Anyone who reads it will come away with a solid understanding of how to manage their own stress and create stronger, more connected teams for sustainable success."

Debbie McGrath, CEO, HR.com

"The perfect companion to start or evolve your mindfulness journey! From Joe's highly relatable personal story to the comprehensive research and practical and easy-to-implement approaches, *Creating Mindful Leaders* has everything professionals need to start positively impacting their personal and professional lives today!"

Patti Clark, Global Chief Talent Officer, Havas Group

"Joe Burton is a mind reader, trendsetter, or whatever you call someone who realized, long before mainstream media, that mindfulness is important. Here's proof that all leaders have the ability (and responsibility) to support employees in their general wellness and happiness. The concept's here are simple, actionable, and powerful. *Creating Mindful Leaders* is an extension of Joe's vision of mindfulness for professionals-and the world is a better place because of it."

Laura Agostini, Global Chief Talent Officer, JWT

"There has never been a better and more needed time for *Creating Mindful Leaders*! This book is essential for any person wanting to lead in today's stressful and highly competitive world. A mindful approach and attitude is essential for success in a fast paced world. With this book, Burton gives you the tools and knowledge to succeed in business and in life."

Chris Bertish, Professional Speaker, Best Selling Author, Big Wave Champion, SUP World Record Holder, Ocean Pioneer

"*Creating Mindful Leaders* captures what every professional in government, education, and business needs to know-times are changing fast and we need to adapt to thrive. We can all become more resilient, compassionate, and effective with the practices, tools and techniques shared here."

Greg Fischer, Louisville, KY

JOE BURTON

CREATING
mindful
LEADERS

How to **Power down,**
Power up,
and **Power forward**

WILEY

Published by John Wiley & Sons, Inc., Hoboken, New Jersey.
Published simultaneously in Canada.

For general information about our other products and services, please contact our Customer Care Department within the United States at (800) 762-2974, outside the United States at (317) 572-3993 or fax (317) 572-4002.

Wiley publishes in a variety of print and electronic formats and by print-on-demand. Some material included with standard print versions of this book may not be included in e-books or in print-on-demand. If this book refers to media such as a CD or DVD that is not included in the version you purchased, you may download this material at http://booksupport.wiley.com. For more information about Wiley products, visit www.wiley.com.

Library of Congress Cataloging-in-Publication Data:

Names: Burton, Joseph, 1968– author.
Title: Creating mindful leaders : how to power down, power up, and power forward / Joseph Burton.
Description: Hoboken, New Jersey : John Wiley & Sons, Inc., [2018] | Includes bibliographical references and index. |
Identifiers: LCCN 2018000461 (print) | LCCN 2018007548 (ebook) | ISBN 9781119484776 (pdf) | ISBN 9781119484790 (epub) | ISBN 9781119484783 (cloth)
Subjects: LCSH: Leadership.
Classification: LCC HD57.7 (ebook) | LCC HD57.7 .B873 2018 (print) | DDC 658.4/092—dc23
LC record available at https://lccn.loc.gov/2018000461

Cover Design: Wiley
Cover Image: © Manuel Breva Colmeiro/Getty Images

Printed in the United States of America

10 9 8 7 6 5 4 3 2 1

CONTENTS

Top performers aren't looking for
"enlightenment." They just want to lighten up a bit.

—Joe Burton

For Sarah, Jackson, and Will. You've made cherishing every moment my life's work.

For the Whil team. Thanks for all you do to help people to live healthier, happier, and more engaged lives. And thank you for helping me to make my dream a possibility.

For the reader. Everything's gonna be alright.

ACKNOWLEDGMENTS

This book would not have been possible without the help of many special people in my life. I can't list them all here, but I would like to thank my wife, Sarah Burton; my team at Whil, especially Mak Akhtar and Jenna Pascal for their research and support and Izzy Sanchez, Maya Edelman, and Eunice So for their beautiful design work; Chip and Shannon Wilson for investing in my dream and for showing me what commitment and integrity truly mean.

To Jeanenne Ray, Danielle Serpica, Barath Kumar Rajasekaran, and the rest of the Wiley team. Thank you for your interest in Whil and your belief in me. To Josh Bersin for his expertise, industry leadership and willingness to share the foreword to this book. To Dr. Tara Cousineau, Whil's Chief Science Officer, for her amazing commentary in the editing process. To the rest of our Science Advisory Board at Whil, Dr. Jeffrey Durmer, Dr. Paul Friga, and Dr. Robert Graham; our lead Whil teachers for your trust and ongoing commitment; Mark Coleman, Pascal Auclair, and Ali Smith; and Atman Smith and Andres Gonzalez from the Holistic Life Foundation (go Steelers!). Steve Morris, Greg Healy, and our partners at The Eventful Group and the American SAP Users' Group (ASUG), for giving me a platform as a keynote at so many of your excellent events; Jim Gimian Publisher of *Mindful* magazine for your mentorship, advice, and sarcasm; the Boys & Girls Clubs of America for giving a poor kid from Pittsburgh the hope, confidence, and pride to strive to "be great." To my family: growing up wasn't perfect, but we had love and we had each other; my brother John and my sisters, Sue and Sherry; my sister Mary and my twin sister, Julie. Your deaths caused me to take a new direction in my life; and my mother, Shirley Burton. Mom, you're the original Mindful Leader in our lives. I love you every day.

I'd also like to thank the researchers, academics, authors and leaders that I drew inspiration and insights from, including Dr. Dan Goleman, Dr. Dan Siegel, Dr. Rick Hanson, Dr. Alia Crum, Jon Kabat-Zinn, Josh Bersin, Daniel Pink, Tony Hsieh, Dr. Tara

Cousineau, Martin Seligman, David DeStefano, Daniel Khaneman, B. J. Fogg, Gary Hamel, Peter Drucker, Fred Luskin, Rudy Wolfe, Dr. Jim Loehr, Jane McGonigal, Dr. Liz Stanley, Peter Salovey, John Mayer, Jenn Lim, John Eaton, Jack Zenger, Joseph Folman, Albert Einstein, Chris Bertish, Dr. Barbara Fredrickson, William James, Henry James, Andy Lee, Dr. Jeffrey Durmer, Victor Frankl, Mark Bertolini, Steve Zaffron, Dave Logan, Eileen Fisher, Bill Moyers, Donald Hebb, Ramon y Cajal, Richard Branson, Sigal Barsade, Olivia O'Neill, Raj Sisodia, David Wolfe, Jad Seth, Douglas Stone, Bruce Patton, Sheila Heen, Barry Schwartz, Charles Darwin, Bruce Feiler, Bill George, Christin Carter, Brene Brown, John Barth, Neel Doshi, Lindsay McGregor, and Les Brown.

Most importantly, thank you, Reader. May you find what I found.

Foreword, by Josh Bersin

I Wish I had Read this Book Earlier in My Career

Leadership is one of the most complex and difficult roles in business. You are constantly under pressure to perform, people watch every move you make, and your entire success is based on your ability to motivate, align, and support others. How do you take care of yourself in the process?

Over the years, I've studied leadership and HR, meeting with the world's leading CEOs and talking with HR teams about their need to develop better leaders. I've come to a very simple conclusion: Leadership is not a job, it is a career – one that requires each of us to do a lot of thinking about ourselves.

As I got to know Joe Burton and read his book, my immediate reaction was simple: "I wish I had read Creating Mindful Leaders earlier in my career." We all lead in unique ways, but when you bring it all together, "mindful leadership" really is the destination we all seek.

Great Leadership is an Enormously Complex Topic

Let me start by saying that "being a great leader" is a complex and heavily researched topic. There are thousands of books and workshops on the subject, hundreds of leadership models to follow, and billions of dollars of consulting, assessment, and coaching spent on this issue. And yet, many companies still end up with toxic work cultures.

Why? Because being a good leader is difficult, success can be fleeting (a great leader in one situation often fails in another), and people approach the problem in different ways. As we've studied leadership development over the years, the biggest thing we found is that "environment" matters more than almost anything else. We, as leaders, have to be very sensitive to the team, company, business situation, and culture of those around us. And when your environment involves constant change and disruption, this critical need to be a good listener and good observer of the world is only possible if we are resilient and mindful.

To make this whole topic even more difficult, the expectations of leaders keep changing. When I entered the workforce in 1978, working originally for Exxon and then IBM, people moved into management in a slow and predictable way, and managers were essentially "the boss." You had years to prepare for management and leadership, and once you made it you had established rules and practices to follow. Companies were stable during those times, so people were patient to wait their turn, and once you were in a management role you were suddenly part of the club and everyone gave you a little extra deference.

It wasn't always easy to move into leadership, but the patterns were clear: Companies promoted people who were well liked, people who could rally teams to succeed, and people who were committed, hard-working, and often workaholics by nature. I call this the hero leadership model, and it demanded a lot of grit and toughness to succeed.

In the 1980s and 1990s, the theme of leadership started to shift. The labor market became more competitive, we entered the "War for Talent," and leaders had to take on a new role. Suddenly leaders were not expected to direct and allocate resources but rather to inspire, empower, develop, and support our people. It now became okay for leaders to show their vulnerability ("Authentic Leadership" was the rage) and we expected leaders to be more open about their company financials, their personal challenges, and their strategies to succeed.

Today the world has changed again, and, so too, has the nature of work. Every employee is asked to be a leader in almost every role, and we found that 40% of us now work for leaders who are younger and perhaps less experienced than we are. Each one of us leads a team, a project, a meeting, or some group of people at work, and our behavior and activities are easier to monitor than ever. Imagine a situation where you are just tired and stressed out and inadvertently say something you regret: It might be captured on video, and could be shared in a private employee chat room or online with the entire world. The expectations for leaders are higher than ever before, making it even more important to slow down, relax, and think before you act.

MY LEADERSHIP JOURNEY

In my case, I started my career as an engineer, then worked for years in sales and marketing, and didn't aspire to be a leader for many years. I had the opportunity to work in some great companies, so I could observe, learn, and model myself after many great managers and executives. My boss at IBM, for example, was such a wonderful manager (he ran a sales operation on the West Coast) that he felt like a father figure for most of us. When he passed away years later almost the entire sales organization showed up at his funeral. He was mindful in a very traditional way: He would sit in his office with his suit coat on (we all wore suits and ties in those days) and often gazed out the window, thinking hard about a situation and then speaking slowly before he would react.

In my case, I was thrust into management early in my career (before I felt ready), and tried to learn the ropes by watching others, reading books, and taking some classes. As an engineer I thought I could decode the job and make sense of it, but years later I learned that much of leadership is just being a holistic person. So I bumbled along for a while, and I was probably not nearly as mindful as I could be.

In the year 1997, at the age of 41, I learned about the importance of mindful leadership in a big way. I had taken a new job as VP of Marketing at a small software company and within a few weeks the CEO had a heart attack and had to step down. The founder, who lived 120 miles away, had no interest in running the company so I was asked to be the virtual CEO overnight. A job I never wanted was thrust upon me, and the stress level was higher than I could have imagined.

While I have always been a calm person on the outside, I am competitive by nature, so my passion, energy, and fear of failure suddenly came to the surface – transforming me into a workaholic, stress-filled executive. With the new volume of issues to manage I found myself struggling to find enough hours in the day, and as a result worked very long hours and hardly slept for over a year. We managed to sell the company and I then went into an even more stressful job as an executive at the acquiring company. I'd slip into being the kind of "commanding" leader that Joe describes in his research. Was I mindful? Not at all – and in retrospect it was one of the most difficult times in my career. Like so many leaders, I had never been trained (and was not intuitively equipped) with the right tools, techniques and mindset to be calm, focused and resilient in the face of ongoing adversity.

Over the 20 plus years since, I have had the opportunity to start and run my own company, meet with hundreds of leaders around the world, study leadership in detail, and learn from an amazing set of leaders at Deloitte. Looking back and now reading Joe's book and the impressive bevy of supporting research and clinical studies that he presents, I would say that learning to be mindful is perhaps the most important life skill any leader can acquire.

Enter Mindfulness and Meditation

I read "The GE Way" by Jack Welch many years ago and there is a quote I always remembered: "Face reality as it is, not as it was or as you wish it to be." He was referring, of course, to the many businesses at General Electric he was trying to turn around, and how important it was for his leaders to have an unbiased perspective of the market changes and competition they face.

But I now read this quote in a very different way: Great leaders really do "face reality as it is," and that means they have a very mindful way of being. They actively cultivate emotional intelligence. They have an uncanny ability to listen, they pick up signals about what's going on, and they sense how to bring out the best in people (including themselves). They are often quiet, they may tend to speak slowly, and they often pause and think before they act. As Joe would say, they act out of choice rather than compulsion.

Some of this is based on physiology and psychology, but much of mindfulness comes from practice and experience. For most of us, leadership is a new and constantly changing beast; we are always a little bit off-center, so we have to cultivate the ability to pause and reflect (take a breath) so we don't react in the wrong way.

No matter how much experience you have, being a leader can also be vexingly hard. When a situation goes sideways or someone is underperforming, you are often at a loss about what to do. Some of us react quickly, become loud and aggressive, and feel we must control a situation to make things better. The "I" versus "We" leader syndrome explored in Chapter 18. We wake up in the middle of the night, we ruminate obsessively about problems, we are pressured by our stressed-out superiors, and we worry about our personal reputation. I believe these pressures explain why an increasing number of senior leaders seem to do unethical things: The personal pressure to succeed, especially if you are competitive by nature, coupled with the implicit power we have, can create bad behavior.

Underneath it all, of course, leadership is about people. If we as leaders (and this means everyone, not just those of us in formal managerial roles) can't give other people a feeling of energy, clarity, and alignment, we simply are not doing our jobs. And we cannot do this if we are not taking care of ourselves. This is what Joe's book is all about - cultivating the skills to be resilient in the face of ongoing pressure and the ability to apply those skills to improve your own mental and emotional wellbeing, relationships, and performance.

Over the past five years I've been studying wellbeing at work, and I have become a huge fan of meditation and mindfulness myself. While I am certainly not an expert, I now take time to go for walks, I avoid the elevator and take the stairs, and I relish my time alone to read, listen to music, or exercise. I now understand the importance of downtime to allow the brain to power down, so that I can power up and power forward. Has it made me a better leader? I certainly hope so, but I wish I had read Creating Mindful Leaders long ago. Without any doubt, the practices presented here create the foundation for a sustainable competitive advantage for leaders at any stage in their career.

Remember as you read this book that taking care of yourself has an enormous "force-multiplier effect." Everyone at work observes how you behave, so your ability to be mindful, emotionally intelligent, listen, and be calm will also have a calming and focusing effect on others. That creates a more healthy high-performance culture. If you work hard (as most of us do) we must understand the impact we have on our colleagues, families, and children – they need us to be healthy and happy. And of course our customers, stakeholders, and business partners are impacted too – so taking care of yourself is vital.

I want to thank Joe for writing this timely, useful, and very readable book. I hope the powerful and actionable insights presented here help you to "face reality as it is," and be more present, healthy, and effective in your own leadership journey.

Josh Bersin
Oakland, California

Josh Bersin is Founder and Principal at Bersin™, Deloitte Consulting LLP, a leading provider of research-based membership programs in human resources (HR), talent and learning. He is an author, global research analyst, public speaker, and writer on the topics of corporate human resources, talent management, recruiting, leadership, technology, and the intersection between work and life.

Introduction:
Being a Leader Is Amazing.
And It Kinda Sucks

The problem with being a leader is that you're
never sure if you're being followed or chased.
—Claire A. Murray

I spent a 20+-year career as a global COO in high stress, high performance Fortune 500 companies. Like so many professionals, decades
of high stress took a toll on my health and mental wellbeing. According to the World Health Organization, stress is considered a worldwide
health epidemic.[1] The American Institute of Stress links stress to the
six leading causes of death (heart disease, accidents, cancer, liver disease, lung ailments, and suicide).[2] If you're concerned about your own
wellbeing, you are not alone. The stress business is booming. And it's
getting worse every year.

At the beginning of this decade, I started a mindfulness and
meditation practice to help manage my own stress. Shortly thereafter,
I was brought in by a venture capitalist to turn around a startup called
Headspace, a now-famous app to help individual consumers learn to
meditate. It was an odd career turn for me, going from public company
life to running a tech startup that featured a former monk with a
"learn to meditate" training program based in Tibetan Buddhism.
That unexpectedly put me on a path to go beyond a simple consumer
app and into understanding more about the human brain than I ever
thought possible. It also led me back to my corporate roots with a
mission to help other professionals boost resilience and improve their
mental wellbeing to get more out of life.

In August 2014, I founded Whil Concepts, Inc. ("Whil," pro-
nounced Will). The name comes from a mixture of **Where** are you

going and what **Will** you create? Whil.com was also a four-letter URL I could afford to buy when I started the company (don't tell anyone). Our mission is to help professionals live healthier, happier, and more engaged lives. After 20 years of corporate life, I hit a wall and my health, wellbeing, and attitude began to fail in my early 40s. What I share here literally saved my life and changed the course of my career. May it do the same for you.

Whil has become the global leader in digital wellbeing training. Today, we feature 250-plus targeted training programs and 1,500-plus unique video and audio sessions from top MDs, PhDs, and trainers to help professionals reduce stress, be more resilient, and improve their sleep and performance. Our training system is based in the neuroscience, adult learning theory, mindfulness, emotional intelligence, and positive psychology practices shared in this book.

Whil's training apps are now used in over 100 countries by hundreds of companies like Intuit, Express Scripts, Havas, Sharp Health, Square, Harvard Business School and Reading Health. We partner with and integrate into every major EAP, LMS and employee wellness platform including Virgin Pulse, Castlight, Limeade, Viverae, and so on. We're in five clinical research studies, inducing three National Institutes of Health (NIH)–funded projects. And we're helping the world's top payers and providers to improve their members' health.

In late 2016, I undertook a seven-city research tour with Steve Morris, cofounder of The Eventful Group (TEG). TEG is one of the top live event companies, owning some 40 conference events around the world. We met with leaders in major cities to hear their business challenges and learn more about the need for resilience and mindfulness training in business. That research culminated in a new event, *The Mindful Business Conference: A road map for high performance, leadership, and culture in the age of disruption*. A mouthful, I know. The event drew 250 leaders from over 30 countries. We featured speakers including Congressman Tim Ryan; U.S. Army General Walt Piatt; Howard Behar, the retired president of Starbucks; and leaders from the Seattle Seahawks; Mondelez; McKinsey; Google; SAP; Starbucks; Plantronics; Volvo; Microsoft; BASF; PeoplesBank; Harvard University; Accenture; Snap-On; the Chicago Cubs; Intel; Harvard Pilgrim; GE; Royal Bank of Canada; Aetna; GlaxoSmithKline; the University of San Francisco;

and more. We learned that resilience and mindfulness training is good for people and it's good for business.

The event sparked a fire in our clients and planted the seeds for what would become Whil's *Creating Mindful Leaders (CML) Workshop*. In early 2017, Whil's clients began asking for a live training experience to introduce their leaders to the importance of stress resilience, mindfulness, and emotional intelligence (EQ) skills. That led me to create a one-day live training program, a deep dive for resilient and mindful leaders. We've now visited dozens of cities, trained over 500 companies and thousands of leaders in our live *CML Workshop*, and an ongoing webcast series. We've worked with over 50 industries, including advertising, insurance, healthcare, automotive, law, education, government, consulting, professional sports, technology, pharma, entertainment, retail, CPG, cosmetics, finance, utilities, oil and gas, and news. We have not yet worked with the "fake news" media.

We never expected the success that followed. It's been rocket fuel for the Whil team and, more importantly, changed the lives of the participants.

How to Use This Book

All of that amazing activity has led me to create this book. Consider it a personal reference guide. It's intended as a "state of the nation" to help you better manage stress, change, and disruption. Each chapter highlights approaches to transform your mental and emotional well-being, performance, relationships, career, sleep, and physical health. And best practices and techniques to do the same for your team and your company culture. I'll share the latest research on the key factors driving more professionals to stress out, burn out, and opt out. You'll experience actionable techniques to learn what resilience and mindfulness training is, how to do it, and immediately apply the techniques to benefit your life. You'll also learn first-hand why the *Harvard Business Review* calls mindfulness the "must-have skill for executives."[3]

We Get Better at the Things We Practice Most

Our brains learn from experience. We get better at the things we practice most. Research tells us that most of us are practicing stress, anxiety, insomnia, anger, and so forth to the point at which we're becoming black belts in the wrong things. It's impacting our health, happiness, and performance. A recent report by Willis Tower Watson found that 75% of U.S. employers ranked stress as their top health and productivity concern.[4] I'd like to help you before you hit the stress wall. I did. And it wasn't easy to bounce back.

Just like Whil's digital training apps, this book is activity-based learning. You'll learn and then immediately apply skills to use throughout your day. I've incorporated exercises covering mindfulness meditation, reflection and planning, emotional intelligence, expert communication, sleep practices, and more. Key resources from top brain-training experts are shared as "Pro Tips" throughout. Consider it a road map outlining the specific science-based tools and techniques to directly impact the quality of your life and tangible business outcomes. You'll learn how to implement mindfulness into your existing routines and work processes without creating new work and what mindfulness looks like in small, practical, day-to-day applications for yourself and your team.

You're Not Alone and It Doesn't Really Suck. The challenges facing leaders across industries, geography, and cultures are shockingly similar. If you feel like you're experiencing life at the rate of several WTFs per hour, you're not alone. It doesn't matter what line of work you're in. There is a universal truth: It's getting harder to manage the pace of modern business and the related impact that stress is having on our lives. Once you accept this starting point, you can change your mindset from "This sucks" to "This is normal. I just need the right tools to cope and then thrive."

PROFESSIONALS AREN'T LOOKING FOR ENLIGHTENMENT

This book is meant to be a counterbalance to the abundant supply of hokey, woo-woo concepts out there. There's a McMindfulness movement that's pushing sparkly rainbow solutions, healing stones, and how being mindful can put you on the path to enlightenment. In my experience, professionals aren't interested in hipster monks or mystic hokum. And we aren't looking for "enlightenment." We're looking to lighten up a bit. There's a big difference. When it comes to improving your mental and emotional wellbeing, the right approach for professionals, by professionals makes all the difference.

It's been said that worry is the interest paid in advance on a debt you may never owe. The approaches I share in this book are an invitation to turn a new page in your life and career, debt free.

This Book Is a Call to Action. You have the opportunity to change the unhealthy and negative routines in your life. You can get back to the things you love most. You can be more resilient through the ongoing change, disruption, and challenges in your life. In fact, you have to. They aren't going away. The pace of life is only going to pick up. Commit to doing the practices in this book and get ready to be happier, healthier and more engaged in your life. This is happening.

As Yoda wisely said, "You must unlearn what you have learned.... Do or do not. There is no try."

I hope you have as much fun experiencing the book as I did in writing it. This is my life's work and I'm happy to share it with you.

Enjoy! From one formerly stressed-out leader to another.

PART I

FOR YOU

WELLBEING

PERFORMANCE

RELATIONSHIPS

CAREER

SLEEP

MOVEMENT

CHAPTER 1

What Is Mindfulness and Why Should I Care?

> Begin doing what you want to do now. We are not living in eternity. We have only this moment, sparkling like a star in our hand—and melting like a snowflake.
> —Francis Bacon Sr.

The answer to this chapter's question changed my life, my approach as a leader, and the direction of my career. May it do the same for you.

This is why I care.

I grew up in Pittsburgh, Pennsylvania, the youngest of six kids, and a twin. Our father was an unemployable alcoholic. Our mother has a form of muscular dystrophy and a walking disability. An older sister married a construction worker come drug dealer. Three generations lived under the roof of my grandfather's home. Early on, we had alcohol, drugs, and occasional violence in the home. I learned to be a fighter. I was the first person in my family to go to college. I started my career at Price Waterhouse (now PricewaterhouseCoopers). I thrived on their up-or-out culture; survival of the fittest. When it came to fight or flight, I always chose fight. That mentality helped me to achieve more in my career than I ever thought possible. Being a fighter served me well. Until it didn't.

Figure 1.1   The author (more handsome as an illustration)

When I was 32, I herniated the L5-S1 disk in my lower back while playing basketball. At 35, I herniated both the L4-L5 and the L5-S1 discs again. Not by playing sports, but by—wait for it—picking up luggage. By the time I turned 40, I'd been suffering from eight years of chronic back pain. I was stressed out, traveling constantly (50 countries, yippee!) and routinely worked 12-hour days and weekends as a badge of honor. And my health and mental wellbeing was slipping fast. Sound familiar?

Following my second back injury, I was using a cane, limping into my well-appointed office at Ogilvy & Mather and closing my office door several times a day so that I could lie on the floor, sometimes crying through the pain. Over time, chronic back pain lead to insomnia. Insomnia lead to asthma. Constant pain, failing health, and family challenges lead to anger, fear and a bad attitude. At 37, I lost my sister Mary, a long-time drug user, to a heart attack. At 38, my twin sister, Julie, committed suicide. She had been a long-time addict. I had another kind of addiction but I didn't know it at the time. At 40, I was the global COO within a division of Interpublic, a $7.6 billion public company in advertising and personally responsible for managing over $500 million in annual revenue. My declining health and wellbeing were not a good recipe for success. The worse I felt, the harder I worked. I wasn't in survivor superdrive mode. But being a workaholic is how

I'd handled setbacks in my life. I was frustrated, angry, competitive, and hurting. I wasn't mean or taking it out on others, but I was certainly commanding, impatient, and not much fun to be around.

None of my training had equipped me to think about my own emotional and mental wellbeing, let alone that of our 50,000 employees around the world.

I was making over $650,000 a year. In my mind, the promotions, bonuses, and stock rewards confirmed that I was great at what I did. But I knew I couldn't continue. So did my amazing wife, Sarah. After our first son was born, instead of being elated, I was a stressed-out, deeply unhappy workaholic, who was in constant pain and missing out on my life. I had hit a wall.

It impacted my performance to the point at which I was basically being paid to fly around the world to stress people out. Try putting that on a business card.

Skip the Hippy Dippy. At the time, Dr. Alex Eingorn, a chiropractor in New York City, recommended that I try meditation to help manage the pain. As a Type A personality, this just made me angry. The idea of mindfulness or especially "meditation" conjured up the worst woo-woo images in my mind. It took me many years to escape Catholic guilt. I wasn't looking to replace that with what I mistakenly thought were healing stones or a membership card to the local neighborhood Buddhist society. Other doctors were recommending spinal fusion, drugs for pain management, and a myriad of Band-Aids you don't want to hear about in your early forties. Ultimately, I was desperate. I would have tried anything. I did. And then I tried my doctor's prescription for mindfulness. It changed my life.

It can change yours too. Together, we're going to discover how the right mindfulness practices can open up health, happiness, and a more engaged life even for the most skeptical and driven professional. We'll explore practices to improve every aspect of your life and career. Don't worry. You don't have to join a cult, say "Namaste," sit in lotus position, get a spirit animal, wear Birkenstocks, or find a new religion. We're going to learn how mindfulness relates to the natural functioning of the brain: what you think about, you become. Not only will we avoid the woo-woo, I've found that a modern attention training practice can create a competitive advantage for yourself and your company culture. You can become the leader you aspire to be: happy, confident, committed, energized, connected, charismatic, lovable, intentional, compassionate, and purposeful. For your team or company, you can be the driving force in creating a sustainable high performance culture.

Will you commit five minutes a day to change your life?

I Love My Work and It's Really Hard

We like to start off our *Creating Mindful Leaders (CML) Workshop* with a discussion. Attendees pick a partner and they speak for five minutes on two topics: What do you love about your work and what are some of your biggest challenges?

I highly recommend doing this exercise with your own team. It's an eye-opener into what brings joy to your team as well as what's weighing the company down or just plain driving people nuts.

Here's a summary of responses from our recent *CML Workshops*.

What I Love About My Work		Some of My Biggest Challenges	
Accomplishment	Excitement	Always-on mindset	Egos/Narcissism
Affirmation	**Fast pace**	Ambiguity	Emotions
Autonomy	Flexibility	Bad/dumb bosses	**Fast pace**
Breakthroughs	Freedom	Bureaucracy	Fear of change
Challenge	**Fun**	**Change**	**Fun (lack of)**
Change (driving it)	**Growth**	**Clients**	Generational conflict
Clients	Helping others	**Competition**	Getting buy-in
Collaboration	Human interaction	Compliance	**Growth demands**
Competition	Humanity	Conflicting priorities	**Innovation (pace)**
Connecting	Impact	Cost cutting/ layoffs	Lack of alignment
Creativity	**Innovation**	**Culture**	
Culture	Interaction	Distance	Lack of compassion
Discovery	Laughter	Distractions	
Empowering	Learning		

What I Love About My Work		Some of My Biggest Challenges	
Making a difference	Teaching	Meetings	**Technology**
Mission	**Technology**	Naysayers	Time/Resources
Money	**Training**	**People**	**Training (lack of)**
Opportunity	**Transformation**	Politics	
People	**Travel**	Poor communi- cation	**Transformation**
Positivity	Trust	**Problems**	**Travel**
Purpose	**Unpredictability**	Proof/ROI	Uncertainty
Recognition	Values	**Recognition**	**Unpredictability**
Relationships	**Variety**	Resistance	Unrealistic deadlines
Solving problems	**Work/life balance**	Safety issues	**Variety**
		Secondary trauma	Volatility
		Stagnation	**Work/life balance**
		Stress	

There's a tremendous amount of overlap (see the bolded areas in the table above) in what leaders both love and find challenging in their work. Different leaders can perceive similar or "normal" work demands in very different ways. By normal, I mean facing constant change, innovation, and disruption. That is today's norm. The pace of modern business requires a new way of thinking. Our mindset and reactions to these norms determines the impact on our mental and emotional wellbeing, leadership style, relationships, and ultimately, our success. Together, we'll explore two recurring themes for leaders around the world:

1. We get better at the things we practice most.

2. You're training your brain all the time. Why not be intentional about it?

When it comes to training our brains, too many of us are practicing and training the wrong things. Add to this the brain's natural default instincts for survival (feeling anxious; constantly scanning for threats) and it all contributes to our stress, illness, and propensity for disease. It's freeing to learn about the brain's normal and basic survival functions. It takes awareness and effort to engage the higher-order thinking functions of the brain—and mindfulness is a great way to do this. Attention training helps us build stress resilience, manage our emotions, and avoid the human tendency to make things worse through ongoing negative ruminations, unconscious biases, and lack of self-awareness.

WHAT IS MINDFULNESS, ANYWAY?

Mindfulness is awareness and attention training that helps you create daily habits to calm and focus your mind and relax your central nervous system. It's brain training to improve your focus, mental and emotional wellbeing, and enhance just about every aspect of performance. What I learned over the past six years is that we're training our brains all the time. There's an expansive field of brain research called "neuroplasticity" that dates back to the early 1900s. In short, it's the brain's ability to change based on experience. Your brain is like any other muscle. You get better, stronger, and faster at the things you do the most. You form and strengthen neural pathways. You actually change your gray matter.

Here's the "CliffsNotes" history leading to over 4,500 peer-reviewed research studies on the health and performance benefits of mindfulness training.

- 1906: Ramón y Cajal, a Spanish neuroanatomist, spent years making painstaking drawings of brain anatomy, mapping neural pathways. He was one of the first researchers to postulate that we change the makeup and function of our brains based on how we use them. He wrote, "Any man could, if he were so inclined, be the sculptor of his own brain."[1]

- 1949: Donald Hebb, a Canadian psychologist, was influential in the area of neuropsychology. He sought to understand how the function of neurons contributed to psychological processes such as learning. Hebb's work confirmed that "neurons that fire together, wire together" is now famously known as the *Hebbian Theory*. It was first introduced in his classic work *The Organization of Behavior*, with the idea that we create and strengthen neural pathways (both for good and bad behaviors) based on experience.[2]

- 1979: Jon Kabat-Zinn founded the Stress Reduction Clinic at the University of Massachusetts Medical School. He subsequently structured an eight-week course called Mindfulness-Based Stress Reduction (MBSR) and was one of the first researchers to place mindfulness training into a scientific context.

- 1993: Brain training was introduced into popular culture with Bill Moyers's influential documentary, *Healing and the Mind*, igniting a new field of study.[3]

Since the early 1980s, countless studies have confirmed that our brains are malleable like plastic. They change, adapt, and mold based on how we use them. Dr. Rick Hanson does an excellent job of explaining the latest research in his book, *Hardwiring Happiness*, "Neurons that fire together wire together. Mental states become neural traits. Day after day, your mind is building your brain. This is what scientists call experience-dependent neuroplasticity."[4]

The field of neuroplasticity research has become so advanced that the biggest brains in the world (and me) come together to talk "plasticity" at the annual Brain Futures conference.[5]

Have you've ever described yourself as a "numbers person" or "good with people?" Beyond your inherent ability lies thousands of hours of training your brain to be good at specific skills to the point at which you can do amazing things without even thinking about it. You actually become that kind of person.

For example, after thousands of hours of training, Tom Brady throws a 50-yard touchdown. Steph Curry drains three pointers. Itzhak Perlman plays a mean violin. They've practiced to the point at which the brain just takes over. The neural pathways have been created to process information seamlessly to allow them to perform without even thinking about it. That's amazing if you're practicing rewarding and valuable skills —and we can all get better at what we choose to focus on.

We're Practicing the Wrong Things

The problem is that most of us are training the brain and getting *tons* of practice doing the wrong things. We practice worry, regret, anxiety, and

Figure 1.2   Are you a worried, easily distracted goldfish?

conspiracy theories. We practice distracting ourselves with social media and the same old news feeds that we read five times a day. We train ourselves to fill every waking minute with activity. We're addicted to busyness and toxic Twitter streams; the greatest hits of our friends' pretend lives on Facebook; and we ruminate on negative things that happened years ago. We feed worries that may never happen. More of us train ourselves to be experts at insomnia, lying in bed until we exhaust ourselves into mediocre sleep. Our brains are strengthening neural pathways to make us better at the things we practice most.

When it comes to training ourselves to be distracted, we've gotten to the point at which a Microsoft study estimates that human beings now have the attention span of 8 to 12 seconds.[6] That's about the same that a frickin' goldfish has. In case you drifted off, I said a frickin' goldfish.

Multitasking Is a Myth. Stressed out professionals tend to multi-task. It gives us the feeling we're getting more done. Research indicates that multitaskers are actually less likely to be productive.[7] However, the illusion of productivity helps them feel more emotionally satisfied with their work. Multitasking isn't really a thing. The brain focuses on one thing at a time. What we're actually doing is task switching, and the cost is high. It takes more time to get tasks completed if you switch between them than if you do them one at a time. You make more errors when you switch than if you do one task at a time. In fact, researchers found that a lot of switching in a day can add up a 40% loss of productivity.[8] I call it "multislacking." Moreover, studies have shown that switching tasks leads to more stress. People with high rates of impulsivity and neuroticism tend to switch tasks more than others.[9] To recap, our best go-to strategy for dealing with being overwhelmed actually causes more harm than good.

Here's the point. What you spend your time thinking about matters. You're training your brain all the time. Why not be intentional about it?

> Pro Tip: Your stress, fear, anger, and anxiety are 100% dependent on your mental approach for their survival. Multi-tasking feeds stress. Mindfulness training helps you to be aware of the brain's natural and trained unhealthy routines and to correct them by focusing on one thing at a time for optimal performance. Single-tasking is part of the antidote. Think "Quality over Quantity."

How Does It Work?

Power Down. Power Up. Power Forward.™

Mindfulness training helps you to notice when you're distracted and come back to a single point of focus. You can increase your ability to focus with practice. There are dozens of techniques to do this. One is to meditate, using your breath as the focus of your attention. Focusing on your breath is a mindfulness fan favorite because it's always with you.

You can also train your attention on things like your heartbeat, pressure points in your body, a spot on a wall, even music. In fact, you can train your attention using almost any soothing point to calm the mind and relax the central nervous system. Even 5 to 10 minutes of practice a day on a fairly regular basis can be transformative.

There have been thousands of studies on the health and performance benefits of mindfulness. Don't worry, you don't have to read them. We've got you covered in my favorite study. That comes out

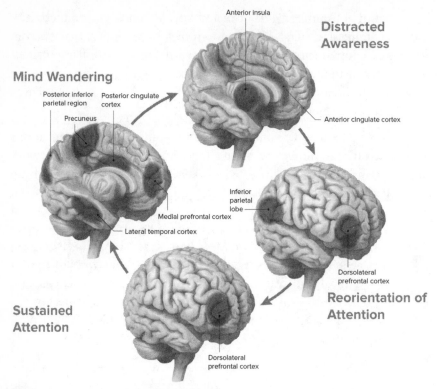

Figure 1.3   Natural cycles of the brain

Source: Modified with permission on a one-time basis. Copyright © 2014 Scientific American, a division of Nature America, Inc. All rights reserved.

of Harvard University. One of the reasons it's my favorite is because saying, "Harvard University" makes me feel smart.

In their research, Harvard shares that the human brain cycles through normal states of awareness and neural activity (Figure 1.3). They estimate the average person spends about half their time with the mind "wandering."[10] By wandering, we mean worrying about the future. Worrying about the past. Is my boss out to get me? Fantasizing, fretting, conspiracy theories. Did I leave the oven on? You name it. Most of us have trained our brains to cycle through a myriad of thoughts, except what's actually happening in the moment.

Obviously, this much unproductive time is terrible for business. But it gets worse. They further estimate the average person spends another 20% of their time in "distracted awareness." This is when you're kind of listening, but not really. Anyone who's married may recognize this state of mind. The research from hundreds of universities, insurance companies, healthcare systems, and think tanks indicate that these natural tendencies for the mind to wander are also terrible for your health. It can cut years off of your life.

There are two analogies I like to use. The first is that our brains are like refrigerators. The equipment is running at various levels of effort all the time. But if you leave the door open, they work nonstop, the equipment breaks down faster and what's inside ends up spoiling. The wandering mind is causing our minds to burn out from overactivity while spoiling the quality of our emotions, moods, and thought patterns. What's worse, much of that overactivity is negative and recurring.[11] That means we have a tendency to think about the same unhealthy nonsense all the time. It's the human condition. And because of neuroplasticity, our brains become experts at processing and revisiting the things we think about most. A double whammy.

This tendency to ruminate on the negative can feed self-doubt, turning us into our own worst critics. That leads to my second analogy. As a kid, I remember Pluto, Daffy Duck, and other cartoons where characters would have a devil on one shoulder and an angel on the other, representing two sides of their conscience. Two inner critics. Pixar took it to the next level with the movie, *Inside Out*, in which all five primary emotions (joy, sadness, anger, fear, and disgust) took turns tugging at the lead character's conscience. When it comes to the wandering mind, you likely already realize that it's not very quiet in there. In fact, many leaders feel like we have an entire board of directors in our head. The critic. The worrier. The fraud. The savior. The conspiracist. The hot mess. The regretter. The hero. The second-guesser. Left unchecked, an overly active board of inner critics can feed the constant distraction that has a detrimental impact on your health and performance.

The wandering mind and tendency to constantly worry are the root causes of professionals getting stressed out, burnt out, and opting out at earlier ages and at record numbers. Getting stuck in negative thought patterns creates stress. Stress impacts your health, wellbeing, and performance. That impacts relationships and teams. And that impacts entire company cultures.

Don't let this get you down. The inner critics or voices arise as ways to protect you from fears, failure, or shame. It's an illusion. Often they just need your permission to stop working so hard on your behalf. There are many techniques to reverse the mind's natural tendencies and let them know the job's over.

Pro Tip: In the TV show *Dexter*, the lead character was a vigilante serial killer. He had an ongoing dialogue in his head (the Wandering Mind), which he called his "Dark Passenger." Mark Coleman, Whil Master Trainer, recommends that you give your group of inner critics nicknames so you can have a friendly way to dismiss them when they distract you. "Hello, Pessimist. I don't need you right now. Goodbye." But don't kill anyone.

It's Brain Training

By training the brain to sustain attention on a single point of focus like your breath, you can create new neural pathways and strengthen your ability to pay attention to the rest of your day. By focusing your

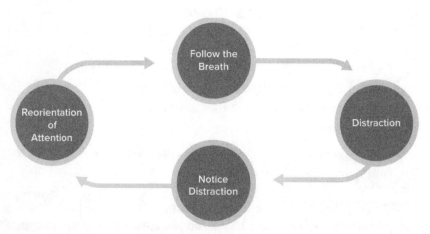

Figure 1.4   Basic routine for training your attention

attention time and again, you're creating muscle memory. You can then become better at noticing when you're distracted anytime, and then direct your attention back to a single point of focus. Over time, present, focused and attentive can become your normal (default) way of being. Doesn't that sound better than training yourself to be constantly distracted while ruining your health, happiness, and performance? One or the other is happening. You get to choose.

ATTENTION TRAINING

Let's give it a try using a one-minute practice from the Whil training library.

The instructions are simple. Set a timer. Close your eyes or relax your gaze. Set an intention to make your breath the sole focus of your attention for one full minute. Take deep breaths in. Hold each for a moment or two. Then fully exhale.

As you do this, you'll likely notice that other thoughts also enter your mind. This is the distracted mind doing what it does. As this occurs, label each thought with one word and kindly let it disappear (e.g., Worry, Job, Boss, Kids, etc.). Then come back to focusing on your breath.

By doing this time and again, you're building muscle memory: the ability to notice when you're distracted and then come back to a single point of attention. As you train your brain to become better at this skill of focused attention, you can apply it throughout your day. It can become your default way of being.

What's the Difference Between Meditation and Mindfulness?

Meditation is the practice of training your attention. This can be done in short bursts. At Whil, we recommend 5 to 10 minutes a day on a fairly regular basis to enjoy the greatest benefits.

Mindfulness is the goal of attention training. It's a lifestyle. It's applying your ability to be focused, aware, kind, intentional, open, curious, nonjudgmental, and compassionate in the other 24 hours of your day. Meditation is just one form of practice. Mindfulness is applying what you learn during game-time.

Start with Tiny Habits

Dr. B. J. Fogg is a professor at the Persuasive Technology Lab at Stanford University and one of the world's leading experts on human behavior change. Just like any habit, meditation gets easier to do if it's part of your daily routine. We recommend following B. J.'s advice to start a new "Tiny Habit."[12]

1. **Get specific** as to what new behavior you want (meditate five minutes per day). Translate target outcomes into behaviors (for example, I practice every day at 3 p.m. no matter where I am).

2. **Make it easy.** (All I need is my phone app and a place to sit.) Simplicity changes behavior.

3. **Trigger the behavior.** Some triggers are natural (I meditate when I lie down to sleep every night). Others you must design (I schedule time on my calendar and receive notifications from my Whil app). No behavior happens without a trigger.

WHY IS EVERYONE TALKING ABOUT MINDFULNESS?

In case you haven't noticed, the world is stressed out. In 2017, the *Stress in America* poll reported a significant increase in national U.S. stress.[13] More of us are reaching the point at which we'll try just about anything to alleviate the pressure. There are three key reasons why mindfulness is taking center stage as the antidote of choice.

Mindfulness Has Gone Mainstream

It's in the news. *60 Minutes* even did a special covering it with Anderson Cooper. There's a new book on the topic every week (you're reading one now). It's on the cover of every major magazine, ranging from *Cosmopolitan* to *Fast Company* to *Wired*. *Time* magazine did a special edition on Mindfulness, featuring Whil.[14] Pretty cool. The *Wall Street Journal* and *New York Times* cover mindfulness (and stress) like any other important business news topics. Our friend, Congressman Tim Ryan, even wrote the book, *A Mindful Nation*, covering how mindfulness is changing schools, business, the government, and even the military.[15]

In the documentary, *On Meditation*, Tim describes finding mindfulness as his own antidote to stress. "I was a congressman at 29 and doing alright. And then in 2008, after being in congress for about six years and my life getting more and more hectic, more and more responsibilities, more and more burdens - I had a lot of negative thoughts, a lot of self-criticism of 'you can do better' or 'why didn't you do this or that.' Really beating myself up to where I felt I was going to be burnt out. And I was 35 years old ... I really wanted to jumpstart a daily meditation practice. It changed my life. I got a taste of what it's like to have your mind and your body synchronized ... After I got a taste of it, I though we really have to introduce this into the healthcare system in America."[16]

It Benefits Every Aspect of Life

You can find help on just about any topic ranging from improving focus to managing back pain to PTSD to mindful parenting to recovering from cancer.

Basketballers from Steph Curry to Michael Jordan are doing it. Footballers from Tom Brady to Joe Namath. Musicians from Katy Perry to Paul McCartney. Actors from Kristen Bell to Hugh Jackman. Comedians from Russell Brand to Jerry Seinfeld. Ellen to Oprah. Mark Zuckerberg to Steve Jobs. Martin Scorsese. Judd Apatow. Eddie Vedder. Tony Robbins. George Lucas. CEOs like Mark Bertolini, Marc Benioff, Ray Dalio, Les Moonves, Eileen Fisher, Bob Shapiro, Roger Berkowitz, Robert Stiller, Nancy Slomowitz, Rick Goings, and Marnie Abramson. The list is endless. Top players in every field are looking for a better quality of life. And they're looking to maintain their competitive edge.

Sadly, I've found that too much of what's written comes from novices who ignore the research and science that correlates recognized practices with improving health outcomes.

There's Been an Explosion in Scientific Research

The American Mindfulness Research Association alone maintains a database of more than 4,500 studies on the health and performance benefits of mindfulness training (Figure 1.5).[17] The first research study occurred in the early 1980s. In 2017, there were more than 80 research studies per month.

As a skeptical numbers guy, the science behind these practices was a major factor in my giving it a try.

Stress and the resulting impacts of illness and disease are a global crisis. When you dig into the details of these studies, you quickly understand why mindfulness is the new must-have life skill for leaders. Studies are even showing that mindfulness and meditation can be as effective as medication. But unlike medication, mindfulness has no pill

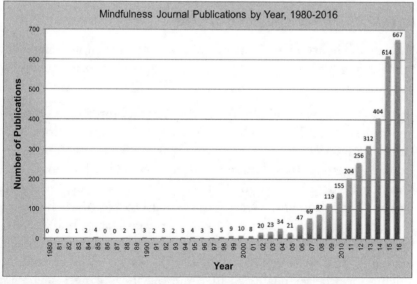

Figure 1.5   The stress business (and related research) is booming.

Source: American Mindfulness Research Association, 2017; goAMRA.org.

form. It takes practice and I'll share the most relevant research and techniques throughout. But I won't keep you waiting. Here are 10 of my favorite research studies for leaders.

1. **Increase Focus.** Professionals trained in mindfulness were able to concentrate better, stay on task longer, and remember what they'd done better.[18]

2. **Manage Your Triggers.** People with greater meditation training had less activity in the amygdala (the fight-or-flight trigger in the brain) during negative distractions. The more hours of training, the lower the triggering effect.[19]

3. **Improve Chronic Stress.** Veterans with Post-Traumatic Stress Disorder (PTSD) had improvements in symptoms such as depression, behavioral activation, and experiential avoidance.[20]

4. **Reduce Pain.** Just three days of brief mindfulness training was effective at reducing pain ratings and sensitivity, producing analgesic effects.[21]

5. **Strengthen Immunity.** Practitioners showed decreased anxiety and significant increased activity in the parts of their brains associated with positive emotions. They also developed more antibodies to the influenza vaccine.[22] Another study linked training to a 50% decrease in cold and flu symptoms and a 76% decrease in absenteeism.[23]

6. **Lower Your Blood Pressure.** Mindfulness can lead to lower risk of heart attack and stroke. Patients who received training had significant decreases in systolic and diastolic blood pressure.[24]

7. **Be Happier and More Energetic.** Professionals who practiced mindfulness reported less emotional exhaustion and greater job satisfaction.[25]

8. **Improve Cardiovascular Health.** Mindfulness improves heart health, particularly shown in risk factors such as smoking, body mass index, fasting glucose, and physical activity. Practitioners were 83% more likely to have good cardiovascular health.[26]

9. **Sleep Better.** Two weeks of mindfulness practice produced steady improvements in both sleep quality and duration.[27]

10. **Reduce Your Error Rate.** Practitioners were able to reduce their personal error rate and increase control over the distribution of limited brain resources to process more data.[28] It's like getting more Random Access Memory (RAM) in your brain.

It's no wonder that the leading universities, think tanks, hospital networks, and insurance companies are all focused on mindfulness practices. Large companies are even adding c-level officers to focus on employee wellbeing, including our friend Andy Lee, Chief Mindfulness Officer of Aetna.

Work (and Life) Requires Performance

Mindfulness training is being embraced by organizations ranging from big business to universities to healthcare systems to the military. In 2016, the National Business Group on Health (NBGH) estimated that 45% of the Fortune 500 would bring mindfulness training to their employees within a year, mostly through extended live training and increasingly, through digital training solutions like Whil.[29]

It's even occurring in sports in a big way. The last three winners of the Super Bowl, the World Series, and the NBA Championship all practice mindfulness. Here in San Francisco, the championship Golden State Warriors practice mindfulness. I don't think the beleaguered San Francisco Forty-Niners practice mindfulness. Until recently, we were starting to wonder if they even practice football.

For you New England Patriots fans, your perennial Super Bowl championship team does mindfulness training. Tom Brady has been meditating for years. And when he focuses on his breath, he needs a little less air than anyone else. Sorry, that's a "Deflategate" joke from a bitter Steelers fan.

You get the picture. Coaches are looking to help their players to be able to focus and perform under pressure. They're looking for an edge. They want their athletes to be "in the zone" more regularly.

Figure 1.6   Mindfulness is the new breakfast of champions.

Sound familiar? As leaders, that's exactly what we want for our corporate athletes: to perform under pressure. The ability to calm and focus the mind and perform under pressure is a valuable skill for leaders, and provides a competitive advantage when enough team members apply the related techniques to their work, relationships, communication style, and in creating your company's culture.

MINDFULNESS IS ABOUT AS RELIGIOUS AS RED WINE

Even as the business and sports worlds rapidly embrace mindfulness training as a tool for productivity and performance, I still sometimes hear the concern that meditation is considered too spiritual or religious to give it a try. I've even had a few folks in the bible-belt suggest that meditation is "evil", leaning on the old English proverb, "An idle mind is the devil's workshop." It's hard to say, "that's just stupid", mindfully. Instead, I share that allowing your mind and thoughts to be largely out of your control should be the bigger concern.

As someone who was raised Irish Catholic, I certainly wasn't looking for a new religion when I found mindfulness. I was looking for a way to stop stressing out about every little thing in life (and especially at each quarter's end). I was looking to sleep better. I was looking for help dealing with chronic back pain. I wanted to stay at the top of my game. I didn't want to be angry all the time. And since I'd hit a wall with my health and my decreasing level of patience, I realized I needed help. Separately, my wife was looking for the guy she married and a husband who was more present with the family.

To calm any fears that you may have, I've learned that mindfulness training is about as religious as red wine. Wine has been used for some 9,000 years in a wide array of religions dating back to ancient Egypt, Greece, and Rome. This included having a starring role in the Last Supper. As an adult, I was delighted to discover that red wine is also good on its own. Like, really good. Try it with a steak. It just works.

Just like red wine, mindfulness meditation has also been around for a long time (some 5,000 years). Sure, it's been used in every contemplative tradition in prayer, sitting in silence, or actual meditative practices to calm the mind and sometimes bring focus to a higher calling or being. But, just like wine, a mindfulness practice is also really good on its own. Try it with stress. It just works.

I'm not particularly religious these days. But I like red wine. I like mindfulness. And mindful wine drinking ain't bad either. I almost said wine "tasting," but let's be honest.

Pro Tip: If you regularly drink wine to manage your stress, that's not mindfulness. Sometimes, that's called alcoholism. Everything in moderation, my friend.

It's About Improving Life

I've found what millions have discovered through mindfulness practice: greater happiness, improved wellbeing, and better sleep. My back pain dropped from a constant 8 of 10 to a manageable 3. My resting heart rate dropped 20 points. My blood pressure is down. I've learned to tame the wandering mind. Entrepreneur and author, Jim Rohn said, "One of the greatest gifts you can give to anyone is the gift of attention." Learning to focus and to not take things personally has made me more kind, calm, and compassionate with the most important people in my life (including myself). And my wife got what she deserved—I'm back to being the guy she married before extreme stress became my unwanted mistress.

A modern mindfulness practice also cultivates many of the community aspects that can be found in contemplative traditions. Beyond the personal desire to have continuing success and a healthier and happier life, I've also experienced the unavoidable side effects of thinking more about my team, our community, and living life with purpose. Being a better parent, partner, and person come first. All of that has created a foundation for improving my performance as a more caring and compassionate leader.

CHAPTER 2

What's Stressing People Out?

So now you know what mindfulness is. And you know it doesn't have to be creepy or new age-y or spiritual. But why do you need it? Let's start with a few high-level questions to get to know one another. Do you suffer from back pain? Insomnia? Stress? Annoying co-workers? If you answered yes to any of these, you're in the majority of professionals having a similar life experience. Increasingly, that experience is contributing to poor health, declining performance, and toxic work cultures. We'll get to that in a moment. For now, let's dig into the details around what's stressing us all out. Then, we'll work on the antidote.

WELCOME TO WORK

Think back to when you were being recruited for your current role. The conversation with your suitor probably went something like this: "You're going to love it here. The company is great. The CEO is brilliant. Our culture is awesome. We have our mission, vision, and values on the wall! You're going to fit right in. Look at how cool our offices are. Have I told you about the snacks? OMG, the snacks are amazing!" As a candidate, you can almost hear the birds singing and see butterflies surrounding Bambi as he prances across your new work campus. We tend to put the best face on everything when we're recruiting.

Figure 2.1 Is distraction your default mode?

WELCOME TO WORK, TAKE TWO

Once you start work, the reality is a bit different. How did conversations in your first week at the new job go? "Welcome back. We forgot to mention that the pace of business is relentless. Ongoing change and disruption is the norm. On any given day, you'll be dealing with globalization, innovation, and transformation. Actually, we're dealing with all the *-ations*. Expectations and inundation may lead to frustration, speculation, and aggravation. But we still expect you to be amazing! The table stakes are high. And there's a lot of confusion and concern with robotics and artificial intelligence. Have fun! You'll be great."

The truth is: work is hard. Every now and then there's a forest fire and sometimes Bambi's mom gets shot. Oh, and we're out of snacks. Are you equipped to deal?

ARE YOU SENDING MIXED MESSAGES?

We need leaders to help avoid mixed messages in the business world. Most companies tell employees, "You are our most important asset!" But what happens next? According to *The Economist*, 90% of companies cite offshoring as crucial to their growth and to reduce costs.[1] In 2013, 43% of the global IT sector had been outsourced. Today, it's 72%.[2] So, "We love you, but we love less expensive employees more." The rapid changing nature of global economics also has offshoring changing to "nearshoring" and sometimes to "backshoring." We love you. We love you not. Oops, we love you again.

More companies are acquiring companies as their de facto innovation strategy. Or worse, they outsource innovation to third parties because they can't keep pace with change. Once again, a mixed message. We love you, but we're giving a lot of the cool work to other folks. My bad. You understand.

THE FUTURE IS NOW

Our fascination with robotics has moved from *The Jetsons* to being real, son. We used to think about robots as big mechanical arms helping to build cars. Now, self-driving cars are paving the way for self-driving trucks. Machines are already asking, "Do you want fries with that?" Throughout Asia, hotels are replacing their desk clerks with robots (Figure 2.2).[3] You have your choice of checking in with an attractive lifelike female robot, a T-Rex robot, or a super-cute kid's toy robot. Drones will go from delivering our packages to delivering our persons. For anyone familiar with commercial aircraft, you know planes already are robots. Pilots are there for taking off and landing. Everything else has been automated for decades. The World Economic Forum estimates that some five million jobs will be replaced by technology by 2020.[4] That estimate goes up as much as threefold depending on which futurist you believe.

Not Even Pizza Is Safe. In September 2017, Ford and Domino's announced a partnership for self-driving cars to deliver pizzas. Not to be outdone, Little Caesars announced their robotic "Pizza Portal": You text and the robot makes your pizza. Employees have ongoing low-level concerns about robotics and AI usurping their jobs. But when you start messing with their pizza, sh*t just got real. The future is now and it's freaking people out. Employees are asking, "What's going on? Does the company have a plan? Why isn't anyone talking to us? Should I be looking for my next job?" And sites like LinkedIn and

Figure 2.2 Robot desk clerks in Japan
Source: Permission courtesy of © Huiten Bosch

Glassdoor are in business to feed those fears. If you don't believe me, join your collaboration channels at work. These conversations are consuming employee time. Right. Now.

Coopetition Is Temporary. Does your company have any competitors that you also partner with? For most companies, "coopetition" has become the norm. For anyone who has simultaneously partnered and competed, you know the endgame is generally to partner until you can cut your partner out of the picture. Language within the company reflects that, and that sends mixed messages to your employees about how the company does business. If you don't think so, ask the millennials on your team. Coopetition is the new game.

Procurement Don't Play. Procurement moved from being the redheaded stepchild 20 years ago to now having a seat on the board. Their job is to cut 10% to 15% of costs every year, relegating many of your most trusted business partners into your cheapest vendors. That changes how vendors service your company and increases stress for employees who rely on them. When I was the global COO of a $2 billion agency network, we ran a procurement playbook to maximize productivity and reduce costs. Our clients ran the same playbook on us. Wait, what? That's a double whammy when it comes to disruption.

"Faster and Cheaper" procurement decisions can even alter the culture. When I was the head of financial planning at the CBS Television Network, a "cheap" deal to buy a near-bankrupt beauty pageants company in partnership with Donald Trump, resulted in low-cost programing. Sadly, in my opinion, it also resulted in ongoing chatter about sexual harassment claims, needless lawsuits, a decreased regard for the "Tiffany Network," and unnecessary stress and low morale for CBS employees. Cheap filler programming that cost us $10 million for a 50% share in a tiny joint venture became a growing distraction to the Network's other $4.5 billion in annual revenue.

Tech Espionage Is Ramping. The Justice Department estimates that the United States has already lost over two million jobs and hundreds of billions in technology revenue to China.[5] Russia hacked the 2016 U.S. election. For at least two major governments, hacking and espionage has turned into the lucrative business of stealing technology, designs, products, and data and selling them back to the country of origin at a lower cost. Let alone other political efforts to sow confusion and division. The undercurrent of anxiety related to both job security and national security is rising.

The Cool Stuff Is Being Outsourced. There are now nearly seven million people working in technology research.[6] This isn't the Genius Bar at your local Apple store. We're talking about deep technology research. For more companies, the rate of innovation outstrips their ability to manage it in-house. As Gary Hamel wrote in his book, *What Matters Now*, "The world is becoming more turbulent faster than most organizations are becoming more resilient."[7]

And Life Is Hard. On top of all of this, employees have a rising undercurrent of disruption before they even get to work. We're now dealing with global warming and unprecedented destruction from natural disasters. Healthcare, Medicaid, taxes and privacy seem in constant flux. Terrorism has become a norm. Politics have moved to the extreme in developed countries. Some countries are even being run by incompetent egomaniacs and their crazy family members. Thank goodness that could never happen in the United States.

Equifax's hacking created uncertainty for 143 million Americans, including me, who are now facing a serious threat of identity theft for the rest of our lives. Not to be outdone, Yahoo! exposed three billion users and failed to disclose it for three years. Since 2006, sixteen major companies exposed nearly 5 billion consumer records, with many forgetting to mention it until being caught.

At home, many of us parents are dealing with stressed-out children. So, domestic terrorism is in the hizzouse.

Given all we have going on before we even get to work, it's no surprise that it's not turning out great. More employees are feeling that events are out of their control, there's a lack of trust or there's constant exposure to the latest calamity. A lack of job security has put a low-grade, chronic stress response on simmer. When you add in work stressors, the expectation that employees will trust in management or just figure it all out is no longer a sustainable strategy.

It's a great time opportunity for leaders to step in to help, listen, and lead through the issues.

EMPLOYEES ARE SHARING MORE AND TRUSTING LESS

The rise of the sharing economy has us opening up and trusting folks in ways that would've been hard to imagine a few years ago. We trust strangers to drive us around (Uber), deliver our food (Seamless), rent our homes (Airbnb), babysit our kids (care.com), and our pets (dogvacay.com). You can even borrow luxury cars (RelayRide). Kids. Dogs. Cars. Oh, my! The trust and flexibility in these new models requires participants to suspend fear and judgment.

With all the mixed messages, research suggests that the sharing economy is carrying over to employees sharing more with each other about the workplace on external sites (GlassDoor) and internal collaboration tools (Slack, Yammer, and others). But sadly, without the trust factor or willingness to suspend fear and judgment about management.

The 2017 Edelman Trust Barometer revealed a "crisis in trust" with the largest-ever drop reported across all major institutions. Specifically, a minority of people now trust the media (43%), government (41%), CEOs (37%), and political leaders (29%).[8] The study of 33,000 respondents showed the largest gap ever between the 13% of respondents considered "informed" (college educated, top 25% of earners, with significant media consumption) versus the 87% global mass population considered "not informed." The majority of the mass population now mistrusts all four major institutions in 20 of the 28 largest countries.

When the subject comes to trust, employees would overwhelmingly rather hear from other employees over senior management or CEOs. Respondents ranked fellow employees more credible than senior management to share news on culture and treatment of employees by a factor of 2.5 times higher. The same was true for sharing financial results (1.7 times), handling a crisis (1.6 times), and to a lesser degree innovation (1.3 times), understanding industry drivers (1.2 times), and programs addressing societal issues (1.2 times). CEOs fared even worse across the board.

This distrust results in four key themes where leaders with the right approach can make all the difference:

1. Sense of injustice	3. Lack of confidence
2. Lack of hope	4. Desire for change

The report uncovered major trust issues, especially for business:

Change in the Mass Population Landscape:	Feeling that business is stoking societal fears with:
• Rejects established authority	• Lack of training (60%)
• View peers as credible as experts	• Foreign competitors (60%)
• Global concern about losing their jobs	• Low-cost immigrant workforce (58%)
• Feel businesses should also do good in addition to make profits	• Offshoring to cheaper markets (55%)
• Trust in media is at an all-time low	• Automation (54%)
• Rise in protectionism	

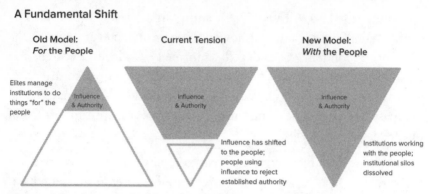

Figure 2.3 Are you making the shift fast enough?

Source: 2017 Edelman Trust Barometer, used with permission of Edelman.

There's a clear movement toward employees wanting leaders to speak with them, not at them. They prefer spontaneous to rehearsed (57%), blunt to diplomatic (54%), and personal experience over data (51%). The mass population also looks more to social media than to advertising (62%) for influence. The old model isn't working. The new model is breaking. It's time for an operating model, with the people, that is mindful of the times (Figure 2.3).

Conversations about these concerns occur in your company daily, openly or in private collaboration channels. While this movement away from "for the people" to "with the people" may feel scary, the time is perfect for leaders trained in mindfulness and emotional intelligence to place people at the center to change the future (Figure 2.4).

Pro Tip: When the subject comes to the sharing economy, you have to play to win. Bringing teams together regularly can help surface employee concerns in a transparent way. Companies including SAP, Salesforce, Google, McKinsey, and Aetna have found that mindfulness training for teams is a great place to begin working "with the people" in this new integrated operating model that puts employees at the center.

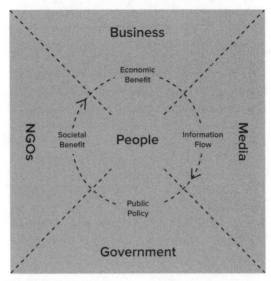

Figure 2.4 "With the People" puts employees at the center.

Source: 2017 Edelman Trust Barometer, used with permission of Edelman.

WELLBEING

CHAPTER 3

The $500 Billion Dollar Slow Leak

The greatest weapon against stress is our ability to choose one thought over another.
—William James

The United States loses over $500 billion annually because of stress.[1] That's up from $300 billion just a few years ago. For companies, this shows up as absenteeism, turnover, lost productivity, and increasing medical costs. For employees, it shows up in more personal ways. They don't feel heard. One in three don't feel trusted (or trust management).[2] They don't feel companies are living up to their missions or values. They feel disrespected by their managers or commanding cultures. They don't feel safe or secure. They quit. Go across the street. And what do they usually find at their new company? Same sh*t, different business card.

The statistics tell us that's not going so well for employees.

- 83% report work as their top source of stress.[3]

- 50% say their stress level is "high" or "overwhelming."[4]

- 33% suffer from insomnia impacting their health and performance.[5]

- 83% of 2014 health cases were due to employee depression, stress, and anxiety (up from 55% in 2012).[6]

- 91% of workplace injuries are due to human error.[7]

  And that's not good news for business or company cultures.

- Turnover rates in the United States have increased every single year since 2011.[8]

- 42% of employees cite "stress" as the reason they leave their job.[9]

- 70% report not being engaged at work. Almost one-third report being intentionally not engaged, meaning they show up planning not to work.[10]

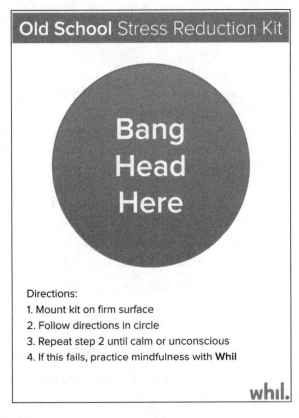

Figure 3.1   The status quo approach to stress.

- 64% feel their employer doesn't provide sufficient resources to help manage stress.[11]

- 35% higher chance of turnover for employees who aren't "thriving."[12]

Stress is shortening our lifespans, reducing our quality of life, and diminishing our potential as professionals. The only good news is that, just like me, most professionals come to a mindfulness practice when they're in crisis. Your employees are highly primed to try new solutions. As a leader, is your business ready to listen? Or do you want to stick with the status quo?

Address the Hidden Cost of Generational Friction

When it comes to company stress, there's an elderly person in the room. And it's probably you. For the first time in history, we have four generations working together. And the fifth, Centennials, are about to enter the workforce.

- Centennials, Gen Z, or iGen: Born 1996 and later (22 and younger as of 2018)

- Millennials or Gen Y: Born 1977 to 1995 (ages 23 to 41)

- Generation X: Born 1965 to 1976 (ages 42 to 53)

- Baby Boomers: Born 1946 to 1964 (ages 54 to 72)

- Traditionalists, or Silent Generation: Born 1945 and before (73 and older)

And guess what? They hate each other. You can't get four generations together for Thanksgiving dinner without all hell breaking loose. It's worse in business. On one end, you have the Millennials thinking, "Who created this mess?" And "What's up with office hours, dude?" On the other end, you have the "walking retired" worried about being less relevant or pushed out at a time when they can't afford to leave. And everything in between. This not-so hidden friction is one of the reasons Bersin by Deloitte reports that "Organizational Design is being challenged everywhere."[13] Your company is not alone.

Good News, Bad News. The good news for business is that we've never had such a rich tapestry of experience in the workforce at one time. The bad news is that, in many cases, these four generations haven't been equipped to accept one another, let alone be happy, willing, and able to work together. Each of these generations has different communication styles, work expectations, aspirations, and belief systems based on how and when they grew up. And Millennials have emojis.

Although Millennials are the most innovative generation, they've also taken the worst reputation beating in this steel cage match. To be fair, each group has their own issues. These aren't glass houses. They're glass neighborhoods.

When it comes to matters of the mind, most companies expect employees to figure it out. But human beings are complex and dynamic. We don't simply "work it out." Instead, we tend to be judgmental of what we don't understand, including other people. With the pace of modern business picking up at an alarming rate, it's important for businesses to address these generational differences to bring out the best in others. In the absence of that, these individual groups tend to bring out the worst in one another—our default mode is to go tribal. Human nature is to pick sides, reinforce one another's belief systems, and draw in support from others. It's Maslow's Hierarchy of Needs.[14] That gives many a sense of safety and belonging, but it can also create a Millennials versus Boomers culture.

It takes effort, awareness, and trust to cross physical, psychological, and cultural boundaries. Training ourselves as leaders and our employees in mindfulness techniques is an excellent way to do this. More companies are looking to mindfulness solutions to cultivate acceptance, collaboration, and create community. If your company hasn't started, now is a good time.

Culture Crossing Practice

Think about other generations in your office that set you off. This week, connect with someone who is completely different from you or that you've been judging. Author David DeSteno suggests that finding even one commonality with another person can nudge people toward trust by establishing a perception of similarity.[15] Invite them out for coffee to find that one point. That can lead to a conversation to explore differences and concerns more openly. Ask for feedback on your own generation's style. My sense is you'll find an interested party who will be happy to share his or her thoughts. Make acceptance a practice and you'll find more work friends and fewer work enemies.

Following are three ways in which leaders can introduce mindfulness to be more open and accepting.

Be Nonjudgmental

Implicit biases are unconscious beliefs and judgments we hold about others. We all have them based on our conditioning when growing up. One study found that just a 10-minute mindfulness practice can reduce age and racial bias on the Implicit Attitude Test.[16] Learning to work with different types of people can reduce your stress while bringing a diverse pool of ideas to the table. That makes any team stronger.

Be Curious, Not Furious

Instead of seeing people as "too old" or "too young" to know better (Don't be ageist, yo!), why not engage in conversation to hear their perspective? Bruce Feiler, author of *The Secrets of Happy Families*, found that sharing intergenerational stories is one of the best ways of learning, in large part because you learn the struggles and triumphs of people like you.[17] The same is true in business, but most leaders don't spend enough time sharing the stories and lessons learned from success and failure.

Pro Tip: You can tell a lot about a person by what they reveal in their life stories. Uncover common ground by asking your colleagues interesting questions. Dr. Tara Cousineau recommends trying, "How do you like to spend your time?" "Tell me about your life." "What obstacles have you overcome in your life and how?" "What are you most proud of?" Then listen and learn.

Use "Just Like Me"

When you come across the youngins or oldins that bother you, try a "Just Like Me" practice. Stop yourself in the moment of judgment. Take a breath. Think of five ways in which this individual is just like you. They probably have similar wants and needs in life. Similar fears and regrets. And the same desire to be loved, respected, and understood. Finding common ground goes a long way to dropping judgment. Then take the next step and open up a conversation. "Just like me" is also a great meditation practice to better understand and get along with difficult family members.

GETTING SPECIFIC ABOUT STRESS AND CULTURE

Peter Drucker said, "Culture eats strategy for breakfast." When the topic comes to your culture, the fight for talent acquisition and retention has never been more competitive. Companies are in an arms race to become the employer of choice. At the same time, in a Gallup poll of 25 million professionals in 189 different countries, only 13% of employees reported feeling engaged in their work. Sixty-three percent reported being not engaged, dialing it in and putting minimal effort into their job.[18] As Barry Schwartz says in his excellent TED Talk, "Ninety percent of adults spend half their waking lives doing things they would rather not be doing at places they would rather not be."[19]

The best organizations create environments that not only engage employees, but sustain high performance over long periods of time.

This includes training them with effective tools to handle ongoing change and the pressure that comes with it.

Stress has become the ubiquitous topic of conversation. We're all "crazy busy" and many of us wear it like a cheap suit. For leaders, it's helpful to understand the specifics of stress when it comes to you and your team. Then develop specific plans and training to help employees not only cope with stress, but be equipped to thrive. Only then can you build a high-performance culture that embraces change and disruption as a given and not something to fear.

Most of us have the occasional sense of feeling overwhelmed. But what specifically is stressing people out? According to the Aon Hewitt *Consumer Health Mindset Study*, it's a bit of everything.[20]

Mental/Emotional Wellbeing	Social Wellness
68%—Managing my stress	70%—Spending enough time with family/friends
65%—Taking time off/relaxing	
Finances/Quality of Life	63%—Balancing work and life
70%—Living within my means	**Work Wellness**
67%—Regularly saving money	40%—Unrealistic job expectations
65%—Paying down credit cards	**Physical Wellness**
Sleep/Rest	65%—Eating healthy
70%—Getting enough sleep	64%—Following medical advice

If we boiled this down to one common theme, it would be the pace of modern living. More of us don't have the time to plan and enjoy life with intention. That's not surprising. Today, Americans take in five times as much information every day as they did in 1986—the equivalent of 174 newspapers.[21] Thank you, Internet. The average professional manages 75 texts and 126 business emails a day (9 and 16 per hour, respectively).[22] Leaders in a global organization can expect two to three times that volume. On a daily basis, the average American sees 5,000 to 10,000 advertisements, consumes 8.5 hours of media, and spends five hours on his or her mobile device.[23–25]

Here's the problem: Science tells us that the human brain hasn't changed much in 10,000 years.[26] Evolutionary changes require slow adaptation over the course of many thousands of years. Society has changed too rapidly in the past twenty years for our brains to adapt. Without the right training, we're not equipped to live in the modern age of technology.

Once again, both the need and the opportunity for leaders to step in has never been more clear.

Ask the Big Questions

When your focus comes to performance and company culture, ask yourself three questions:

1. What challenges and disruptive forces exist in running your business today?

2. How will they get worse in the next 5 to 10 years?

3. Are you and your employees equipped to be resilient in the face of what's coming?

GET CLEAR ON YOUR OWN STRESS

What gets measured gets done. When it comes to stress and its impact on you and your company culture, you need a scorecard to play along and develop a plan. Otherwise, most of us have a secret plan called "I'll deal with it after I hit a wall." Mindfulness training helps you to catch yourself (and your employees) before you hit a wall by training to better understand what's going on in your mind and body.

One of the tools we like to use in our training is the Holmes-Rahe Scale Life Stress Test (Figure 3.2).[27] This oldie, but goodie was initially done in 1967 and updated over the years. The original researchers interviewed 5,000 hospital patients to understand their lifestyles. They came up with 43 life stressors to better understand the drivers behind the causes of illness and disease. The more stressful events you experience in a 12-month period, the more likely you are to face illnesses triggered by that stress. Over time, your reactions to accumulated stressors impacts your lifespan.

I've found the test to be an easy tool to check in on my own stress over the past year. Try it (Figure 3.2) and add up your score.

whil.

The Holmes-Rahe Scale Life Stress Test

In the past **12 months**, which of the following major life events have taken place in your life? Write down the points for each event you've experienced this year. At the end, add up the points for each event.

Event	Impact Score	My Score
Death of spouse	100	
Divorce	73	
Marital separation from mate	65	
Jail term	63	
Death of close family member	63	
Personal injury or illness	53	
Marriage	50	
Fired from work	47	
Marital reconciliation	45	
Retirement	45	
Change in family member's health	44	
Pregnancy	40	
Sex difficulties	39	
Addition to family	39	
Business readjustment	39	
Change in financial status	38	
Death of close friend	37	
Change to a different line of work	36	
Major change in number of marital arguments	35	
Taking on a mortgage (for home, business, etc.)	31	
Foreclosure of mortgage or loan	30	

Event	Impact Score	My Score
Change in work responsibilities	29	
Trouble with in laws	29	
Outstanding personal achievement	28	
Spouse begins or stops work	26	
Starting or finishing school	26	
Change in living conditions	25	
Revisions of personal habits	24	
Trouble with boss	23	
Change in work hours, or conditions	20	
Change in residence	20	
Change in schools	20	
Change in recreational habits	19	
Change in church activities	19	
Change in social activities	18	
Taking on a loan (for car, freezer, etc.)	17	
Change in sleeping habits	16	
Change in number of family gatherings	15	
Change in eating habits	15	
Vacation	13	
Christmas season	12	
Minor violations of the law	11	

Your total score:

This scale shows the kind of life pressure that you are facing. Depending on your coping skills or the lack thereof, this scale can predict the likelihood that you will fall victim to a stress related illness. The illness could be mild - frequent tension headaches, acid indigestion, loss of sleep to very serious illness like ulcers, cancer, migraines and the like.

LIFE STRESS SCORES

0 - 149: Low susceptibility to stress-related illness

150 - 299: Medium susceptibility to stress-related illness

300 & over: High susceptibility to stress-related illness

Figure 3.2   How do you measure your own stress?

Source: Modified with permission granted by the publisher. Taken from "The Social Readjustment Rating Scale", Thomas H. Holmes and Richard H. Rahe, Journal of Psychosomatic Research, Volume 11, Issue 2, August 1967, Pages 213-218, Copyright © 1967 Published by Elsevier Science Inc. All rights reserved.

What Can a Scale Teach Us About Stress?

Were you surprised by your result? The notion behind this research and the survey is this: the higher your score, the more likely you are to cut years off your life. Stress wears on the system, breaks us down, and causes us to age faster. Remember, the brain is like a refrigerator. If the equipment is running nonstop, it's going to break down more frequently.

Daily Hassles Matter, Too. The accumulation of stress from normal traffic, commuting, noise, financial woes, kids, neighbors, regrets, small pains, and so on also takes a toll on our ability to remain optimistic in the face of day-to-day life. According to a study by the Center for Healthy Aging Research at Oregon State University, "People who always perceived their daily life to be over-the-top stressful were three times more likely to die over the period of study than people who rolled with the punches and didn't find daily life very stressful."[28]

Pro Tip: Research has shown that our mindset toward daily hassles determines whether we're continuously flooded with stress cortisol (slow-drip poison) or whether we can regulate our systems. This is the difference between a short life and a long life.[29]

Another study showed that mindfulness practice can produce a 30% reduction of aging at the cellular level.[30] If you're skeptical of that, think about the high school friends whom you're connected to on Facebook, but haven't seen in decades. Sometimes, they connect and you think, "Oh my God, you look amazing!" Other times, you just think, "Oh. My. God." That's stress. How we manage it has a significant impact on how we age.

Common Life Issues Aren't Going Away. They're getting worse. Across the scale, divorce rates are up, illness and disease stats are up, the need for prescription medication is up, and the list goes on. The numbers are all going the wrong way.

Stress Drivers Are Connected and Come in Waves. That's true for what we perceive as bad events: losing a job, financial issues, relationship problems, and so on. This is also true for what we perceive as happy times. We're getting married! We're buying a home! We're having a child! Holy crap, this is stressful.

HSEs Are Impacting Performance and Company Culture. According to the American Psychological Association, the average employer has 35% of workers who are considered High Stress Employees or "HSEs" based on life events.[31] That means they cost three to four times the "normal" stressed employee in terms of health care costs, absenteeism, and so forth. There is no category for nonstressed employees. It's not a thing.

Being equipped to handle these normal life events makes all the difference. Without the right tools to manage their mindset and how they perceive stress, individual employees (and especially HSEs) are the biggest source of disruption in any organization. How they experience life stress and how they bring it into the office every day makes up the culture. Every. Single. Day. Without the proper training, the numbers suggest too many are stressed out, not sleeping, in pain, and unable to focus. That's your company culture. At it's worse, teams begin to operate on a hair trigger. As world renown author and teacher Sharon Salzberg puts it, without some level of training, "The instability of life is so true for each of us. It's like any single one of us can check our cell phone messages and by the time we hang up, we have a different life."[32]

When I was in my early 40s and going through back pain, insomnia, asthma, and the back-to-back deaths of two of my sisters, my Stress Scale score was over 600. Besides the strain of health and wellbeing issues, I got married, changed jobs, moved across country, had our first child and our largest client ($365 million in annual revenue) threatened to terminate our global relationship. I found out later that that's why I was hired. Welcome to the company! All this while managing health issues and the loss of loved ones. I thought working 14-hour days would make it all better. It didn't.

My story is not unique. Professionals at all levels experience the sharp angles of life and work constantly. As a leader, I wasn't equipped to think about and manage my own emotional wellbeing, never mind helping employees around the world. Their mental wellbeing wasn't even a conversation in our board meetings. Sadly, we spent more time discussing exotic locations for our annual meeting.

Okay. Enough about the root causes of stress. Let's talk about the antidote.

Mindfulness Can Disrupt Stress and Unhelpful Routines

Mindfulness practices create a routine to check in with how your body is feeling and how that impacts your emotions, thought patterns, and performance. In the absence of cultivating these skills, more of us destroy our health, relationships, and career potential over time. We move from healthy, happy, and engaged to sick, grumpy, and distracted. That's not good for you. And it's not good for business.

Every day is an opportunity to transform your management style, your health, and your results as a leader.

WELLBEING   PERFORMANCE

CHAPTER 4

Are You Increasing Your Resilience or Decreasing It?

Stand up straight and realize who you are, that
you tower over your circumstances.
—Maya Angelou

The key to managing stress is building up your resilience. When we feel like we're constantly under pressure, we tend to fall into a commanding leadership style. A common reaction to stress is to *increase* the amount of work we do. Being addicted to busyness makes us falsely believe we are productive or working hard. Putting in more hours, sleeping less, and just working through it are fairly common self-prescriptions. Without the proper time to recover from stress, we're really just working inefficiently, wearing ourselves out, and cutting years off of our lives.

Dr. Liz Stanley, Ph.D., is a friend and security studies expert at Georgetown University with joint appointments in their School of Foreign Service and their Department of Government. Earlier in her career, Liz served as a U.S. army intelligence officer in Asia, Europe, and on deployments to the Balkans. She left the service as a captain. Liz speaks, teaches, and writes widely on a variety of topics related to resilience, decision-making in stressful environments, civil-military relations, military effectiveness and innovation, and international security.

Liz is also the creator of Mindfulness-based Mind Fitness Training (MMFT), which has been tested through four neuroscience research studies with the U.S. military.[1] It's not often you get to know your heroes. Liz is my hero. I had the good fortune of attending a seven-day MMFT training in 2015 and it was life changing.

MILITARY GRADE STRESS

Depending upon how much stress arousal we are experiencing, we can think about two types of stress. Eustress is mild to moderate arousal, the kind of stress we experience when we're under pressure and we're prepared and ready to perform. We reach optimal performance and the "flow state" when we're in our zone of moderate arousal—this is a positive kind of stress. Distress, on the other hand, is when we've experienced too much stress arousal beyond our window of tolerance. Distress is what we experience in a challenging situation and we don't feel prepared. The greater our distress, the worse our performance becomes, until we eventually end up paralyzed by overwhelm or procrastination.[2]

As a former military officer who suffered from PTSD herself while she was in graduate school at Harvard and MIT, Liz knows a bit about managing stress and PTSD. She's spent years researching mindfulness practices as they relate to helping soldiers manage and recover from high-stress missions. This is important work. The U.S. military's suicide rate has skyrocketed since 9/11, and for several years since we've been at war, the U.S. military has lost more troops to suicide than to active combat.[3] Beyond suicide, our service-members have suffered from a range of psychological injuries, including PTSD, depression, and alcohol and substance abuse. It's a growing and disturbing mental health crisis.

Dr. Stanley shares that stress, contrary to many cultural beliefs, is not a bad thing. We actually need the energy created by stress to mobilize and to function in the world. The stress we mobilize to accomplish tasks, paired with a full recovery, actually leads to an increased zone of resilience.

To paraphrase her TEDX talk on this topic – a topic she's exploring further in a forthcoming book called *Widen the Window*- resilience is not about being pampered.[4] We actually need to regularly push ourselves outside our comfort zone, and then fully recover from the stress. In this way, we can grow our capacity to be resilient in the face of stress and disruption. Dr. Stanley's research on resilience is both fascinating and intuitive, including the simple formula:

Stress + Effective Recovery = Increased Resilience[5]

When you push yourself and then recover, you can handle increasing amounts of stress over time. The opposite it also true. If you stress the system and do not fully recover, you can take on less and less over time. Over time, you narrow your window of tolerance to stress-and undermine your resilience.

Dr. Stanley sees this phenomenon play out in how military troops function in the face of multiple deployments. After their initial deployment, things tend to be okay. After the second deployment, they may have a drinking issue and problems with their spouse. After the third, there may be violence in the home, a DUI, drug and alcohol use, or suicide.

While most of us are not in active combat, it can sometimes feel like we're on the front lines. And just like soldiers, most professionals tend to block the recovery process. Our work cultures don't tend to value recovery. So, we push until we hit a wall, take a little time out to heal, and then get right back to it. We then tend to rely more on caffeine, alcohol, and other self-medication while not realizing our pain may be increasing or our emotional fuse getting shorter. Too many professionals are being impacted by what I call the "unlucky trifecta": unmanaged stress, mood disorders, and substance abuse. Statistics show that too many of our colleagues turn to alcohol or drugs (including opioids) to self-medicate.[6] That leads to getting sick more often and easier as our systems are being undermined.

I experienced this in my own life. When I first herniated a disk in my back, I worked through it, continuing to put in 12-hour days and travelling constantly. I then herniated two discs again five years later and couldn't function. Once again, I pushed through a semi-recovery, hobbling my way into the office to prove I could do it. I wasn't at my best. In hindsight, I'm certain my colleagues knew that. As the back pain took a toll on my health, it also took a toll on my ability to be an effective leader. I realize now that I had several years of being the kind of leader I wasn't always proud of. How about you?

EDUCATION IS EVERYTHING

I didn't have access to mindfulness or emotional intelligence training at the time. Heck, as advertising executives we'd even half-joke that our clients' taglines were killing our employees. This was especially true as the world moved to ubiquitous brand promises like "Always On," "On Demand," and "24/7." Given what I've learned about injury, stress and the tendency to avoid a proper recovery period, today those old taglines feel like promos for the modern work experience. We go to bed with stress, wake up with stress, and check email in between. Rinse and repeat.

The pace of work has even caused some companies to refer to employees as "corporate athletes"—push it to the limit, win the gold, longer, harder, and faster. Just do it! But the analogy misses the points shared by Dr. Stanley's research.

In contrast to our sports stars, corporate athletes generally follow the same approach that I did. Push until you break. The evidence shows that it's costly in terms of burnout, stress, depression, chronic back pain, injury, pharmaceutical usage, and related healthcare costs. Personally, I pushed hard for two decades. Without understanding the importance of recovery periods, I hit a wall. At the time, I had every (financial and external reward) indication that I was winning, so I didn't care. Now I do.

Pro Tip: Sports psychologists like Dr. Jim Loehr at the Johnson & Johnson Human Performance Institute have long written about the importance of push hard, then recover training

Figure 4.1   The corporate athlete

for top physical and mental performance.[7] The push-recover approach helps build speed, strength, and endurance for professional athletes to expand the limits of human performance and endurance while avoiding injury. A recent University California, San Diego and U.S. Navy study even demonstrated that breathing-based mindfulness training can help professionals develop an "elite performance" brain pattern.[8]

As leaders, we set the pace for others on our team and in the company at large. You also have to take care of the corporate warrior / athlete within yourself. Here are five tips to use mindfulness to help you push and recover throughout the day.

You Work Like an Athlete. Train Like One. Build in micro breaks to recover. Try a few short meditations during the day, and especially before and after tough situations. Find a quiet spot, sit like a normal person, pop in the headphones, and take a one-to-five-minute brain-break to center, calm your nervous system, and clear your mind for what comes next.

Improve Effectiveness with Mindful Meetings. Too many meetings start late, end late, and don't accomplish its goals. That creates stress. Start and end on time. Take one minute to center the room, put devices away, and ask everyone to drop whatever they're bringing to the meeting. Name one to three goals for the meeting, including the decisions that need to be made. Make sure everyone is heard. Use a timer, if necessary.

Let the Team Recover, Too. If you draft emails on the weekend, don't send them until Monday. It may feel good to get things off of your chest in the moment, but weekend emails are simply a way for you to pass the stress baton. Don't do it.

Turn Your Phone Off at the Same Time Each Evening. You may be in a globally connected business, but when it comes to your state of mind and emotional wellbeing, what happens with your family in the short time you spend together is more important than emails after 7 p.m. So is your sleep. Savor and protect your family and recovery time.

Show the Team You Care by How You Listen. When speaking to colleagues, practice "Mindful Listening." Let them speak for two or three minutes without interrupting. Ask them to do the same for you. This creates a recovery time when you're listening, not trying to think or outdo your teammate. We all do it. Small changes in how you communicate will conserve energy, increase connections, and reduce tension in your relationships.

Don't Push Till You Break. Remember, push and then recover. There's a right way to train and a wrong way. Salt-N-Pepa put it best when they said, "Push it good."

CHANGE YOUR MINDSET. STRESS IS GOOD.

In 2017, I had the great pleasure of meeting Dr. Alia Crum, a professor and researcher at Stanford University's Mind & Body Lab, while speaking at the HERO Forum.[9] Dr. Crum's research focuses on stress resilience and what she considers two flawed assumptions. First, that the effects of stress are only negative. Second, the goal should be to avoid, manage, and counteract the effects of stress.

To address these flaws, leaders need to recognize that stress has two sides. Yes, stress has been shown to be debilitating to performance, health, and wellbeing.[10-16] However, it has also been shown to enhance performance, health, and wellbeing by increasing brain processing, improving memory, and focus, quicker recovery, enhanced immunity, physiological, and mental toughening, establishing deeper relationships, and greater appreciation for life.[17-21]

Dr. Crum performed and reviewed research across aging, work, exercise, dieting, and other common stress areas. She found that your mindset matters most.

If you believe stress is debilitating, you're likely to experience those effects. If you believe stress is enhancing, you are likely to experience those effects. This was true both physiologically and mentally.[22-23] Across multiple studies, people with positive mindsets toward stress experienced fewer negative health symptoms, greater work performance, and a greater quality of life.[24] Dr. Crum's recommendation for developing a positive mindset toward stress is perfectly aligned with mindfulness practices. You are what you think.

See it

(Be present to what is happening)

Own it

(You are in control, view stress as an opportunity to ground yourself)

Use it

(Generate the results and possibilities you want in your life)

Mindfulness helps you train this approach, including by being intentional through reflection, planning, and envisioning techniques that we'll try later.

PERFORMANCE   CAREER

CHAPTER 5

What Does "Performance" Mean to You?

Meditation, more than anything in my life, was the biggest ingredient of whatever success I've had.
—Ray Dalio

We're all looking to get better at something. When it comes to performance, I've found that most leaders are looking to be happier and get more out of life versus be Super-Boss or experience some spiritual awakening.

BETTER AT WHAT?

Companies want employees to be better at a range of things, mostly work-related. Employees want to be better in many areas of life, many not related to work. It's an age-old friction point that contributes to more employees feeling that a work/life balance is BS.

Good companies tend to provide expectations and their own definitions of performance. This requires them to make big assumptions, including that most employees are looking to advance, they want to qualify for rewards (pay increases, bonuses, recognition, and so on), and that their corporate culture is enjoyable enough to continue working under the company's norms.

Over the past year, we've surveyed more than 3,500 leaders. Here's what we learned about stress, disruption, and performance.

Companies Do Care

I've never met a company that didn't want their employees to be happier and healthier. Most companies also see that stress is a growing crisis that is negatively impacting their cultures and driving up their turnover; they need help for the good of both the company and employees. Culture has a big impact on individual performance.

Organizations of all sizes are looking for solutions to help employees cope so they can perform at their best. There is universal acknowledgment that the average person's stress is expected to get worse in the next 10 to 15 years.[1]

"Doing More With Less" Is the Language of Business

Whether we like it or not, every business has to compete in the global economy. Doing more with less is table stakes. If you look at the P&L as the usual report card, too many companies are struggling with rising costs and declining productivity. Much of this relates to rising healthcare costs, growing employee absenteeism, and increasing turnover rates. As an employee, if I understand that "faster, cheaper" is the way of the world, I may be open to the idea that my company didn't create the "do more with less" game. But they do have to play in it. It's not good or bad, right or wrong. It just is what it is.

Innovation and Productivity Expectations Aren't Going Away

Companies have to run to keep up with the pace of modern business. Just about every corporate conference in the past two years included the words *disruption, transformation* or *innovation* in their title. The "performance" required to keep up with the Joneses is taking on new meaning in both for-profit and not-for-profit organizations. The World Economic Forum estimates that five million jobs will disappear by 2020 due to robotics.[2] Just robotics. Innovation and productivity

Figure 5.1   How well can you juggle?

trends will continue. Without ongoing communication, these stats rightfully make employees worry—and that impacts performance.

Pro Tip: Bersin by Deloitte points out that too many companies haven't realized that the nature of work has changed. Most employees work on many projects in a given year versus in a fixed job description.[3] Unless employees are aware this is the norm, many wrongly assume, "I have 20 jobs" instead of "my job is project based." One perception is based in frustration. The other in reality.

It's All About Helping the Individual

There are many reasons that people practice mindfulness. Just about everyone wants to be better at something. The majority of employees that we speak with are interested in getting more out of life. They want to stress less, deepen relationships, improve their sleep, be a better parent, and enjoy their hobbies and downtime. And yes, most people would also like to be better at their jobs, too. Living well and doing your job well is all performance. The point is to recognize and enable the individual. What does performance mean to you?

The best companies (most mindful, even) understand that company performance starts with taking care of the individual employee. The following are the most frequently selected goals (performance areas in this context) that our members set when using Whil's digital training.

- **Relax and stress less:** For many of us, stress impacts every aspect of our lives. Science suggests that our brains are actually wired to remember bad things more than good things.[4] Worse, our brain's natural negativity bias tends to reinforce just how bad things are. People want to be better at focusing on the present more and worrying about the past and future less.

- **Sleep better and feel rested:** All that worrying follows us to bed. When things are quiet, bad things can happen in our minds. We worry, and start judging ourselves and others. As you learned earlier, we make our brains highly efficient at the things we process most. Laying your head on the pillow is the perfect way to trigger the mind that it's time to worry, especially if you practice that. All. The. Time.

- **Be happier and enjoy life:** Your colleagues are just like you; they are hungry for a more fulfilling experience, laughter, and purpose.

As leaders, we have the interesting challenge and responsibility of balancing the performance needs of business with the interests of our employees. If we get it right, we'll create unstoppable businesses where people love to work, find human connection, give their all, and find fulfillment in their performance.

Whether you're looking to be a better athlete or artist, parent or partner, executive or employee, mindfulness can help. Anyone who practices solely with the intention of improving their "performance" will also find a more open, joyful, curious, and compassionate approach to life—a great side effect.

Pro Tip: If you're looking to "crush it," "kill it," "not freak out," and so on, you should feel good in doing what's right for you. Just don't hurt anyone. Also, you might like the 1987 movie *Wall Street*. I think you'll love the catchphrases.

What Benefits Can I Expect as A Leader?

I travel the world training leaders on mindfulness and emotional intelligence skills. When I survey professionals in our *CML Workshop* on the question "What does mindfulness mean to you?" the list is inspiring and routinely includes the following:

Calm	Collected	Leadership
Connected	Open	Authentic
Emotional intelligence	Strong	Pragmatic
Culture	Direct	Alert
Present	Insightful	Stable
Aware	Unbiased	Allowing
Inclusive	Kind	Grounded
Accepting	Empathetic	Vulnerable
Engaged	Self-aware	Understanding
Intentional	In control	Management
Peaceful	Thoughtful	Clear
Disciplined	Curious	Resilient
Balanced	In the zone	Adaptable
Nonjudgmental	Reflective	Positive
Centered	Retrospective	Happy
Purposeful	Human	Lower costs
At ease	Nonreactive	Harmonious
Available	Uncluttered	Grateful
Considerate	Heartful	Wellbeing
Transparent	Confident	Inner peace
Self-regulated	Social skills	Change
Motivated	Performance	Metrics
Resilience	Lower stress	Awake
Creativity	Listening	Saving lives

I was recently training 75 leaders in New York City, hosted at J. Walter Thompson's global headquarters. We had a running list of 40 to 50 items. We ended when a doctor attending the training yelled out, "Saving Lives." This is what mindfulness meant to her. She went on to explain to the audience, "Hospital shifts can mean 14-hour days. Doctors and nurses suffer from illness and injury at a rate 30% higher than the next closest industry—manufacturing.[5] We serve patients who wait too long to address serious health issues. By the time they come to us, they're unwilling and unable to participate in their own recovery. Without the right training, compassion fatigue takes years off the average healthcare worker's life." She had tears in her eyes and thunder in her voice. It was a drop-the-mic moment. It was touching, real, and everything else on the list felt cute in comparison. I couldn't have agreed more. We all need this in our lives. And mindfulness is about saving lives. Starting with your own. I've borrowed that sentiment in every live training since then.

This is a powerful list and another reason that leaders and companies are so interested in bringing mindfulness and emotional intelligence skills into their culture. Imagine the kind of leader you can be, and the kind of life you can enjoy, with more of this in your personal arsenal. Let's pause, take a breath, and set that intention. This is happening.

CHAPTER 6

You Versus Technology

Life is what happens between wifi signals.
—Random Millennial

Mobile devices are the best stress delivery mechanisms ever invented. And they get better twice a year. Faster, cheaper, able to stress people out in tall buildings. I can't wait to get the new iPhone XV. It mainlines stress directly into your prefrontal cortex.

According to Deloitte, Americans check their phones eight billion times a day, averaging out to about 46 times per day for each of us.[1] That's up from 33 times per day in just one year. Millennials average 150 times per day.[2] About 81% of U.S. adults have smartphones.[3] That adds up to a lot of time where the average person isn't being present with their friends, co-workers, or surroundings—let alone productive.

We're getting better at distracting ourselves. Addicted even. Researchers from the Network of Addictive Disorders consider cellphones to be one of the greatest addictions of the century. They highlight six types of behavior:

1. Habitual (usage with little awareness)
2. Mandatory (officially required or parentally mandated)
3. Voluntary
4. Dependent (driven by social norms)
5. Compulsive
6. Addictive (the progressive exclusion of other activities)

Figure 6.1   Who's winning?

We've reached the point at which we're actually becoming uncomfortable with any mental downtime. One study even showed that the average adult male would rather experience electroshock therapy than be left alone with their thoughts.[4] Yes—electroshock therapy. C'mon guys! What are you thinking?

Not only are we not giving our brains the time to recover, the excessive attention and uncontrolled dedication to our cellphones is harming our physical, mental, social, and work wellbeing. Here are two ways to reduce distractions to allow your brain to recover.

1.   Set three times during the day to use your device. That will disrupt the automaticity of constantly checking it.

2.   Check email for the final time before you get out of your car in the evening. Then turn it off and focus on your family.

Let your team know they can contact you until a certain time in the evening. After that, 99% of issues can wait until tomorrow. This also sets the tone for their own expectations.

> Pro Tip: Whil's sleep expert, Dr. Jeffrey Durmer, recommends no phones in the bedroom. Charge your phone in another room at night to avoid the temptation for distraction and protect your sleep.

WELLBEING PERFORMANCE RELATIONSHIPS CAREER SLEEP MOVEMENT

CHAPTER 7

Invest Five Minutes a Day to Save Your Life

Who has time for mindfulness?
—Clueless Leader

I occasionally hear from executives asking, "How can I spare 5 to 10 minutes a day for myself to practice mindfulness, let alone for our employees?" Come on, inner peace. We don't have all day!

These folks aren't familiar with how much time the average employee wastes during their day. It led me to create a new faux field of medicine called "Habit Replacement Therapy." Here's how it works. Pick one of the time sucks in your life or company culture and trim 5 minutes off every day. Replace your addictions, er, sorry, habits with 5 to 10 minutes of attention training—enough to produce the health and performance benefits I've shared in this book.

WHERE CAN I TRIM?

Don't stress. We've done a little research on a few areas to free up five minutes. Everyone can find the time.

Gaming. The NPD Group estimates there are 34 million "core" (heavy) gamers in the United States, with the average player spending 22 hours per week.[1] In her book, *SuperBetter*, Dr. Jane McGonigal puts that into perspective. Based on time spent playing, if Candy Crush Saga gamers were "employees," the game would have 3.7 million full-time equivalents (FTEs). Call of Duty would have 8.3 million FTEs.[2]

TV. The average American watches 4.3 hours of T.V. a day.[3] Crazy. At a minimum, record your favorite shows and fast forward through the commercials (that's about 15 minutes for every hour of TV).[4]

Social Media. The average U.S. Facebook and Twitter user spends 42 minutes and 17 minutes, respectively, on their daily fix. Most of that occurs at work.[5] Here's a little secret: it can wait. Cut five minutes from your habit and the same gripes, politics, and curated "best-life-ever" highlights from the people you haven't spoken to since high school will still be there.

Commuting. The average commute in the United States is 25 minutes.[6] If you take public transportation, put the news and your apps down for five. Pop on the headphones and get into a daily practice. If I did this while living in New York City, I could have replaced 20 years of loud-talking, end-of-the-world bible guy on my daily subway rides with peace of mind.

Insomnia. Fellow vampires, I used to be on your crew. But no more. Quit lying in bed for an hour before you worry yourself to sleep. Instead, take five minutes to replace that nonstop crazy with some goodness to ease yourself into rest. It's way better to sleep than to seethe.

B*tching. The walking dead tend to groan. The walking stressed tend to complain. Mindfulness can help with that, too. Imagine taking five minutes back from complaining about your company, your co-workers, your partner, your kids, your in-laws, and your weight, let alone complaining about complainers. Bastages.

Spacing. You know that the average person spends 47% of their time with the mind wandering. That's bad for relationships, raising kids, business, and getting sh*t done. We can all find five minutes out of the daily 676 minutes spent in the twilight zone.

Faux Gyming. You're thinking, "Wait. What? But that's good for me." Planet Fitness averages 6,500 members per gym.[7] However, most of its gyms can only accommodate 300 people. Smart business model.

If your gym is the timeshare you never use, you probably spend five minutes a day thinking about going and then not going. Boom. You just got that back, too. If you're a CrossFitter, take five minutes from the 30 a day you talk about CrossFitting.

It's Not About Trimming

The point of mindfulness is making it part of what you already do, not making it an extra task. The practices shared here can be done in 1-, 5-, or 10-minute increments. Many can also be done when you are focusing on things as basic as brushing your teeth, driving to work, lifting weights, or just listening to a colleague.

As Dr. Dan Siegel, Author and Neuropsychiatrist puts it, "Any individual can learn to focus their attention in a new way. This is a teachable skill. You can learn it at any age. Once you learn to focus your attention in a new way, you're getting the brain to fire in a new way … Your immune system will function in a more optimal way - Your cardiovascular profile, how your cholesterol levels, blood pressure, heart rate - all those things will be improved. Mindfulness meditation has been proven to create these benefits in our life."[8]

Pro Tip: Do a walking meditation each time you go to or from the restroom. Just bring mindful awareness to your breath and each step you take. Make it a practice to calm yourself before you relieve yourself.

Take the Time. Give the Time. As leaders, we should give our teams the time to learn and practice. Trust them to find the time in their day. It's just important to get started. And if you're paying attention to things like your life, your business, politics, global warming, and intergalactic goings-on, you probably have a sense that stress and anxiety issues aren't going to get any easier. Employees are already taking the time to complain and gossip. It's the human condition. Mix in community practices to get them talking about things that create a more healthy culture.

CEO Eileen Fisher is a longtime supporter of mindfulness in business, sharing, "Workplaces are all about people and relationships and how the energy works between people. I've had situations when two people are supposed to work tougher and, if they don't get along, that project is not working. So, the more we do mindfulness practices, what I have seen is the deepening of the work that we do at the company." Adding, "We grow Clothes. We grow people. And we grow business for good."[8]

Mindfulness training isn't about the 5 to 10 minutes of practice itself. It's about developing the life tools to more regularly reduce your own stress and anxiety and be more intentional about the things that matter most. It's about prescribing positivity for yourself, by applying the tools and techniques in the other 24 hours of your day, and especially in your work.

Too many of our habits, addictions, and predilections do the exact opposite. How many habits do you have that keep you revved up, worried, angry, or just escaping from life as the hours slip away? Pick one of your less important habits and try *Habit Replacement Therapy** today.

*Faux trademark pending.

Pro Tip: In her book, *Positivity*, Dr. Barbara Fredrickson shares how experiencing positive emotions in a three-to-one ratio to negative emotions leads people to be happier, healthier, and achieve more in life. Keep an eye on your ratios today.[9]

WELLBEING   RELATIONSHIPS

CHAPTER **8**

It's Not a Religion.
It's a Lifestyle.

> There are only two ways to live your life. One is
> as though nothing is a miracle. The other is as
> though everything is a miracle.
> —Albert Einstein

S aying you can't meditate because your mind wanders is like say- ing you can't exercise because you're out of shape. Just get started. As you cultivate a mindful lifestyle, bring the practices into every aspect of life. Replace the routines that don't serve you with ones that do. Here are some of the questions we get when coaching executives on making mindfulness a lifestyle.

WHAT'S THE RIGHT AGE TO TRY MINDFULNESS?

The short answer is now. Getting into a mindfulness practice is like going to the gym. People generally start when they're going through something difficult (for example, a breakup, putting on weight, bad boss, death of a loved one, sleep issues, and so on), and they want to feel better. When it comes to your mental and emotional wellbeing, don't wait for a crisis.

Mindfulness Is for the Masses

Mindfulness training is for anyone who wants to be happier, reduce stress, increase their resilience, or improve their "performance"— whatever that means for you. You don't have to be a certain height to ride, but we do see trends where people seem most motivated to manage the stress at key points in their lives.

Entering the Workforce. The goal is to get these skills to professionals at the earliest age possible. Living in the age of disruption, innovation, and transformation can suck for new hires or anyone experiencing competition without guardrails for the first time. They're no longer surrounded by teachers, family, and friends who are confirming that they're the best. To the contrary, life is ambiguous in the corporate world.

I recall being 26 at Price Waterhouse and uncovering longstanding questionable financial activity at one of my clients. Following drawn out threats and intimidation, my findings resulted in both the client's President and CFO (as well as my own supervisor at PW) being terminated. Without the right skills to manage stress and regulate

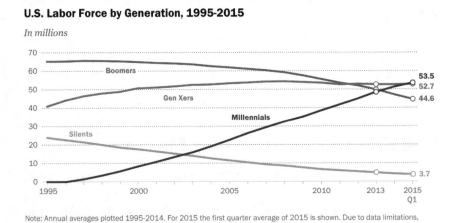

U.S. Labor Force by Generation, 1995-2015

In millions

Note: Annual averages plotted 1995-2014. For 2015 the first quarter average of 2015 is shown. Due to data limitations, Silent generation is overestimated from 2008-2015.

PEW RESEARCH CENTER

Figure 8.1   Millennials are in first place, but iGen is prepping to enter the race.

Source: Pew Research Center tabulations of monthly 1995–2015 Current Population Surveys, Integrated Public Use Microdata Series (IPUMS).

my nervous system, I was a young professional involved in an intense six-month drama where I felt the world was on my shoulders.

Today, millennials report the highest level of "extreme" stress of any generation and it's getting worse.[1] This is particularly concerning since they became the largest part of the workforce in 2015, surpassing Gen Xers (Figure 8.1).[2] To recap—our largest employee population is our most stressed out and they're poised to soon run our companies and our country. Don't forget that Centennials (Gen Z) are right behind them—the "iGen."

Mindfulness can improve a myriad of things like sleep, building confidence as a first-time manager, and being less judgmental of the old heads over 40. Mindfulness has also become a go-to strategy for staying calm when millennials are "adulting."

Pro Tip: As Millennials move into management, get used to more employees popping in their headphones and closing their eyes at their desk for a few minutes each day. Personalized micro meditation breaks like those on Whil will be the norm in the next few years.

When You Get Married or Settle Down. At this stage of life, in addition to settling down, many have bought their first home and/or had their first child. As wonderful as these events are, they're also major stressors. They rank high in the stress scales and they tend to come in waves.[3] These new responsibilities are usually when a paycheck takes on new meaning; when many professionals come to the realization, "Maybe I shouldn't tell my bosses to go (blank) themselves." It's also when many of us start burning out because we haven't developed the right mindset to manage family stress on top of work stress. Attention training teaches us patience, curiosity, and how to regulate our emotions.

People Over 50 or Nearing Retirement. The sandwich generation is both raising kids and caring for aging parents. The things that we pass over when we're younger start to catch up to us at this age, including our physical health, grief, regret, and guilt relating to difficult life experiences. Those over age 50 also start to suffer from insomnia; the mind just won't stop regretting the past and worrying about the future.

After 50, we know that life isn't a dress rehearsal. The realization that we have only a third of our lives still in front of us can be hard. Professionally, hitting 50 is also a critical juncture at which many leaders stagnate. The mistake of having a fixed mindset, or believing that we know everything, tends to catch up to us. It can impact a leader's confidence while simultaneously increasing the propensity to worry. Specific mindfulness practices help maintain a growth mindset, process regret, grief, and anxiety, as well as change sleep habits to quiet the restless mind.

Pro Tip: I don't like funerals. I've made it a practice to visit ill family members in person before they pass. In the past few years, I've said goodbye to my Uncle Bill and my Aunt Pat, both suffering from cancer. In addition to the visit, one of my favorite gratitude practices is writing a letter. It's nice to tell people what they mean to you, but there's something special about committing it to a handwritten note, especially when they are facing the unknown. Leave nothing unsaid or unwritten.

Start When You're Stressed

Human beings experience our greatest stress when major life changes occur. That happens normally when moving from college into the workforce, from single life into family life, and from being a mover and shaker to moving more slowly and shaking our heads at everything that annoys us. No matter your age or stressors, the important thing is to just get started and stick with it. It takes time to build the mindfulness muscle and do mental training. Even small doses will begin to retrain the brain. Consistency matters—these skills are crucial to combat modern stressors. Without them, it's easy for people to become overwhelmed at critical life stages regardless of their generation.

Make It RAIN

Feeling overwhelmed at any stage in life? Try the RAIN technique:

Recognize what is going on

Allow the experience to be there, just as it is

Investigate the feelings or situation with kindness

Non-identify, witness your emotions as though you are a third party. Then plan your way forward with a clear mind.

Stop Trying to Look Good

Teddy Roosevelt once said, "Comparison is the thief of joy." One of the most stressful human endeavors is comparing yourself to others, or trying to look good. As my mother-in-law says, "Caring about what others think is exhausting."

I was at SXSW last year and attended a barbeque reunion for Harvard Business School alumni. I'm a pretend HBS alum, having attended several of their amazing executive programs over the years. But I get the same alumni perks. And I like them a lot.

I walked into the event and immediately awarded the party the "most-tucked in shirts at SXSW," the most blue blazers with gold buttons, and the most Levi Dockers. I found them. All of them.

Like any school reunion, it was equal parts fun and pretentious. There was the required mix of overstating successes and covering up perceived missteps. Awareness training has taught me that most of us work too hard trying to look good. At. Any. Cost. It's part of the human condition, but it also takes the joy out of life. I spent most of my career trying to look good and convince people that I had all the answers. I've learned that being real and authentic (imperfections and all) is more fun, risky, and rewarding.

I worked the patio before joining three (real) MBAs who had graduated together. The conversation was dominated by one gent whose company went public. He'd done *very* well. We knew this because he told us. His bravado sucked the air out of an outdoor BBQ. His personal tale of success was well rehearsed. But he lamented now having to deal with the pains of managing "a real company" post IPO. Ah, hard work. The pain. The injustice.

> Pro Tip: Research shows that happy people avoid the trap of social comparison. Comparing yourself to others and being pressured to keep up with the Joneses is so last decade.[4]

Be Curious, Not Dismissive

As we went around our circle of four, his trying to look good kicked into overdrive. He was dismissive of the Wall Streeter. "Dude, make your money, move on, and do something cool." He was dismissive of the publisher. "People still buy books?" And when I shared that I owned a digital wellbeing training company, he was dismissive of me, too. "I'm so over the world's ridiculous fascination with mindfulness." Everything triggered him.

Try Vulnerability

We'd never met before, but I could relate to how he wore his opinions, emotions, and aggression to establish a facade of confidence. Been there. Done that. Rather than responding in kind, I tried openness and vulnerability, two foundational elements of mindfulness. I find that when I practice vulnerability, it usually results in others responding with the same. Let down your guard and just be yourself. I asked a number of questions to understand his perspective. He shared that in a hard-driving technology company, the last thing he could afford to speak to employees about was stress, let alone brain training, as an antidote. It would make his company look "weak" to talk about it. "Talking about stress stresses people out. And this mindfulness stuff is a fad. It won't last. It feels like it was invented five years ago."

The other members of our group were getting increasingly uncomfortable, sharing the "sorry, he's always been like this" look. They tried to pull the old "let-me-finish my-drink-quickly-so-I can-politely-leave-to get-another-one" trick. As a master of that very move, I called them on it and then asked our confident friend if I could ask some questions. He played along.

Authenticity Rocks

As the conversation continued, he admitted that stress is also a growing trend. He shared that his stress moved from an 8 to a 10 out of 10 following his company's IPO. He actually wasn't the founder of "his" company; that he joined just two years ago; that he was in business development and didn't have any staff; forget speaking to anyone about their stress. He also felt his management team wasn't interested in either his opinions or employee wellbeing. Finally, he shared that he wasn't happy and that he'd be leaving after he fully vested to do "what's next."

We then had a more open and authentic conversation with the rest of the group. We each shared that stress takes its toll and that most big companies tend to ignore it rather than address it. It's amazing what happens when people are open, vulnerable, and authentic. Here was a nice person who was employed, part of his life was good, part of his life was challenging, nothing more, nothing less. Just like the rest of us.

Mindfulness may be a trend. Like stress is a trend. Two long-standing trends that are about as likely to go away as trying to look good at an alumni barbeque.

Be Authentic

I spent most of my life carrying the unnecessary shame and regret of growing up poor and the embarrassment that our father went from welfare at 40 to Social Security at 62.

(continued)

(continued)

In my early 40s, I dropped that shame. I found that sharing my story, warts and all, is a great way to connect with others and a great relief to myself. Openness and vulnerability is generally met with the same.

The next time you're out interacting with a colleague, give it a try. In my case, it's allowed me to deepen relationships and learn more about the people I care about the most. It's allowed them to drop assumptions about me. I've learned to be proud of what I've accomplished, despite a less-than-ideal starting point. It's all made me who I am.

Most importantly, these practices have allowed me to stop trying to look good and just be myself. It turns out that you're way more interesting when you're authentic. Who knew?

LEAVE ROOM FOR THE JERKS IN YOUR LIFE

How many people have you written off in your life because you thought they were jerks? This is something I practiced and developed some expertise with as a C-level executive. Very early in most relationships, I would determine whether someone was worth dealing with. Either they were on my team or they were not. This was generally based on limited interactions. I'm not proud of it, but it's true.

Take Off the Robes, Judge Judy

How quick you are to judge people in your life? What does it take to set you off? If you're like I was, it doesn't take much. Research says that most people make a first impression within the first half a second.[5] I would hope that even the most advanced Type A personalities give others a few full meetings before writing someone off. However, in my experience, too many leaders are quick to make immovable judgments. We think we know someone well enough, based on a limited interaction, to put him or her into a box, permanently. Often times. that box determines how we deal with that person for the rest of infinity. You know the various boxes: jerk, know-it-all, selfish, arrogant, abrasive, d-bag, womanizer, and the list goes on. We're good at making lists when we're judging others. Leaders have an obligation to take a more mindful approach to avoid the temptations.

Pro Tip: We're actually many ways at different points in our day, let alone in our lives. When we're open to others occurring to us as jerks in one moment but as smart, funny, clever, or charming in other moments, then we actually give those moments a chance to appear. We give ourselves the chance to enjoy the many dozens of ways that others can occur, if we're open to it.

Forgiveness Practice

Take a moment to think of the worst person in your work life. Here's a two-minute exercise to change that relationship. Take a piece of paper. At the top, write down "Jerk and … " Under that, write all the other things that you know this person to be. That could include things like parent, brother or sister, runner, Cross-Fitter, tech enthusiast, worried, lonely, grieving, funny, clever, smart, chef, well read, and many more things. Write for two minutes without stopping.

To repair the relationship, take the time to share your reflection. It can be as easy as saying, "Hey Bob, I've been thinking about our working relationship. Our initial interaction didn't go as well as I would have liked. I want to apologize. There's so much I appreciate about you and your work. I know you have a lot going on, just like me. I'd like to give our relationship a fresh start. Are you open to that?"

Practicing Forgiveness and Empathy Is Important for a Few Reasons

Judging Is a Two-Way Street. People are judging you in the same way you're judging them. You had a bad moment or meeting and they put you in a box. You occur one way to them. At all times. It doesn't feel great to think of yourself in one dimension.

Don't Rob Yourself. We lose the opportunity to truly get to know others on a deeper level when we put them into boxes. We actually take away from our own experience when we don't give others some leeway to have a bad moment, bad day, or bad week. And when we do, we can't realistically expect others to do the same for us.

Once we draw the lines of judgment, we tend to gather support from others (join in on the judgment!) to prove that we're right and protect our own egos. It's easy to create an "us versus them" mentality. The next time you want to put someone in a box, keep these thoughts in mind:

Don't Hurt Yourself. Modern business requires dynamic relationships. Those relationships have a better chance of flourishing if you make room for forgiveness, acceptance, and the flexibility to accept people in the many different ways that they show up. Instead of putting others in boxes, start a conversation around what bothers you and how important that relationship is to you. This invites a conversation in which they can see your human side, too.

Look for Common Ground. We all have difficult aspects to our lives. And we all deserve an opportunity for others to experience us as diverse and complex. Allow yourself and others to show up as "flawesome" (flawed and awesome), wonderful, charming, opinionated, and infuriating. This alone can be a point of similarity upon which to build trust. That's the beauty of being human. And it's the obligation of being a leader.

HANDLING DIFFICULT CONVERSATIONS

When you're leaving rooms for the jerks in your life, it's also important not to be one. Every leader's job description should include "handle

difficult conversations with people you believe to be unreasonable."
Too many leaders allow unhealthy dynamics to continue with
employees, vendors, and partners to avoid the friction of difficult
conversations. Here are some of my favorite resources to help.

- In their book, *Difficult Conversations*, Douglas Stone, Bruce
  Patton, and Sheila Heen share that there are actually three
  levels of conversation in each interaction:

  1. The content (what happened?)
  2. The feelings (what emotions are involved?)
  3. The identity (what does this say about me?)

  Only by exploring all three can you truly connect in a
  way that satisfies the other person.[6]

- Author Brene Brown shares a 10-step checklist to know when
  you're prepared to give healthy feedback. When:[7]

  1. I'm ready to sit next to you rather than across from you.
  2. I'm willing to put the problem in front of us rather than
     between us (or sliding it toward you).
  3. I'm ready to listen, ask questions, and accept that I may
     not fully understand the issue.
  4. I want to acknowledge what you do well instead of pick-
     ing apart your mistakes.
  5. I recognize your strengths and how you can use them to
     address your challenges.
  6. I can hold you accountable without shaming or blaming
     you.
  7. I'm willing to own my part.
  8. I can genuinely thank you for your efforts rather than
     criticize you for your failings.
  9. I can talk about how resolving these challenges will lead
     to your growth and opportunity.
  10. I can model the vulnerability and openness that I expect
      to see from you.

> Pro Tip: Our friend, author Michael Landers, shares in his book *Culture Crossing* that the Golden Rule ("Do unto others") is dead. With the Western culture shift from We to Me, leaders can no longer treat employees the way *we* want to be treated. We need to treat people the way *they* want to be treated to bring out personal fulfillment and performance. Understanding that is especially important in difficult relationships.[8]

Taking a mindful approach allows us to slow down and be intentional about important interactions. Even if they're not so important to you, leaders must consistently act in the service of their employees.

MINDFUL EATING PRACTICE

When it comes to a healthier lifestyle, studies have shown that mindful eating strategies help weight loss and treating eating disorders. Awareness training also helps people enjoy their food more and be less focused on controlling their eating. Not only that, but those who meditated more got even better results.[9] This is important if you tend to work long hours, travel, or drink too much. Research shows that lack of sleep and stress lead to unhealthy eating. Our bodies actually crave fatty foods and sugar when our systems are off balance. This can result in obesity, diabetes, and take years off of our lives. When the automaton takes over, it's easier to put on weight, which can also hurt self-confidence.

Over time, mindful eating can bring the thinking brain online to interrupt poor choices, including our tendency to over-consume the "five white poisons"—refined sugar and salt, flour, milk, and rice.

Mindful Eating

Try this short practice with your family tonight. Slowing down to be present can also extend to your meals. Bring moment-to-moment awareness to your eating as well as your

Figure 8.2   Being mindful translates to better food choices

eating habits. Noticing what you select. How much. Each bite. The flavors and textures.

When we're not fully present and aware, we tend to wolf down unhealthy meals to get to the TV or back to work. Use meal times as an opportunity to slow down, enjoy food, connect with yourself, and intentionally give your mind a break. Slowing down also helps the body to recognize when it's full.

Pro Tip: Doing good is good for you. Research has shown that people who volunteer their time to help charitable causes increase their level of optimism, connectedness to humanity, and ultimately, their health.[10]

MINDFUL WALKING PRACTICE

Ever spend a day running around and when it ends you can't really remember what you did, who you met, or even if you ate lunch? On these days, we're just going through the motions without really being present to what's happening. Going through life distracted becomes our lifestyle.

You can interrupt this tendency to be a zombie by doing a daily mindful walking exercise. Don't worry. You don't have to walk slow or look weird. It can be done formally or informally as you walk anywhere.

Mindful Walking

Put your phone away. Pay attention to each step and movement. Bring attention to the body, breath, thoughts, feelings, and the experience of walking in the environment. Take in each smell, sight, and sound.

Feel each step hitting the ground. Notice how different parts of your body feel as you move. As distracting thoughts come into your mind (and they will), label them with one word and let them pass. Set an intention to do one or two mindful walks every day. Build them into your existing routines to and from the office, on the way to the bathroom, and so forth. Get your steps in and train your ability to focus at the same time. Make giving your mind a break an intentional part of your lifestyle.

Pro Tip: Sitting is the new smoking. Rather than destroy your health or turn into a keyboard hunchback, set your smart watch or a timer to get up and move at least once every hour. In his book, *Brain Rules: 12 Principles for Surviving and Thriving at Work, Home, and School*, biologist John Medina shares that our ancestors averaged 12 miles a day walking. 12 miles! Humans used to be cardiovascularly fit! Exercise keeps us mentally alert. It doesn't take much, walking a few times a week at a modest clip - 30 minutes will do.[11]

If Journaling Is for Teenage Girls, Buy Me Some Hairclips

In my early 40s, a friend recommended that I try journaling when I was suffering from burnout. My response was literally, "Do I look like a teenage girl?" This was meant to be funny. I looked like a teenage girl's middle-aged father.

When I looked into the "science" behind journaling (not realizing that was even a thing), what I found was fairly surprising:

- Writing can boost immunity for those battling terminal or life-threatening diseases.[12]

- People writing about traumatic, stressful, or emotional events are significantly more likely to have fewer illnesses and be less affected by trauma.[13]

- Gratitude journaling can improve sleep.[14]

- People who were unemployed and started journaling found work 68% faster.[15]

From Skeptic to Scribe

Since my skeptical introduction to journaling, I've found it to be an incredibly powerful life reflection and planning tool. I can work through difficult thoughts or prepare for hard conversations. It allows me to anchor back to what's most important in my life; something we could all use a little more of. And I enjoy capturing future plans. There's something about writing them down and committing that makes them come to be. Commit and the universe moves in your favor. Intentions matter.

The primary benefit isn't having the written history. It is instead an active training tool to help me more intentional in managing a busy and sometimes stressful life.

In preparing to write *CML*, I was flipping through my journals and came across an old post. This is from the night I first met my wife. At the time, I had been single in New York City for 10 years. While I enjoyed dating in the Big Apple, I often found it lonely and unfulfilling. I was at high risk of becoming one of those middle-aged, used-to-being-on-my-own, stuck-in-my-ways kinda guys. Until that night, I'd never journaled about a relationship.

> Tonight, I met a woman named Sarah Swanson. She is a beautiful South African and I believe that she will steal my heart.
>
> We talked, laughed, and danced at Kevin's birthday party. I asked her out to dinner within five minutes of meeting her. She is smart, has the most beautiful smile, incredibly honest eyes, and the grace of a dove (despite falling off her stool and into my lap!).
>
> I learned that she is at the tail end of a breakup. I told her that although I'm sorry for that, I am also happy for me—assuming she'd accept my dinner invitation.
>
> Well, she did. And I can't remember ever being so excited to meet someone again. Fingers crossed. After having known her for only a few hours, I knew that I have never felt this way about someone before. I believe I may have just met my wife. Thank you, Fate (and to Kristin for putting in a good word for me).

Over the time we dated, I journaled often to explore why past relationships hadn't worked out. I even saved our email correspondence and letters and compiled them into a book—the journal of my relationship with Sarah. Two and a half years later, we were married. In hindsight, it was cathartic to capture intentions, work through my own limitations as a long-time bachelor, and explore another person in writing. Living with intention has become part of my lifestyle. Journaling supports that by enabling active reflection and planning. Planning creates growth and outcomes.

Pro Tip: Try journaling to work through all manner of life's challenges and opportunities. For Type A professionals, you may find the biggest benefits to be (1) managing with more intention, and (2) forcing yourself to focus on very specific topics a few times a week. Try writing for five minutes each morning on goals for the day. It's a great way to relax and help the brain recover. Science suggests that watching news, TV, and social media produce the opposite effect.

Balance the High Cost of Outsourcing Your Brain to Apps

If you want to outsource some of your brain's cognitive functions, there's an app for that!

In the wonderful world of technology, we've seen many apps have increasingly freed us of the need to think. It's amazing. And somewhat concerning. We've replaced the need for cognitive functions related to driving directions and remembering addresses, phone numbers, and restaurants (love me some Yelp!). Our news is curated by RSS feeds. And forget the full news—reading headlines is the new well-read. Even doctor visits are 50% young nurses feeding your answers into a computer. Thanks. I could have Googled my symptoms at home. Goodbye bedside manners. So long having to learn new things. Short-term and long-term memory are no longer needed, and comprehension and, to a large degree, human interaction skills are being sidelined like Colin Kaepernick.

What Have You Replaced That Time With?

The good news for the business world should be that all these apps have freed up a significant amount of thinking time. We now have more time to dedicate to higher-purpose endeavors. The bad news is that most of us haven't filled that available cognitive space with anything of value. In fact, we've filled that excess capacity with lifestyles anchored around checking news feeds, playing video games, worrying about the past, surfing porn, worrying about the future, checking feeds, regret, anxiety, checking feeds, and a full range of distractions that are detrimental to our health. Let me check my feed. Oh, and cat videos. Though my friend Mak points out that some cat videos can actually boost energy and positive emotions.[16]

Increasingly, we're outsourcing our abilities to remember, recall, and connect the dots to the basic information that drives our lives. We're also no longer using the brain to do these things. Remember that Microsoft study that suggests the human attention span has decreased to the level of a goldfish?

Apply digital wisdom to use your apps mindfully. Don't over-rely on them. Most importantly, find new ways to keep your brain sharp. You know, for when the robots take over. Attention training does that by creating new neural pathways and building up muscle memory in areas where we need it most. This also keeps our brains functioning at their best for things like memory, recall, and self-regulation.

As we outsource more of our cognitive abilities, brain training helps keep our cognitive abilities intact. We also need to stay active to ward off things like Alzheimer's, dementia, and a range of mental disorders.

Outsourcing feels great. You know there's an app for that. But maintaining a mindful lifestyle requires insourcing other experiences to keep you and your employees' cognitive abilities active. The mind is still a terrible thing to waste.

WHAT PART DO YOU PLAY IN OFFICE POLITICS?

Politics can bring out the worst in us. Especially when labels are used to manipulate or do harm. The United Kingdom's Brexit vote and the 2016 U.S. presidential race presented two low points that seeped into the corporate world. Candidates were masterful at touting their amazing records and ignoring the reality of the highs and lows everyone experiences over time. They used labels to create false praise for themselves, while simultaneously damaging the reputations of their competitors.

Save Labels for Envelopes

The same politics, manipulation, and labeling happens in the corporate world all the time. These behaviors are a cornerstone for employees who don't feel heard and thrive on politics, insecurity, creating winners and losers, and protecting their turf.

If members of your team become masters at labeling others in order to do damage, it's time to take stock. These kinds of character attacks are subtle but deadly in the corporate world. If you're like me, you'll recall co-workers whose reputation labels preceded them. There's the guy who didn't care because he has family money. The backstabber who couldn't be trusted. The one who didn't do any work, but took all the credit. Or the person who slept their way to the top. These labels require little thought, but can do tremendous harm.

Corporate politics, rumors, and innuendos are used to make someone look good and someone else look bad. Over time, they can turn individuals, departments, and teams against each other. They become part of the company's culture. They divide teams, create blind spots, and play into the hands of insecure managers.

I've seen this play out a staggering number of times. I'm also guilty of playing the game. It's isolating, stressful, and removes the joy from teamwork.

Here are five tips to create more kind, open, and honest work environments:

1. **Use Personal, Mindful Labels.** Rather than labeling colleagues as wasteful, lazy, or untrustworthy, practice labeling your own emotions. Train yourself to notice anger, resentment, fear, and so on. Science shows that the simple act of labeling your emotions engages the thinking brain. The PFC filters your thoughts, words, and actions while preventing the emotional brain from taking over and b*tch

slapping someone before you can register what happened. Make self-compassion a practice to avoid heated action without thought.

2. **Filter Your Words.** What if everything you said went through a three-step filter: Is it true? Is it kind? Is it necessary? If you're like me, you'd probably say a lot less. What you do say will be received more willingly and produce better outcomes.

3. **Monitor Your Actions.** Business professionals are trained to identify and fix problems, look strong, and respond quickly. What if you trained yourself to stop, breathe, notice, reflect, and *then* respond. Instead of jumping right in, you might stop to notice: Why am I angry? Is this related to me? Do I even need to respond? This sacred pause can change how you react to and treat others.

4. **Expect the Same from the Team.** Lowering the bar for professionalism and decency isn't a slippery slope—it's a jagged cliff. Tolerating politics, insecurity, bigotry, or labeling from some team members sets the tone for everyone. The best teams are able to have strong opinions while maintaining respect and a safe environment.

5. **Come Together.** At Whil, our team comes together every day at 3 p.m. for a 10-minute mindfulness practice (Figure 8.3). We cycle through one training program per week led by a different teammate. It's an opportunity to learn, build trust, and to truly get to know each other. It's become a foundational part of our culture - so much so that we now offer digital team programs for our clients around the world.

Pro Tip: The state of politics around the world may have your employees stuck in unhealthy discussion and social media battles. With some patience and compassion, this could be a teachable moment to bring out the humanity in your team.

> Getting stuck in a culture of us versus them is all too easy. Real discourse requires patience, openness, and curiosity. Is your business having an impact on society or simply being impacted by it?

Next are three mindful tips to do your part in healing relationships for a more kind, open, and connected culture.

Apologize to Someone Today. We all carry around unresolved issues. Over time, that resentment does harm to the person carrying the resentment, not the one being resented. Author Christin Carter recommends a three-step process: "(1) Tell them what you feel, (2) Admit your mistake and the negative impact that it had, and (3) Make the situation right."[17] Dr. Amit Sood at the Mayo Clinic also recommends

Figure 8.3   Daily 3p.m. mindfulness practice with the Whil team.

making forgiveness an ongoing practice to improve your health. If you could pick one issue in your life to apologize and forgive, how much would that be worth? Imagine a calmer, happier you every day.

Expect and Offer Transparency. Let others know what is upsetting you in the moment. Expecting them to guess while you seethe silently prolongs pain and division. It's okay to have differences. In fact, recognizing differences makes the world interesting. We can love family and friends regardless of their opinions and political affiliation. Unless they support the Green Party.

Wish Your Enemy Well. Rather than making pretend enemies, pick the one Facebook or Twitter friend who has turned you off with their politics to the point at which you're about to unfriend their stupid @ss. Now, instead of doing that, take a minute to silently wish them well. Simply say to yourself, "May you be happy. May you be open to others. May you find joy. And may we be friends." Research has shown that a Loving-Kindness Meditation produces positive emotions and a wide range of personal resources, including increased awareness, purpose, social support, and decreased illness symptoms. These, in turn, predicted increased life satisfaction and reduced depressive symptoms.[18] It pays to make acceptance and compassion a practice.

The past few years in global politics have confirmed that it's easy to spread fear and division. As leaders, we have an obligation to spread acceptance, kindness, and compassion if we expect to build sustainable and healthy cultures. With practice, it can even become part of our lifestyle.

PART II

FOR YOUR COMPANY

CHAPTER **9**

Reality Check: How Toxic Is Your Work Culture?

The key to being a good manager is keeping the people who hate me away from those who are still undecided.

—Casey Stengel

The *Harvard Business Review* defines *culture* as "consistent, observable patterns of behavior in organizations."[1] It's how we work, speak to one another and treat each other. How we make decisions, what we tolerate, and how we feel day to day. You'll notice that this definition does not include snacks, free lunch, or unlimited vacations. Those are perks that help people tolerate a crappy culture.

As a company, it may sound great to be driving ongoing disruption, transformation, digitization, and innovation. But if the average employee isn't equipped to meet the challenge, then not so much. Companies all over the world tell us they feel like they're losing their culture. Increasing stress is turning more work cultures into a worsening mix of *Hunger Games*, *Lord of the Flies*, and *Office Space*.

I recently attended a Bersin by Deloitte *Impact* conference. They drew over 1,000 top human resources executives from around the world. In one panel on culture, I posed the question, "Would you agree that the majority of companies are experiencing toxic cultures?" The panel debated that for about 10 minutes. Ultimately, four of the top strategists in the world not only agreed, they estimated that 80% to 90% of companies they advise suffer from toxic cultures.

This wasn't surprising to the audience. We've already covered the stressors and trust issues. If you were to ask your employees in one or two words to describe your company culture, what would they say? More than a few might answer high-stress, low morale, overload, insecurity, no control, no loyalty, or no community. Some may even use one long F-bomb as it relates to the pace of business. It can be easy for leaders to get caught up in the grind and kick into autopilot, or what social psychologist John Bargh calls "automaticity," in which the brain locks into unhelpful routines without even being aware of it.[2] Or what I call, "same sh*t, different day" syndrome. What's feeding your company culture?

EMOTIONAL CULTURE MATTERS

In over a decade of research, Sigal Barsade and Olivia A. O'Neill, professors at Wharton and George Mason University, respectively, found that emotional culture influences everything from employee satisfaction, burnout, and teamwork to hard measures like financial performance and absenteeism. "Countless empirical studies show the significant impact of emotions on how people perform on tasks, how engaged and creative they are, how committed they are to their organizations, and how they make decisions."[3] Positive emotional cultures were consistently associated with better performance, quality, and customer service. Likewise, negative emotional cultures were associated with group anger, sadness, fear, poor performance, and high turnover. Early in my career, I experienced this first hand as the CFO of a division of a public company that changed CEOs five times in six years. Gulp. Talk about stress. It was like building on quicksand. Emotional culture matters.

STRESS AND THE COMMANDING LEADER

When the subject comes to company culture, ongoing stress and negative emotions translate into people not treating each other well. In his book, *Emotional Intelligence*, Daniel Goleman researched six different leadership styles. We each have a desired way of being. That could be coaching, visionary, affiliative, pacesetting, or democratic.[4] Each is self-explanatory and descried in the Figure 9.1. It's no surprise that when leaders get stressed, they tend to adopt the sixth leadership style, "Commanding." That sounds like "No excuses. Hit the numbers. Get it done. Ship the product. Just make the client happy."

If company culture is made up of consistent, observable patterns of behavior, then enough stressed-out managers make for a highly commanding culture. The shorthand for this commanding management style is what most would recognize as "faster, cheaper." In my experience, this is table stakes in most companies. You have to be running a more-with-less playbook to keep pace. That doesn't mean it's fun. But it's important to balance this necessity by developing a culture with the right communication, training and intention.

> Pro Tip: Stanford Business School estimates 120,000 deaths result from stress each year because of an accumulation of long hours and perceived lack of job security, fairness, and control.[5] To balance the stress created by "Commanding" managers, build employee wellbeing into the foundation for your company culture.

It's Easy to Slip

I've fallen victim to the commanding style on too many times to count. In my late 20s, I was the youngest divisional CFO in Young & Rubicam's history. And a little full of myself. In the early days of hacking, the FBI contacted our company to inform me that we'd been hacked. Our payroll records were accessed and sold to criminals. That resulted in certain employee bank accounts being compromised. We met with the FBI and the impacted employees. As the FBI approached a breakthrough in their investigation, they asked us not to alert others because it could compromise their investigation. We agreed. Immediately following that meeting, one employee took it upon herself to send out a blast email to the company. It compromised

The Six Leadership Styles

	Commanding	Visionary	Affiliative	Democratic	Pacesetting	Coaching
The leader's modus operandi	Demands immediate compliance	Mobilizes people toward a vision	Creates harmony and builds emotional bonds	Forges consensus through participation	Sets high standards for performance	Develops people for the future
The style in a phrase	"Do what I tell you."	"Come with me."	"People come first."	"What do you think?"	"Do as 1 do, now."	"Try this."
Underlying emotional intelligence competencies	Drive to achieve, initiative, self-control	Self-confidence, empathy, change catalyst	Empathy, building relationships, communication	Collaboration, team leadership, communication	Conscientiousness, drive to achieve, initiative	Developing others, empathy, self-awareness
When the style works best	In a crisis, to kick start a turnaround, or with problem employees	When changes require a new vision, or when a clear direction is needed	To heal rifts in a team or to motivate people during stressful circumstances	To build buy-in or consensus, or to get input from valuable employees	To get quick results from a highly motivated and competent team	To help an employee improve performance or develop long-term strengths
Overall impact on climate	Negative	Most strongly positive	Positive	Positive	Negative	Positive

Our research found that leaders use six styles, each springing from different components of emotional intelligence. Here is a summary of the styles, their origin, when they work best, and their impact on an organization's climate and thus its performance.

Figure 9.1   What's your default leadership style?

Source: Modified and reprinted with permission. Goleman, Daniel, "Leadership that Gets Results," Harvard Business Review. March-April 2000 p. 82-83.

the investigation. Sitting in my office, she made it clear that she didn't care. This was frustrating for me. I thought I was a big deal. I was the CFO. I had a small sofa in my office and everything. My emotions got the best of me. Dropping into a commanding style, I stood and pointed to the door, "Get out of my office." She said, "No." I didn't really have anything else to say. So I left. It was a sad day for emotional intelligence skills. But a great learning experience for me.

Fun with the Internet

If you'd like to see an example of what happens when leaders let their egos and a commanding style get in the way, do a Google search for "Eddie Izzard and Death Star Canteen sketch."[6] You'll find an incredibly funny Lego Darth Vader modeling the exact opposite of emotional intelligence. It happens more than most leaders are willing to admit. You're welcome!

Pay Attention to Culture

In the face of a tough culture, all leaders can slip into styles that may not serve them. Here's a five-minute reflection and planning (journaling) practice to help bring those issues to the surface. Set a timer. Move on to the second writing prompt at the midway point.

Your first prompt is: What I don't like about our company culture is …

Your next prompt is: To make a better culture, I will …

Throughout Whil's training, we encourage members to not only explore issues, but also resolution. That includes taking personal responsibility and accountability. Each of us

(continued)

(continued)

creates the culture we operate in. Complaining and negativity can quickly become the culture. And because of neuroplasticity, it can become an ingrained personal habit. This is especially important for leaders. Research by Gallup shows a clear link between employee engagement and wellbeing. When leaders become wellbeing cheerleaders, engagement drastically rises.[7] The opposite is also true.

REARRANGING DECK CHAIRS

Unless you're actively addressing the primary drivers of employee stressors, you might describe your culture as "We demand faster, cheaper and ignore systemic market forces in the face of increased evidence that employees don't like it here. And we have good snacks."

If your culture is simply accepting disruption, speculation, and frustration as the norm, you may have a culture problem that a PR spin won't help. Negative emotions are part of a company's emotional culture. Here are a few ways to manage them effectively:

- Look for ways to emulate the companies showcased in Raj Sisodia, David Wolfe, and Jag Sheth's book, *Firms of Endearment: How World-Class Companies Profit from Passion and Purpose*. In it, they describe humanistic companies that "seek to maximize their value to society as a whole, not just to shareholders. They are the ultimate value creators: They create emotional, spiritual, social, cultural, intellectual, ecological, and, of course, financial value. People who interact with such companies feel safe, secure, and fulfilled in their dealings."[8] Employees enjoy working for these companies. Customers enjoy buying from them. And communities enjoy having them as neighbors. Of the 76 companies showcased, all have incorporated mindfulness training programs into their culture. This includes Adobe, Costco, Disney, Southwest

Airlines, Whole Foods, REI, Trader Joe's, USAA, BMW, IKEA, Unilever, and Honda. As a group, they outperformed the S&P 500 stock performance by eight times. More proof that humanistic, mindful, and emotionally intelligent business practices create a competitive advantage.

- Bring people together to create community. Whether it's monthly happy hours, celebrating big wins with team karaoke, or offsites, a team that bonds with one another builds a healthy company culture that is imperative to sustainable high performance.

- Add mental wellbeing to your quarterly staff surveys. When in doubt, ask. Check in on the level of employee stress in an open and transparent way with the intention to open up the conversation instead of ignoring it.

- Recognize the numbers. One in five Americans suffers from depression or anxiety.[9] That's at least two members of your 10-person board of directors. That's 10 people in a 50-person sales department. You may not know who they are, but you can create a culture that supports mental wellbeing.

When things get busy, the first thing that goes is that we forget to take care of ourselves. Performance suffers when wellbeing slips. Find what the biggest issue is first and focus on that for a quarter. Then move on to the next big thing. Remember the old African proverb, "If you want to go fast, go alone. If you want to go far, go together."

Pro Tip: People don't leave jobs; they leave managers. When the subject comes to your culture, start with your own wellbeing as a leader and you'll have a better chance of improving the inner workings and emotional culture of your team and organization.

SLEEP

CHAPTER **10**

Sleepless Nights and the Walking Dead

People ask me if I sleep well at night with
all of the competition. I tell them I sleep like
a baby—I wake up every two hours and cry.
—Roberto C. Goizueta

Zombies are slowly killing your company culture. Are you one of them? According to the Centers for Disease Control and Prevention (CDC), one-third of us suffer from insomnia.[1] A growing body of work indicates that poor sleep is a killer. In fact, if you took the CDC map of U.S. sleep issues and overlaid it with their maps for heart disease and poor mental health, you'd find nearly perfect correlations across states.[2-4] People suffering from insomnia are 10 times more likely to suffer from depression, at 60% greater risk for obesity, and miss 11 more days of work annually because of absenteeism and presenteeism.[5]

Beyond taking years off of people's lives, insomnia also takes a toll on culture. Remember our definition of culture—consistent, observable patterns of behavior. If one-third of your workforce (leaders included) have sleep issues, they also struggle with focusing, productivity, and generally being nice to co-workers. Insomnia turns us into zombies looking to kill fun and rip the flesh from the joy around us. When you don't sleep, you may as well wear a T-shirt that says, "Leave me alone. I'm a jerk today." You don't have to imagine one-third of your company experiencing this. It's already happening. #TheWalkingDead

Worse, for workers in jobs like construction, manufacturing, utilities, or oil and gas, the lack of sleep is the equivalent of being hung over. Even one bad night can reduce your motor reflexes significantly.[6] Now, imagine you're behind the wheel of a tractor trailer or forklift, or operating in dangerous conditions. It's like going to work drunk—skip 20 to 25 hours of snooze time and you'd be well over the U.S. legal driving limit at 0.1%.[7] In these cases, the lack of sleep can also place bystanders in harm's way. In 2014, a Walmart truck slammed into comedian Tracy Morgan's limo, killing a passenger. The driver fell asleep at the wheel in the middle of a 14-hour shift, having been awake for 28 hours.[8] While the $10 million dollar settlement grabbed head-lines, similar issues happen every day in business and go unnoticed. In fact, AAA estimates that sleepy drivers account for 328,000 accidents every year in the United States.[9]

WHY AM I SO DAMN GOOD AT INSOMNIA?

We're training our brains all the time. We get better at the things we do most. Think about your sleep patterns. What do you practice constantly? Are you training good sleep habits? Or are you like one-third of Americans who train themselves to be *zombies*, great at insomnia?

As leaders, we have to protect our own sleep to ensure we're at our best. Most of us don't. That led the Whil team to create a four-week digital sleep training program with FusionHealth and Dr. Jeffrey Durmer called *"Synchronize Your Mind and Body for Better Sleep."* I'm borrowing from Dr. Durmer's work here with his permission. Jeff is a systems neuroscientist, neurologist, and sleep medicine physician. He's also one of the coolest peeps I know. On top of ridiculous credentials, including working with the Fortune 500, the Atlanta Falcons, and the Federal Aviation Administration (FAA), he's also annoyingly good looking. Our team calls him, "super hot sleep Doc." They call me Joe.

Dr. Durmer has worked with thousands of professionals to address the impact of sleep on their physical, mental, and emotional health, their performance, and their overall quality of life. In his work with everyone ranging from truck drivers to CEOs, Jeff tells me, "I've found that people who 'suffer from their sleep, rather than savor it' don't really know why. That results in years of misperception, sloppy sleep behaviors, or easily treatable sleep disorders."

Dr. Durmer uses the science of sleep and circadian neurobiology to improve the quality of life for professionals suffering from sleep issues. He trains strong leaders to be "strong sleepers." This is important. Too many of us actually train to be terrible sleepers. By the time we lie down at night, our daytime activities have already set the stage for an awful night's sleep. Then we feed the insomnia beast. We start with a hint of strong worrying, add a big dose of regret, sprinkled with anxiety and a splash of grief, longing, and maybe a few conspiracy theories for dessert. We cycle through our to-do lists for the next day. Or next week. Or next year. The more we do this, the better the brain gets at revisiting these thoughts. It becomes a routine. A habit. We become increasingly efficient at driving ourselves nuts. The more we train ourselves to be experts at insomnia, the more it limits our ability to be effective leaders.

REM And Non-REM Sleep Both Matter

Sleep is so natural that it works like hunger and thirst. Your brain builds up a "hunger" for sleep (like a zombie wants brains) when it's awake for too long. When you expend enough energy, you experience sleepiness. This trigger starts your mind and body on a well-choreographed "change of state" from being awake into being asleep. This "sleep dance" includes two distinct types: rapid eye movement (REM) sleep and non-REM sleep.

For most, our sleep switches between REM and non-REM every 90 to 120 minutes throughout the night. The first half is dominated by non-REM sleep, providing your body and brain with essentials to restore function, fight disease, and inflammation. It is also why you feel rested even if you've slept only a few hours. Basically, your brain clears out what you don't need at night, giving you that "refreshed" feeling when you wake. Dr. Durmer calls it, "Taking out the trash."

This is also the time your body heals itself by lowering blood pressure, heart rate, body temperature, blood glucose, and insulin levels. Without non-REM sleep, your brain and body would be unprepared for life.

REM sleep is distinct from non-REM sleep because it comes and goes. REM sleep is associated with dreaming, memory, and emotion. If non-REM is housekeeping for the brain, REM sleep is housekeeping for the mind.

When you feel the stress of the day in your mind or through body tension, it pulls you out of the natural process of programmed sleep. Because of that, being a bad sleeper often correlates to being a less effective leader. Jeff points out, "The rate of sleep disorders is very high. And most go untreated because individuals don't know what to look for. But there is good news. Just as you can learn to control your emotions with mindfulness, you can also learn to control the mind-body synergy that leads to sleep."

Turn Off the "Wake"

It's important to know how the brain produces wakefulness so that you can learn to turn it off when it's time for bed. We build up a "sleep hunger" throughout the day as we burn energy. This is satisfied (reversed) by sleep. There is also a system in your brain that creates wakefulness, and it's unique because it also responds to light.

The wake system functions a bit differently from sleep, in that there is no "hunger" that accumulates. Instead, wakefulness happens because we have a cellular switch deep in a part of the brain called the hypothalamus. It's like a 24-hour pacemaker for wakefulness. This neural pacemaker, known as the Suprachiasmatic Nucleus (let's just call it the SCN) synchronizes wake-promoting hormones, neurochemicals, and shuts down sleep "hunger" when you wake up.

Because it is directly linked to light detection in your eyes, it becomes active when you see light. This is why getting light exposure in the morning and throughout your day is very effective for staying awake. It helps shut down sleepiness—much more effectively than caffeine, and it doesn't hang around in your brain for six to eight hours, either.

Figure 10.1   Sleep for success

Mindfulness can also help when you're sleep deprived. One study found meditators who sleep less actually had less of a decline in cognitive function than nonmeditators who don't sleep well.[10] Other studies have shown that mindfulness results in what scientists call the "relaxation response"—a physiological state of deep rest induced by practices like meditation and yoga. So even if you're not getting enough sleep, meditation helps you experience the deep rest your body needs for processes like energy metabolism and immunity.

UNDERSTAND YOUR SLEEP ENVIRONMENT

As your knowledge about sleep increases, you'll be able to look around your bedroom and identify problems like light. Light is the most important element to control when you're trying to synchronize your mind and body for sleep.

Here are 10 other fundamental principles from Dr. Durmer to develop a healthy sleep lifestyle:

1. Temperature: research shows that sleep is induced by a cool sleeping temperature (below 68 degrees Fahrenheit).

2. Noise: sounds that are continuous and monotonous can "mask" background noise that may wake a light sleeper.

(continued)

Try a ceiling fan, white noise generator, or nature sounds like water, wind, or waves.

3. Food: eating signals the brain and body that we have more energy to use and we should be awake. Large meals are to be avoided in the hours before sleep. You literally want to be "hungry" for sleep.

4. Alcohol: Ben Franklin once said, "Beer is proof that there is a God." But what Ben did not say is that alcohol is also a potent REM sleep suppressant. Avoid it whenever possible.

5. Nicotine: sitting may be the new smoking, but smoking is still cancerous life-altering stuff. It also kicks the wake system into overdrive through receptors for nicotine in the brain.

6. Drugs: this is a huge category that includes over-the-counter sleep aids (they're all basically antihistamines), prescription drugs, illicit or recreational drugs, and even vitamins. If you are regularly using some kind of substance to help you sleep, you could use some help. The very nature of sleep (like hunger, remember), means there's no need for supplements. Do you take a drug so you can get hungry? No.

7. Exercise: using up energy increases the signal for "time to sleep." Regular exercise is key to accentuating your "sleep hunger," but try not to jump right into bed immediately after exercise, because your nervous system may continue to be "stoked" for a couple of hours.

8. Unhealthy patterns: What do you do when you lie down to rest? Experts suggest turning off the TV and doing stuff to calm the mind, like reading a book. Too many of us spend our bedtime watching TV or surfing the web under the bright light of a mobile device. Both tend to keep us awake and excite neural pathways versus relaxing them.

9. Make the bedroom a sacred place: the bedroom is for sleeping and for occasional sexual activity. And if you're

married, increasingly occasional sexual activity. Use it for its intended purpose. *Do not* have a work desk in there.

10. Focus on your breath: mindfulness training helps you sleep by calming and relaxing you. One study found that insomniacs went to sleep 30 minutes faster and slept 22 minutes longer thanks to mindfulness training.[11] Focusing on your breath removes distractions. It's the equivalent of telling those negative board members in your head to take the night off.

Pro Tip: Dr. Durmer recommends you carve out at least 30 minutes to prepare for sleep to engage in "downshifting" activities for your mind and body. Put away the phone. Put down the remote. Pick up a book.

How Much Sleep Have You Lost? Let's pressure-test how you're building up your insomnia expertise. Over the past five years, how much sleep have you lost due to anxiety? There are 365 days in the year. On average, a person takes 10 to 20 minutes to fall asleep.[12] An insomniac can take one to two hours to get there. If that's you, in the past you may have "practiced" staying awake for hundreds of hours. In five years, that's approaching 3,500 hours. Most insomniacs suffer for years. It's not hard to see how easily we put in those 10,000 hours from Malcolm Gladwell's book *Outliers* to become top-notch experts at insomnia.

Having spent 30 years as a corporate road warrior, I learned the hard way. Prolonged insomnia reached the point of affecting my mood, my focus, and my judgment. As we age, sleep becomes increasingly more important for both our physical wellness and our mental wellbeing. For leaders, good sleep also has the intense side effects of decreasing grumpiness, snarkiness, and just being a jerk.

In patients with insomnia, mindfulness training improved both the quality and duration of their sleep.[13]

Treat sleep the way kids treat Pokémon cards: young kids quickly develop an expertise and understanding of the value of the individual cards. Early on, they may get tricked into trading a valuable one for a "chump" card. They quickly learn better. What if we all treated sleep as a precious object not to be traded away for another glass of wine, cup of coffee, or piece of cake? We'd train ourselves in new ways to protect what we value most. As I get older, sleep has moved way up on that list.

Don't wait to learn this later in life. Start treating sleep like your life depends on it. Because it does.

Pro Tip: Research at the Mayo Clinic shows the power of gratitude to improve your health.[14] Introduce a gratitude practice into your sleep routines. Name one or two things you're grateful for when lying down to sleep each night and do the same each morning when you wake up.

A Word of Caution. If your sleep is not improving, or if you're concerned about specific sleep symptoms such as snoring, restlessness, or nightmares, please see a specialist for an evaluation. Dr. Durmer says that nearly 80% of adults with sleep disorders suffer in silence not knowing they have a medical condition that needs attention. Don't be that person.

Sleep for Success Practice

This sleep meditation practice from the Whil training library will help you feel and release tension in your body using a body scan and breathing practice. It'll help prepare you for sleep.

Find a comfortable lying-down position. As you close your eyes, feel the whole body and its weight on the bed.

Feel your breath flowing gently in and out. Notice any thoughts that may be present. Allow them to fade into the background.

Slowly cycle through the entire body, piece by piece. Notice any particular places of tension or tightening, as well as any places of spaciousness and comfort.

Start by bringing attention to your face, jaw, and neck. Notice if you are holding any tension here. Behind the eyes, in the throat, and so forth. If you come across tension, feel it and notice if your attention causes it to release.

Then move your attention to the back of the head and neck, then the upper shoulders. Once again, notice any tension and bring soft awareness to your experience, allowing any tightness to melt and release.

Moving down, sense both arms and hands. Tighten your fists and release. Sense a quality of weight and comfort in your body as it releases tension. As you continue, check in with your breath. Allow it to flow with lightness and ease.

Now, sense the whole torso and any tightness or contraction in your chest or abdomen or back. Release any tension into the bed. Allow any thoughts and images to come and go. Bring attention to your heart center, then down to your belly. Each time, taking the time to experience how your body feels and releasing any tension you may experience.

Moving down to your upper legs, lower legs, and then into your feet. Notice your body feeling heavier and relaxed.

Close by again bringing attention to your whole body. Let go of any remaining tension. Feel into a sense of comfort and ease. Allow the breath to flow effortlessly in and out. Allow any thoughts to fade away and continue to focus on your breath as you drift off into a deep and restful sleep.

CHAPTER 11

Look, A Squirrel!
Distraction and the
Growing Safety Crisis

It is better to be careful 100 times than to get
killed once.

—Mark Twain

E very day in America, 13 people go to work and never go home.
Every year, 3.3 million suffer a workplace injury from which they
may never recover.[1]

Safety isn't just a major issue at companies in manufacturing, construction, utilities, and oil & gas. Injury rates are up in every major
sector. Even white-collar companies are having a significant increase
in on-the-job injuries. So what's causing it?

We already know that the average person spends about half of
their time with the mind wandering. Researchers estimate that 90%
of all workplace accidents are due to human error.[2] Connecting the
dots here isn't hard. When people don't pay attention, bad things can
happen. And the stats are getting worse in just about every industry.
It's become a crisis and ignoring it won't make it go away.

> More Stress + Less Focus = More Injuries

I've had the pleasure of speaking on the topic of safety at conferences around the world, including *Mainstream, Best Practices for Oil & Gas,* and *SAP for Utilities. SAP for Utilities* brings together the world's leaders in maintenance, reliability, and safety in industries like oil, gas, and power. I joined my good friend, Rudy Wolf, on stage for the utilities event to address 1,500 executives. Rudy heads the safety organization for Electric Transmission and Distribution Operations at Pacific Gas and Electric Company, a $15 billion annual energy company.

We were asked to speak on "leadership, stress, and safety." As a driven perfectionist, it's a topic I know well. And as a COO inside of public companies, I'd driven my fair share of stress.

I accepted the invitation for two reasons. First, the opportunity to work with Rudy. He's an accomplished and inspiring leader. Second, speaking to an oil, gas, and utilities crowd about the role of mindfulness in the workplace kicked my judging mind into overdrive. Surely, the starting point for this crowd would be "Mindfulness training is a bunch of hippie bullsh*t."

Yup. Check. Confirmed. The crowd was skeptical. That eased when Rudy and I got started. We both had a lot in common with the audience. Blue-collar beginnings. Learning to ignore stress, work through pain, and do whatever we needed to in order to succeed. Humor, long hours, and tenacity were common weapons.

To connect with the skeptics, I shared that I was one. I had to jump three hurdles before trying mindfulness training. The first was data. I wanted the science. Second, I wasn't looking for a new religion. Third, who else was doing it? Even in my 40s, I still wanted to be with the cool kids.

I saw the science. I saw that a secular, pragmatic approach was possible. I saw that the top performance-driven cultures were already embracing it, including professional athletes, universities, and Fortune 500 execs. I shared that studies have also shown that even four short sessions of meditation training reduced fatigue, anxiety, and significantly improved visuo-spatial processing, working memory, and decision making.[3] All important when it comes to safety. That went down well.

Rudy had the crowd from the word go. A tall, muscular, and imposing figure, he looks like he could pull a utility pole out of the ground and replant it across the street. Rudy's got a commanding presence and the crowd could tell he knew how to roll up his sleeves. He was one of them.

INJURIES DON'T HAPPEN WHEN YOU THINK THEY DO

Rudy is a great storyteller and shared statistics from various industries. When it comes to utility companies, you might expect more worker injuries to occur in lightning and thunderstorms. Rudy shared that you'd be wrong, "Injury rates under dangerous weather circumstances are actually similar to normal working conditions. When workers know they are at risk for injury, they tend to be laser focused to ensure that doesn't happen. Surprisingly, just as many injuries happen on beautiful sunny days when workers don't have a care in the world. When it's just another day on the job, it's easy for the mind to wander into distraction. That's when people get hurt." He called it the "blue sky effect."

This is just one of the challenges that impacts safety. Most industries are facing increasing competition, cost pressures, increasing regulation, and the need to replace aging assets. Add to this maturing workforces and the difficulty in hiring young, skilled workers to service demanding consumers and you get increasing stress. It all feeds the more-with-less and faster, cheaper routines, which also impact employee stress and safety.

Traditional Solutions Aren't Enough

Industries have popped up to analyze the issues and help prevent injuries. Most companies have picked the low hanging fruit: training programs for workers, maintenance policies for equipment, machinery, tools, and technology to drive process improvement. Billions are spent on consultants and to address theories of accident causation models and map out correction plans to avoid future injury. Billions more on helmets, gloves, and special clothing. There's even a multi-billion dollar signage industry reminding workers not to get hurt.

Figure 11.1   Be mindful. Avoid injury.

Pithy signs like "Don't get hurt today!" "Watch out for the other guy," and "Be alert! Expect the unexpected!" have their place and these traditional approaches are important. But all of these solutions and all the exclamation points on bright colored metal don't address the core issue. Most humans spend about half the time with their mind wandering and 90% of all accidents are caused by human error. We need to train people to improve their ability to focus.

THE NUMBERS ADD UP

Beyond employee health concerns, injuries also impact productivity. Rudy shared, "If your business has 10,000 employees and you increase productivity by 1%, that's the equivalent of adding 100 full-time equivalents (FTEs), or about $20,000,000 annually. The opposite is also true if injuries cause you to lose 1% of productivity."

Fatigue and injury rates are impacting business:
Manufacturing Example

Annual Injuries*
(per 100 Employees)

Annual Direct Costs*
(Average $38k, each)

Revenue Needed to Cover Direct Costs
(Assuming 10% profit margin)

Figure 11.2   The high cost of distraction.
Source: Occupational Safety and Health Administration, 2014.

When you dig into the statistics related to the cost of injuries, the numbers get big fast. Here's an example: according to the Occupational Safety and Health Administration (OSHA), if you're in the manufacturing sector, the average injury rate per every 100 employees is 3.9.[4] You might think that 3.9% of people getting injured doesn't sound so bad. The national average in the United States is 3.2%. But here's the rub. U.S. businesses pay over $1 billion every week in direct injury costs (worker's compensation, medical, and legal expenses) with an average expense per injury of $38,000. For 3.9 injuries per year, you'd have $148,000 in injury-related costs (3.9 × $38,000) for every 100 employees. This does not include indirect costs (lost productivity, hiring, and training replacements, investigations, and so forth), which are two to 10 times higher, depending on the type of injury.[5]

Now, let's assume you're in a 10% profit margin business. For every, $148,000 in costs, you'd need to make $1,480,000 in revenue ($148,000 / 10%) to make enough profit just to cover these expenses. Again, that's for every 100 employees. If you have 10,000 employees, multiple that by 100. If you have 100,000, multiply by 1,000. And if you're in a 5% margin business, double your numbers. It's a crisis.

I've shared a number of other industries in Figure 11.3. Unless your company has professionals that sit behind a desk all day, employee injuries have become a hot topic for good reason. Both the human and financial impacts are big and growing.

Industry	Average Injury Rate per 100 Employees	Direct Cost per 100 Employees (at direct cost of $38k per injury)	Revenue Required to Cover Direct Costs
Professional Services	1.5	$57K	$.6M
Leisure/Hospitality	3.6	$137K	$1.4M
Retail	3.6	$137K	$1.4M
Manufacturing	3.9	$148K	$1.5M
Construction	4.2	$160K	$1.6M
Food & Beverage	4.4	$167K	$1.7M
Transportation	5.0	$160K	$1.6M
Government	5.0	$190K	$1.9M
Agriculture	5.5	$213K	$2.1M
Airlines	7.5	$285K	$2.9M
Hospitals	8.7	$331K	$3.3M

Figure 11.3   What's (left) in your wallet?
Source: OSHA, 2014, assumes $38,000 direct cost per injury.[5]

IT'S ALL FUN AND GAMES UNTIL SOMEONE GETS KILLED

These numbers always grab the crowd's attention. Then Rudy dropped the mic. He asked the audience the question, "How many of you have had to go to an employee's home to inform their spouse that they wouldn't be coming home?" As hands went up in the audience, more than a few teared up. Employees being injured or dying on the job have spiked in a lot of industries. Forget about innovation and transformation. That's disruption.

By the time we wrapped our talk, the crowd appreciated that mindfulness has also gone mainstream. Hearing that the last five Super Bowl champs and all five branches of the military also use mindfulness training to be "in the zone" and perform under pressure also resonated with the manly-man crowd.

I Don't Need Mindfulness Training, But the Guy Next to Me Sure As Hell Does

During the evening social, I was struck by the openness of the attendees. Here were executives dedicated to the safety and reliability of the industrial plants and machinery that largely keep the world running. Their collective mission is to serve customers and protect their people. They operate in high-stress industries where, if something goes wrong, communities are impacted and employees could be seriously injured or worse.

I used to find it easy to joke about oil & gas folks being fat, rich, and happy. I can now tell you that most are not. These are normal people, just like us, pushing the ball uphill in public companies. They work hard in highly competitive, stressful industries. Most were knee deep in R&D, investing in alternative energy solutions. Their future depends on it.

It doesn't matter how much you spend on the plant and equipment if the individual doesn't show up calm, focused, and in the right mind. They were surprisingly open about the elephant in the room. Despite their focus on the reliance and reliability of "assets," there was an open recognition that they didn't focus on employee stress. It was accepted as a given. Over drinks that night, one executive lamented, "Man, do we need this. The stress on oil rigs is crazy. We lost two guys just last week. We're running teams into the ground with double shifts and no one seems to care. This is a dangerous business. It's not f*cking accounting."

Later, a CEO of a well-known utilities company summed it up over beers. "We could all use mindfulness training. It's a stressful business. Most of our guys probably think 'I don't need attention training. But the guy next to me sure as hell does.'" We laughed. We worried. We drank. And his company is now a client.

Attention training helps employees concentrate better, be more situationally aware, react faster, stay on task longer, and retain more information. That means being more alert and aware of themselves, their co-workers, and their surroundings. It's a skill that makes the billions invested in other safety solutions work better—an all-natural performance enhancer.

Shift Kickoff

If you operate in a potentially dangerous field, here's a grounding practice from Rudy and the Whil training library to remind your crew to keep a clear mind. Use the S.T.O.P. practice when you need to ground and disengage in reactivity:

Stop whatever you are doing

Take three deep breaths

Observe and name what is happening. Describe it to bring your thinking brain online, focus your mind and relax your nervous system.

Proceed with more balance and awareness

WHY TOUGH GUYS LIKE MINDFULNESS TRAINING

While we're on the topic of safety, I should address the misconception that practicing mindfulness is "for women" (or if you follow the recurring cover images of *Time* and *Newsweek*, healthy, fit white women). This simply isn't the case. Within our business, we cover millions of lives. The breakdown of male and female users is almost 50/50. These coping and resilience skills have countless benefits, no matter your gender, ethnicity, age, or profession.

In our experience, men enjoy digital mindfulness training better than attending typical coaching sessions or live training experiences. This is especially true for leaders when expectations run high.

There Are Several Reasons Why Men Like Digital Mindfulness Training

We Don't Have to Tell Anyone. Us guys fear all kinds of things. Failing. Looking bad. Having our masculinity challenged. Perhaps more than anything, we fear talking about our emotions. Remember that study about how men would rather go through electroshock therapy than sit alone with their own thoughts? It doesn't come easy to speak to our partner, our colleagues, or our boss about stress, anxiety, and our mental wellbeing in general.

We Can Fit It in Around Our Schedules. Mindfulness training offered up through a mobile device provides efficient and easy, on-the-go access for the busy, stressed-out business executive. This provides the opportunity to step away, find a few minutes to reset. Whether it's on the train to work, before an important meeting or kicking off a dangerous job.

We Have Anger Management Issues. According to the American Psychological Association, more of us are dealing with "extreme stress" than ever.[6] With that comes an increase in anger management issues. In fact, 37% of people reported being angry most of the time.[7] Research shows that men have been conditioned to show their anger.[8] However, when you're dealing with anger issues, it's hard to focus, let alone be a connected and empathetic leader. It's been said, "He who angers you conquers you." Leaders can't afford that. With time, you'll find that you can manage anger more skillfully while experiencing it less frequently. Thanks neuroplasticity.

We Want to Win. Look, us guys are a competitive group. We like to be, look, and feel at our best. We like to believe we can be competitive no matter what the situation. As we age, sometimes it's hard to deal with the loss of our physical abilities and mental edge. But it doesn't have to be. Mindfulness not only makes us more resilient, it opens up deeper learning into a growth mindset, being less judgmental and more accepting (including of yourself).

It Helps Reduce Pain. In one study, just three days of brief mindfulness training was effective at reducing pain ratings and sensitivity and producing analgesic effects.[9] When the topic comes to focus and performance, pain hurts our sleep, moods, and ability to focus. Sleep good. Pain bad.

It Ain't Therapy. All leaders could use a little help with our mental and emotional wellbeing. There's no shame in that. But for many, including myself, the idea of lying on a couch and pouring out our heart to a stranger just ain't happening. Of course, there's nothing wrong with therapy. But most men are looking to build coping skills that they can learn quickly and put to use immediately without an over-reliance on others. We're fixers, so we like to be the ones with the solutions.

Myth dispelled. Leaders come in all shapes, sizes, and genders. So does the need for training and life skills to help us be at our best.

Chapter **12**

Turn Depressing Data Into Healthy Employees

We're entering this era where if you don't have an outcome, you're not gonna have an income.
—Sandra Nichols, AstraZeneca

One of the most exciting aspects of healthcare technology is the increasing opportunity to leverage real-time data. The annual employee Health Risk Assessment (HRA) snooze fest can now be supplemented with connected devices including wearables, biometrics, and healthcare claims. We've entered into a new era in which an individual employee's needs can be evaluated and solutions (especially digital training programs) "prescribed" in the moment.

Way Beyond Wearables. Data sources go well beyond consumer wearables like Fitbit. Medical device wearables are being developed to target the four most prevalent chronic illnesses: congestive heart failure, diabetes, hypertension and chronic obstructive pulmonary disease. Roughly 72 million wearable devices were shipped in 2015. That's expected to grow to 156 million by 2019.[1]

DATA RICH BUT INSIGHT POOR

Most large companies collect tremendous amounts of data on their employee populations. Until recently, it generally just sat on a shelf.

With connected devices and the resulting data, we can now prescribe the right solutions for individual employees when they are needed.

Although the data-enabled human race is just kicking off, I predict that digital training programs incorporating mindfulness and emotional intelligence practices will lead the way. Both have been correlated with improving conditions across a myriad of illnesses, disease, and performance issues. The opportunity is to help professionals improve their lives and careers with both preventative resilience programs as well as targeted curative solutions. The body of scientific research is rich, and early wearable and biometric measurement opportunities are a custom fit for changing health outcomes. Following are a few examples.

Improve Sleep. Let's say your wearable tells you that your sleep sucks. Tomorrow it will do the same. And the day after. And so on. But it never recommends the right training program to help with your sleep. Digital training products like Whil are filling that gap by recommending the right training programs in real time based upon the user's needs.

Lower High Blood Pressure. Modern high blood pressure devices are Bluetooth enabled. They can remind you (and your doctor) on a daily basis that your resting heart rate or blood pressure is too high. We can now recommend the right training to help you relax to reduce your blood pressure as well as your resting heart rate. Both are leading indicators of health issues down the road.

Recovering from Illness. In May 2017, Whil produced a four-week program with Dr. Tara Cousineau to help young adults recovering from cancer to reduce stress and anxiety. In 2016, we did the same for patients suffering from IBS.

The Connected Human

The digital revolution in healthcare means that thousands of connected medical devices are providing hundreds of things to measure about the human body and performance. There are four main areas in which this is occurring to better connect doctors to their patients, including (1) activity trackers, like the Apple Watch, (2) medical wearables, like insulin pumps, (3) stationary devices, like CPAP breathing machines, and (4) devices embedded in your body or under the skin, like pacemakers, neurostimulators, and birth control.

In the past, we'd have to look at the devices to see our progress (or problems). We are already starting to connect these Bluetooth-enabled devices, feeding more data into centralized training apps so that you know when you have a problem and when to start recommended digital training solutions instead of, or in addition to, prescribed medications.

The medical system is moving from occasional crisis management to ongoing care relationships with patients. As companies are looking at targeting their biggest healthcare cost drivers, companies like our friends at Validic and HumanAPI are providing single-point access to more than 300 connected devices through application programing interfaces (APIs).[2] That makes targeted mindfulness training programs a superpower for fighting stress, illness, and disease.

Employee Wellbeing: Then and Now

With all the numbers going the wrong way, the explosion of interest in employees' mental wellbeing could not come at a better time.

Traditional corporate wellness programs have largely focused on employee engagement and physical wellness. This progress has been important in the early stages to help employees understand their options and to encourage them to play an active role in managing their own health and wellbeing. Early players largely laid the groundwork to get employees engaged with points and rewards programs. Do your health risk assessment. Get points. Connect your activity tracker. Get points. Read about nutrition. Get points. Here's a stress ball. Please don't throw it at anyone. People like tchotchkes, rewards, and gamification and that's a good way to get them started. Many programs even convert wellness points into cash. Folks like cash. Carrot programs are plentiful. The problem is that 40 years of research from psychologists like Edward Deci, Richard Ryan, and Mark Lepper have shown that monetary (external) rewards actually undermine intrinsic motivation—your own satisfaction at making progress.[3-5]

More programs are predictably moving into the stick phase, increasing deductibles and other costs for employees who are not taking care of themselves. Engagement programs have made it easier to identify and segment high stress employees (HSEs) and those at high risk for illness and, therefore, higher medical costs.

While the early approaches have been important, there are a few limitations with these programs.

1. Passive programs are helpful, but they are not training employees repeatable life skills.

2. The programs tend not to be personalized. Research shows that generic, one-size-fits-all approaches tend to lose engagement fast.[6]

3. They uniformly missed the need for stress resilience and mental wellbeing, which is intrinsically linked with physical wellbeing. Taking care of the mind matters just as much, if not more than taking care of the body.

4. They have limited impact on culture. Step programs and corporate challenges go only so far. If much of your workplace stress is driven by a commanding culture and a faster and cheaper way of working, a focus on bringing employees together will help improve connections and communications.

These are key drivers in Bersin by Deloitte's research pushing employers to move beyond merely focusing on wellness and into programs focused on employee "Wellbeing and Human Performance."[7] Mindfulness training is the key to the employee engagement stack. It covers some of these limitations with personalized, activity-based learning with which employees can learn repeatable life skills and then apply them when they need them the most. Mindfulness training also provides an ongoing opportunity to bring teams together to practice. This creates a common language and opens up a transparent conversation around challenging issues.

We've seen that all of this can lead to real change for individual leaders as well as how teams interact in some of the largest companies on the planet. This ladders up to impacting the entire culture of an organization. In recent studies:

- 94% of leaders said mindfulness improved their overall wellbeing.[8]
- 83% improved their cardiovascular health.[9]
- 50% experienced a decrease in cold and flu symptoms.[10]
- 30% saw a reduction of aging at the cellular level.[11]

In Whil's digital training, 93% of training sessions are rated as helping users with their wellbeing and in accomplishing their goals. That gives us tremendous insight into what's working and not working for each employee in hundreds of global clients. This is important when the most played training sessions relate to reducing stress, calming anxiety, managing insomnia, improving difficult relationships, and managing chronic pain.

Various studies also have shown that these practices are equally transformative for the bottom line and company culture, including:

- 76% decrease in absenteeism[10]
- 46% reduction in employee turnover[12]
- 12% increase in productivity and performance[12]
- Aetna even released a study showing a $2,000 annual decrease in healthcare costs per employee and an additional $3,000 annual increase in productivity per employee going through mindfulness training[12]

Aetna has been a clear leader in driving research, including training over 13,000 of their own employees in mindfulness skills. Their CEO, Mark Bertolini shared, "We saw dramatic drops in heart-rate variability. We saw 69 minutes more of productivity a month. Actually, that following year, we had a 7.5% drop in the company's healthcare cost...All of a sudden, all of these other companies started coming out and talking about mindfulness in the workplace and how important it was. And that sort of broke the log jam of corporate America talking about it. And now if you don't talk about it, you're just not cool enough to be a CEO."

Whil conducted six of our own case studies over a 12-month period and the results were similar. This included decreases in turnover up to 44%, increases in employee satisfaction scores and reductions in absenteeism of two days per employee compared to the prior year.

What's more is the opportunity to impact other leaders in the company. Studies have shown the impact of mindfulness training as it relates to building emotional intelligence skills. One study with the Institute for Mindful Leadership found all of the following:[13]

- 43% reported improved decision making ability.
- 86% listened to themselves and others better.
- 68% could respond with clarity, even under pressure.
- 93% reported being more innovative.

Research has shown that happy employees are 12% more productive while unhappy ones are 10% less productive than the control group.[14] That's a 22% swing in productivity. Do the math with your own company's average salary. Even at the national average salary of $46,000, the value of a productivity shift for happy employees is staggering. Most companies are dealing with a staggering shift in the wrong direction.

Creating a data-driven, balanced employee wellness *and* wellbeing program pays for itself many times over. This is particularly true when combining live and digital training approaches to serve your workforce by creating both community and convenience.

It's no wonder the top high-performing companies are embracing mindfulness training. This includes the early adopters in Silicon Valley like Apple, Google, Facebook, LinkedIn, and Salesforce. But don't be fooled into thinking this is some New Age-y tech industry fluff. NIH estimates that 8% of all U.S. employees are now meditating, some 18 million adults.[15] That includes traditional giants in every category like GE, Procter & Gamble, Target, General Mills, Lululemon, Ford, Dow Chemical, American Express, Aetna, J&J, PWC, McKinsey, Intel, Havas, and 45% of the Fortune 500. The leading companies want to improve the health and happiness of their employees. They want to improve performance and productivity. This is not your grandfather's mindfulness.

Pro Tip: Mark Bertolini, Chairman and CEO of Aetna credits mindfulness with saving his life following a near-death skiing accident which broke his neck in five places. As he put it, "A healthy individual is productive. A productive individual is spiritually, socially and economically viable. And viable people are happy. Wouldn't we be a better place if everyone was a little more happier and a little more viable?"

PART III

EMOTIONAL INTELLIGENCE (EQ) FOR EVERYONE

PERFORMANCE   CAREER

CHAPTER **13**

Building Emotional Intelligence (EQ) Skills for Yourself

What you do speaks so loud that I cannot hear
what you say.
—Ralph Waldo Emerson

We've covered the crash course in stress, disruption, and the pressures on ongoing change management. Now, we're moving into my favorite part of the *CML Workshop*, emotional intelligence (EQ). The ongoing impact of stress on individuals and company cultures is why *Fast Company* calls EQ the fastest-growing, must-have skill for leaders.[1] This is also why the World Economic Forum Future of Jobs Report lists EQ as one of the top 10 job skills for 2020.[2]

EQ Is the New IQ, Only Better. Every leader, organization, and family works in a constant state of change. When it comes to helping individuals and company culture, mindfulness and EQ training help create a tectonic shift in the norms of how you do business.

At Whil, we talk about this shift as moving from the ordinary to the extraordinary. According to the research I've shared so far, the ordinary is the state of affairs that most individuals live in and that most companies tolerate. It's the negativity, gossip, politics, and lack of clarity and trust that drags leaders, teams, and company cultures down.

The Ordinary	The Extraordinary
Stressed, anxious, and angry	Calm, focused, and kind
Disconnected	Collaborative and creative
Overwhelmed	Empowered
Reactive (EAPs)	Proactive
Sleepless and tired	Rested and energized
Distracted and injured	Situationally aware and safe

The following table can help you determine what percentage of your time is spent in each set of behaviors. Attention and awareness training helps you to be more present. Once you're focused and aware, you can't help but shoot for being extraordinary.

According to the leaders in our *CML Workshops*, Ordinary is ...

Drama	Blame	Loose language
Untrusting	Unclear goals	Meeting driven
Concealing	Us versus them	Feeling threatened
Overwhelmed	Defensive	Too serious
About right/wrong	Gossip	Polarizing
Ego driven	Risk averse	Coasting
Political	Avoiding conflict	Stressed out
Taking credit	Disconnected	Negative/sarcastic
Indecisive	Scarcity	Impulsive
Rationalizing/Justifying	Disengaged	Tolerating the ordinary
Controlling	Speculation	Frustrated

Extraordinary is ...

Compassionate	Humble, but kick-ass	Revealing
Transparent	Proud	Wildly fun (and funny)
Simple/authentic	Honest	Vulnerable/courageous
Direct	Focused	Driven
Empathetic	Growing/learning	Opportunistic
Gracious	Best in class	Encouraging
Sincere	Committed	Hungry
Collaborative	100% accountable	Healthy
Decisive	Data-driven	Diverse
Present	Curious	Mindful

We all slip into the ordinary several times a day. Mindfulness improves the ability to know when you've slipped (when you're distracted) as a leader and it gives you an anchor to come back to a point of focus to lead with specific intentions and values.

It's not easy to be a leader and even harder to be extraordinary. But making it a lifelong pursuit, a lifestyle, changes the way you think about yourself, your employees, and your mission.

Next, we'll cover what EQ is, why it's necessary, and how to begin learning the skills yourself. The nature of today's complex work requires leaders who value employee wellbeing, identify and mentor emerging leaders, and who model effective business and interpersonal and intrapersonal skills. Only then can organizations establish a strong foundation for sustainable success.

EMOTIONAL INTELLIGENCE DEFINED

Although Daniel Goleman brought EQ into public consciousness, the concept is attributed to Professors Peter Salovey and John Mayer in 1990. Professor Salovey is provost of Yale University, and the Chris Argyris professor of psychology. John Mayer was a postdoctoral scholar at Stanford University and is a professor of psychology at the University New Hampshire. They define EQ as "The ability to monitor one's own and others' feelings and emotions, to discriminate among them, and to use this information to guide one's thinking and actions."[3] Let's look at three aspects of this definition.

1. *Monitor* means being aware and clear about your own feelings and emotions. That alone is a tall order. Too many leaders run through their day on autopilot. They're not in touch with their own thoughts and emotions; forget about monitoring others.

2. Being able to discriminate, or separate, your own perspectives and emotions from those you're interacting with. That's another superpower. Too many leaders get drawn into emotional battles and pick a side without understanding what's going on. Humans are tribal. When things get heated or we get challenged, we like to enroll others to help prove we're right.

3. Using this information to guide your thinking and actions gets to the heart of leadership; using data (not emotions) to make informed decisions.

Being mindful, present, and aware is the key building block for EQ. We'll cover five other aspects of EQ, building on this foundation.

First, let's cover the need for emotional intelligence. When we hire leaders, we expect them to show up prepared. Luke Skywalker, ready for anything. A Jedi Master calm, cool, and collected. Great hair. Ready for battle. The Force Is Strong in This One.

SLIPPING TO THE DARK SIDE

After a few decades of dealing with constant change and disruption, it's easy for leaders to slip into the dark side. We can become Darth Vader without even realizing it. Over time, we wear it. Do not piss me off. I'm in a bad mood. I'm hot. I'm tired. I'm wearing black. I'm just looking for an opportunity to take someone out. I live on the Dark Side, man.

After 10 or 20 years it's not hard to see why so many slip into being angry, frustrated, and competitive. You live and die by the quarterly numbers. You occasionally feel like killing someone. It just happens. "Disease states" like diabetes, obesity, and heart disease result from decades of micro traumas to the body (over-eating, binge drinking, smoking, and so on). Years of physical stressors take their toll. We find the same tends to happen in what we call "career states." Most professionals have analogous and ongoing micro traumas in their work. In sales, that may be managing constant rejection. In healthcare, it's compassion fatigue from dealing with daily patient crises or death. In manufacturing or construction, it may be ongoing pain management, and so on. Years of stressors take their toll on mental wellbeing. A tipping point moves us to the Dark Side; a line we cross when our coping skills and resilience have worn too thin. It's often imperceptible because we adapt to stress levels over time, but it happens in every career.

This happened to me. I had sh*t to do. My back hurt. I wasn't sleeping. After years of the same old routine, I wasn't trained to care much about others' feelings along the way. I had numbers to hit.

As it turns out, the Dark Side isn't much fun. On the way to and from the Death Star every day, things can get heavy. Leaders tend to feel the weight of their team, projects, decisions, and sometimes of the full company. It can feel lonely. It can destroy your health and mental wellbeing. Remember, Darth Vader had a wicked case of asthma and some major skin issues. Oh, and no friends.

ON THE FRONT LINES

Leaders are corporate warriors and more companies are using the acronym "VUCA" to describe the global business landscape. This term was introduced by the U.S. Army War College in the 1990s to describe the more Volatile, Uncertain, Complex, and Ambiguous world that resulted from the end of the Cold War. VUCA has also found a fitting home in describing the current work experience. Change happens rapidly and on a large scale. The future cannot be predicted with precision. Challenges are complicated by many factors and there's little clarity on both problems and solutions. Welcome to work!

Figure 13.1   The corporate warrior

So, this is our work life. But a VUCA existence is also impacting our home life in a bigger way with global warming, politics, terrorism, data hacking, identity theft, and more.

It's hard being a leader. It's hard being an entrepreneur, parent, or just being a human. Our brains are wired with a negativity bias—a quirky survival characteristic. We're primed to constantly scan for danger in our surroundings. It's necessary for survival under harsh conditions but quite a nuisance in contemporary life. It fuels our inner critic. Ongoing stress can result in a growing perception that the demands in life exceed our ability to cope. We're also the only creatures born knowing that we're going to die. That's another bummer.

For many companies, the world is changing faster than they can reasonably adapt. As a global COO, I recall the onslaught of 300-plus daily email messages coming in from 115 offices around the world. I'd clear them every day and 200 more would be waiting for me the next morning. I remember starting too many days thinking, "You have got to be frickin' kidding me." Most of us aren't dealing with just our own companies. We're operating in ecosystems that include clients, vendors, regulators, and family members who are all operating in their own global, connected VUCA worlds that are constantly bumping into ours. Just thinking about it can trigger anxiety, back pain, and insomnia.

Inspirational Leaders

It takes a fairly special leader to be resilient through the shifting norms of today's work environment. When we survey leaders on the qualities of the most impactful mentors in their own careers, the list is inspiring.

Inclusive	Actionable feedback	Informing
Respectful	Involved	Co-creator
Integrity	**Knowledgeable**	Collaborative
Patient	Visionary	**Expertise**
Caring	Relatable	Open minded
Positive	Forgiving	Stable
Listener	Unbiased	Selfless
Communicator	Level-blind	Composed
Inspires	Present	Genuine

Direct	Honesty	Humble
Initiative	Personable	Authentic
Supportive	No ego	Motivates
Kind	**Qualified**	Proactive
Empathetic	Benevolent	Reliable
Compassionate	Self-confident	Hard working
Self-aware	Coach	Fun/funny
In control	Decisive	**Analytical**
Transparent	Builds relationships	Mentor
Vulnerable	**Strategic**	Engaged
Always learning	Human	Supportive
High EQ	Resilient	Accessible
Leads by example	Open	Influence
Excellence	Nonreactive	Results oriented
Trust	**Smart**	Knows the limits
Ethical	Diplomatic	Admits mistakes
Deep values	Non-micromanager	Accountable
Articulate	Good social skills	Walks the talk
Focused	**Can spell**	
Fearless	Calm	
Concise	Curious	

I don't know about you, but I want to work for this person. This is an impressive list that all leaders can aspire to. As an aside, I generally like to add a few things, including: can spell, doesn't shame (or fire) coworkers on Twitter, and so forth. But I digress.

If you look at this list, how many of these qualities relate to IQ? I've placed them in **bold**. Eight out of 84 qualities. Just 10%. You'll also notice that "Kicks ass in Excel" and "Knows their way around a budget" do not appear on the list. Although important, they never come up.

While our live *CML Workshop* survey results do not represent a controlled study, they are consistent with formal research. In his book, *Emotional Intelligence*, Daniel Goleman cites data from over three hundred companies and the EQ traits that distinguish their star performers from average employees.[4] When it came to intellectual abilities, star performers had 27% higher ratings on cognitive skills than the average employees. I'm not saying intellect doesn't matter.

But the gap in emotional intelligence competencies was twice as great, with top performers scoring 54% higher than the average employees. This was consistent across roles ranging from management to sales to technical roles.

To drive this point home further, Goleman found intellectual and technical abilities to be threshold competencies. In other words, you need to meet a certain threshold to be able to contribute in any role. Gotta be smart, dude. But once an employee meets that threshold, gains in performance tend to come more from emotional competence (EQ) than from building additional cognitive or technical competence (IQ).

In another study, Goleman surveyed tech companies to ask what traits they found distinguished top performers from those who were average. He found that four of the top six (67%) of the top competencies related to EQ:[5]

1. Achievement drive and standards
2. Influence
3. Conceptual thinking (IQ)
4. Analytical ability (IQ)
5. Initiative
6. Self-confidence

Similarly, researchers Jack Zenger and Joseph Folkman surveyed over 300,000 professionals on the skills they believed had the greatest impact on their success. Nine of the 16 skills (56%) related to EQ:[6]

Character:

1. Displays honesty and integrity

Personal Capabilities:

1. Exhibits technical/professional expertise (IQ)
2. Solves problems and analyzes issues (IQ)
3. Innovates (IQ)
4. 4 Practices self-development

Getting Results:

1. Focuses on results (IQ)
2. Establishes stretch goals (IQ)
3. Takes initiative

Interpersonal skills:

1. Communicates powerfully and broadly
2. Inspires and motivates others
3. Builds relationships
4. Develops others
5. Collaborates and fosters teamwork

Leading change:

1. Develops strategic perspective (IQ)
2. Champions change
3. Connects the group to the outside world

This stuff even applies to the manliest of manly men. A 1988 study by Wallace Bachman showed that the most effective U.S. navy commanders had higher EQ than their lower-rated counterparts.[7]

The Playing Field Has Been Leveled

All of this makes sense. Internet search engines have leveled the IQ playing field. We expect employees to be smart when we hire them. You could walk into a conference with 500 other people and know nothing about the topics being discussed. Within 10 minutes, you could Google yourself into having a quick understanding of the top issues, pros and cons, recognized research, best practices, and so forth. You'd be at some threshold to perform.

This is the primary reason that EQ skills are in such high demand. Does your company hire dummies? No? What if you could hire dummies for 30% less than smart employees? Still no? Of course not. We expect our leaders to be smart. There's an abundance of IQ. But we need leaders to possess the wide array of emotional intelligence skills to move beyond basic performance to be able to lead under pressure,

Differences in Twentieth-Century and Twenty-First-Century Leaders

Characteristics	Twentieth-Century Leaders	Twenty-First-Century Leaders
Image	Charismatic	Purpose-driven
Focus	U.S.-centric	Global vision
Motivation	Self-interest	Institution's best interests
Experience	Perfect resume	Learning through crucibles
Time frame	Short-term	Long-term
Organizational approach	Hierarchal leadership	Distributed leadership
Greatest strength	IQ	EQ
Personal measurement	External validation	Intrinsic contribution

Figure 13.2   Differences in twentieth-century and twenty-first-century leaders (from George, 2015, p. 186).
Source: Printed with permission of Bill George and Wiley.

understand and cooperate with others, be good listeners and open to feedback, make thoughtful decisions, and inspire by example. As Bill George covered in his book, *Discover Your True North*, there's been a tremendous shift in the types of leaders we needed from the twentieth century to what we need in the twenty-first century (Figure 13.2).

Given the state of the world, there is a demand for leaders who are self-aware, more skilled in managing their emotions, motivating teams, and relating to others as valued human beings. The bad news is we have a shortage of supply today. The good news is EQ skills are trainable.

CHANGE YOUR ATTENTION TO CHANGE YOUR LIFE

The British philosopher Alan Watts once said, "This is the real secret of life—to be completely engaged with what you are doing in the here and now. And instead of calling it work, realize it is play." This a lovely way of saying stay curious—treat each moment as though it will never occur again. Too many of us see the stars every night and take them for granted. We do the same with our experiences, partners, and colleagues. Each and every day human beings try to connect, they cry for help, and reveal their souls. And we look away to check our phones. What if we could train ourselves to live in the moment, be a bit more curious, and experience things fully as they are happening? As Albert Einstein wrote, "The important thing is not to stop questioning. Curiosity has its own reason for existence. One cannot help but be in awe when he contemplates the mysteries of eternity, of life, of the marvelous structure of reality. It is enough if one tries merely to comprehend a little of this mystery each day."[8] Mindfulness and EQ skills allow us to do just that, a little bit each day ...

Pro Tip: Innovative research on "social baseline theory" shows that relationships shape our emotions. Social proximity and peer bonding stimulate cardiovascular health, reduce anxiety, inhibit the release of stress hormones, reduce amygdala activation, and promote health and longevity.[9] Even facial expressions and verbal communication help us adjust our emotions and conserve energy (versus jumping to erroneous email conclusions). Conversely, social isolation in business settings (think email, texts, and Slack messages) causes stress and compromised health. Spend your time more directly interacting with people.

Looking at something with a curious, childlike mind can help you experience it anew each time. You can look at your hand right now and notice things you've never seen in it before. Perhaps that you're aging, or injured. Now, imagine a different single point of focus. Your child is trying to share they were bullied at school. A coworker had a miscarriage. A teammate is worried about his or her job. If you're not in the moment, these things come and go. People in our lives suffer without help or connection. Or worse, they remember that you weren't there for them; your interaction is like a hundred others where you couldn't wait to shift your attention back to your phone or some other distraction versus what is happening in the moment. As leaders, we have constant opportunities to send the message that we care, we're here for you, we hear you, and want to help. But how often do we step out of automaton mode, or mindlessness, to really connect with co-workers?

Developing EQ skills radially shifts the moment-to-moment meaning of our lives and more importantly, what we can mean to others.

NOTICING THE WANDERING MIND

William James was an American philosopher and psychologist. Before his death in 1910, he was one of the leading thinkers of the late nineteenth century. Some even call him the Father of American Psychology.

James explored mental processes imperative to understanding how the mind works. One of his key areas of focus was on "attention." He described it as "taking possession of the mind, in clear and vivid form."[10] This is beautiful imagery. Too often, the mind is like a broncing bull taking us wherever it wants to go.

He also explored the idea of "meta-attention." This is the "Attention of attention; the ability to know when your attention has wandered." Meta-attention is the secret to concentration. When you develop the ability to recover a wandering mind, you create and strengthen neural pathways to improve your ability to sustain your attention anytime. You become good at concentration. The more you practice, the better you become.

Being aware of our attention helps settle the mind and keeps us relaxed and alert. Otherwise, our default is a wandering mind. Once again, the refrigerator door is left open. The equipment keeps running and what's inside isn't very good.

Catching ourselves when we're distracted is equivalent to closing the refrigerator door so that its motor isn't working so hard. We cool our emotions while conserving energy. This ability to calm and focus the mind and to choose your thoughts is key to your health and happiness. As James said, "The greatest weapon against stress is our ability to choose one thought over another."

Personally, my biggest enjoyment from mindfulness and EQ training is actually enjoying each day more as it unfolds. Walking and enjoying a walk. Being in nature and enjoying it. Completely giving myself to play when I'm with my kids. Or actually connecting with work colleagues; listening, and giving my full attention to the interaction. All of this becomes easier, natural even, when you're able to focus on one thing at a time.

Five Key Things

There are five key areas to Goleman's famous research on emotional intelligence.[11] We'll explore each of the following with specific exercises and applications for business and life.

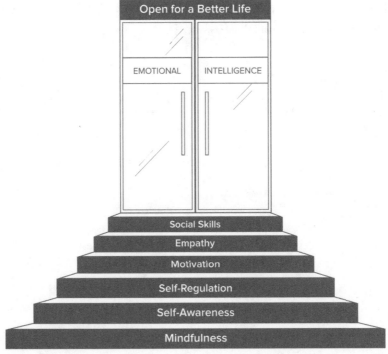

Figure 13.3   The stairway to Heaven or, at least, emotional intelligence

1. Self-awareness

2. Self-regulation

3. Motivation

4. Empathy

5. Social skills

These five elements build on mindfulness, the foundation to being present, focused, and ready to perform. Each is like a step up the stairs to a healthier life (Figure 13.3), with self-awareness being the next step. As you develop skills in the other steps, you become a more complete leader.

While each of these steps can impact all aspects of your life, I like to think of the first three steps as EQ to benefit yourself and the last two as EQ to benefit others. In other words, clients, colleagues, your direct reports, and friends and family will benefit most from improvements in your empathy and social skills.

WELLBEING   PERFORMANCE   RELATIONSHIPS   CAREER

CHAPTER **14**

Increasing Self-Awareness

Life has never given me lemons. It has given me
anger issues, anxiety attacks, a love of alcohol, and
a serious dislike for stupid people.
—The Internet

In *Working with Emotional Intelligence*, Daniel Goleman describes self-awareness as "Knowing one's internal states, preferences, resources, and intuitions."[1]

Self-awareness goes beyond simply knowing yourself. For leaders, it is about developing the moment-to-moment insight into your emotional experience as well as understanding your own strengths, weaknesses, biases, and intuitions. It's like having a camera lens to zoom in and out on your emotions and abilities.

"Internal states" gets to the heart of the mind-body connection. Before I started learning EQ skills, even hearing the phrase "mind-body connection" brought the worst hippy-dippy images to mind. It was a trigger for me – here come the sandals. As I got older, back pain opened up a new willingness to drop my judgmental attitude and blue-collar sensibilities. Now I accept that how your body feels, affects your moods, thoughts, patience, and what comes out of your mouth. It's common sense. If you're in pain, you probably have a shorter fuse. If you haven't slept, you're probably ill-tempered. If you're hungry, it's easy to become angry or "hangry" when you

---

combine the two. Accepting the basic understanding that how your body feels affects your mindset, decision-making and an ability to focus opens up new possibilities as a leader.

Reflect and Plan

Here's an eight-minute Whil journaling practice to help explore your own self-awareness. Set a timer and spend two minutes per topic. Remember, don't stop writing till the time is up.

Things that agitate me include ...

My weaknesses include ...

Things that bring me joy include ...

My strengths include ...

Take a few minutes to reflect on what you wrote, your triggers and weaknesses. As a leader, it's easy to fall into the false belief that you're good at everything. Or that you have to be good at everything.

Pro Tip: Abraham Lincoln kept a journal about the highs and lows of his presidency during the Civil War. When you think about your weaknesses and the things that annoy you, be easy on yourself. Keep a journal and think about Honest Abe. What you're going through probably isn't as bad as you think.

The goal of building self-awareness skills is to develop clarity into your own emotions as a leader. When it comes to how you see events, circumstances, and people, consider it going from standard definition TV (SDTV) to high definition TV (HDTV). When it comes to what you hear and perceive, consider it going from low fidelity to high fidelity. By increasing the clarity at which you experience your emotions, you can better manage them as they arise and recognize when they change. This gives you greater insight into your emotional life and how it impacts your thoughts, moods, and performance. It empowers you to manage your emotions more effectively in real time.

Imagine you're talking with an employee who's not at their best. Under normal circumstances, you might be tired from a poor night's rest, managing pain, or carrying something that set you off in your last meeting into this meeting. Your normal interaction with this employee (and others) might be short or unfocused and you may miss out on important elements of the conversation. Sure, you might get the content, but if you're focused solely on what you need, you may miss the employee's emotions, what they feel is at risk in the conversation, and how their ego is being impacted. From your perspective, you might think you got everything. From the employee's perspective, you may have missed everything.

If this conversation is about travel plans or signing documents, maybe it's no big deal. The employee is probably used to you not being at your best for the mundane. But what if this is a highly valued employee and they're thinking about quitting? What if this interaction would make up their mind? What if it were your child and they were just bullied at school. Or they just had their heart broken. Or a person who was considering taking his or her own life? I still recall my last conversation with my twin sister. The point is this: Each interaction we have with the people in our lives is important. Each interaction happens only once. You rarely know how important each interaction is until a later date, if at all.

Self-awareness helps you be present and tuned in more regularly. It helps you be more open and to listen for when your weaknesses may be working against you. It helps you change course in real time. All important skills that can be muted when you're caught in the normal ruminations of the mind.

As you practice, you'll also learn that your emotions, actions, and performance are all interconnected. This is a recurring theme throughout our *CML Workshop*. When it comes to self-awareness, Goleman suggests there is a direct correlation between work performance and

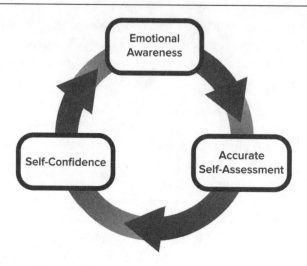

Figure 14.1   The confidence cycle

three emotional competencies. Think of them as a cycle (Figure 14.1). Strong emotional awareness leads to a more accurate self-assessment. This, in turn, leads to higher self-confidence.[2]

The opposite is also true. Limited emotional awareness leads to a less accurate (or nonexistent) self-assessment. This, in turn, leads to lower self-confidence. In my experience, this cycle (positive or negative) has a similar impact on how your direct reports build or lose confidence in you as their manager. As leaders, we tend to consistently practice one cycle or the other. Which one are you practicing? Why not be intentional about it?

Out of Touch Leaders Make Everyone's Job Harder. Too often, we equate a lack of self-awareness with leaders just saying stupid things. It's more important than that. Here's an example. When I was the COO of a division of a public company, our holding company CEO visited just after Barack Obama became president of the United States. In addressing 300 of our global HQ staff, he shared a story that just didn't land. "We have the first African American president. The world is changing. Last month, I sent a gift box to our top 30 clients with a personal note 'It's a new day. Time to play ball'."

He illustrated his remarks by showing one of the gift boxes and pulling out a basketball. Although he had good intentions, it was a great example of implicit bias. We knew he had done this. Our largest client called us a day earlier to let us know they felt it was in incredibly poor taste. Here was an Irishman in his early 60s and widely known as the loud, sexist, out-of-touch account guy who drank too much. He confirmed this at the prior evening's dinner party. He was addressing a team that had grown our top client from $150 million in annual revenue to $365 million in three years. A team that worked around the clock to do it. The most-awarded creative team in the world. There was no "Thank you" or "Congratulations." Just self-congratulatory stories about "the company's growth" and his basketball idea, confirming that he was out of touch. You could feel the energy drop as whispers of "Are you kidding me?" filled the room.

About 50 staff stood and walked out. It was conspicuous and uncomfortable. This included our vice president of human resources, a talented African American woman who was instrumental in managing our culture through rapid growth. She walked past me to exit the room and commented, "I can't stay for this. I'm surprised he didn't send our clients watermelons." The big guy was so caught up in his own ego that he failed to notice his impact. Had he been more in touch with his "internal states, preferences, resources, and intuitions," he would have recognized he wasn't feeling well (hung over from the night before), his implicit biases preceded him, and he needed help in crafting his comments. It wasn't just being stupid in the moment. His lack of self-awareness had a lasting impact on our clients and staff globally. The next day, our top client informed him he was never to visit their offices again. He began to withdraw to a bitter sideline. A year later he "retired."

As leaders, we need to know our audience. Sure, we should avoid saying stupid things. But we also have to understand our strengths and weaknesses and be aware of our conditioning that may lead to entrenched beliefs.

Pro Tip: Feeling compassion for others starts with self-awareness, refocusing and feeling compassion for yourself. As Jon Kabat-Zinn states, "The stories and the narratives we

(continued)

(*continued*)

tell ourselves about my success, my failure, my inadequacies, I-I-I, me-me-me, my-my-my, it's like a little symphony of habitual self-involvement, self-centeredness that is actually imprisoning. When you really see everything through the lens of 'my', you can't really feel the other. Because, the only thing I care about you is how you feel about me. That's a little bit toxic." With self-awareness practices, you can catch yourself and avoid these normal fixations.[3]

Get to Know Your Thinking and Emotional Brain

For decades, neuroscientists have researched the relationship between the amygdala, our "emotional brain," and the prefrontal cortex, our "thinking brain." The Cliffnotes version is that our emotional brain is faster than our thinking brain. The amygdala is the older part of the brain in human evolution; this fight-or-flight trigger kept us safe back in the caveman days. There was fight or flight or freeze, but not too much thinking involved when a saber-tooth tiger was coming your way.

The thinking brain is more advanced than the emotional brain and involves more neural circuitry, so its response time is slower than the emotional brain. When emotional signals are sent throughout the body, it can take a few moments before the thinking brain fully recognizes and interprets these signals. This physiological experience generally occurs before you are consciously aware of your emotions.

This will resonate with anyone who has "lost their sh*t" at some point in their life. Remember my failed "Get out of my office!" story from earlier? Your emotions take over before your thinking brain kicks in. Another physiological example is when you burn your hand on a hot pot. Your amygdala generates the flight response to pull your hand back a few seconds before the thinking brain even knows what happened.

One of the best ways to become more self-aware is to practice bringing mindful attention to your body. How your body feels impacts your emotions, how you process feelings, and ultimately, your preferences, biases, and decision-making. Research show that reducing stress through mindfulness practices correlates with positive structural changes in the amygdala.[4] You can improve your amygdala-PFC connection with specific mindfulness techniques.

This notion has been reinforced by many studies over the years. Here are two of our favorites in EQ circles.

We Feel Emotions in Our Body. A 2013 study exposed over 700 participants in Western Europe and Eastern Asia to different emotionally charged experiences. Participants were asked to color the bodily regions where they felt increasing or decreasing physiological activity while viewing each stimulus. Participants consistently associated different emotions (anger, fear, disgust, happiness, anxiety, love, depression, and so on) with 14 recognizable bodily sensations. The mapping was highly consistent regardless of race, culture and language. Participants felt and experienced emotions through consistent in-body sensations.[5] Emotions adjust not only our mental, but also our bodily states.

Our Intuition Is Faster Than Our Understanding. In Malcolm Gladwell's book, *Blink*, he refers to a gambling experiment known as the Iowa Card Study.[6] This study also showed that emotions drive our decision-making before full-conscious awareness. The research used four decks of cards, two red and two blue. In the game, each card either wins or costs the participants money. But they didn't know the red decks ensured losing while the blue ensured winning. On average, it took participants 50 cards to get a feeling that something was wrong, and 80 cards to figure out the game and be able to explain what was off.

Participants were also hooked up to a polygraph lie detector machine that measured sweat in their hands. These sweat glands don't respond to temperature; they open up in response to stress ("clammy hands"). Researchers found that participants started generating stress responses to the red decks at 10 cards, 40 cards before they had a hunch, and 70 cards before they knew definitively that something was wrong. More importantly, when their palms started sweating, their behavior also changed. Without realizing it, they started avoiding the red decks (like the hand pulling back from a hot pot). A physiological response triggered by the emotional brain caused a behavior change before their thinking brain was even aware of it.

Through mindfulness practice like the body scan discussed earlier, we can increase awareness of how these emotions feel in the body to improve our ability to bring our thinking brain online.

Hulk versus Yoda: You Are Not Your Emotions

A foundational element of mindfulness is learning that you are not your emotions. This is a game changer. As a COO, I can't count the number of times I'd wake up and go to work in a bad mood. I'd get locked onto something and have a visceral bodily reaction. I'm pissed off. I'm stressed. I'm anxious. Conversely, some days I felt great. I'm inspired. I'm happy. It's easy to fall into a mindset that locks us into a certain way of being for a few hours, days, weeks, or years. To the human mind, your emotions can become your very existence.

By developing a better understanding of your emotions, you can move away from the existential experience of "I am" a certain way and into a physiological experience to understand what you're feeling. You can then engage the thinking brain to ask, "Why am I feeling this way," "Are the feelings I'm experiencing necessary?" "Are they true?" and "What can I do about the way I'm feeling?" You can move from feeling, to thinking.

LABEL YOUR EMOTIONS

One of the best tools to use as you practice self-awareness is labeling your emotions. Here's how it works. As negative thoughts come up, stop and take a moment to label the feeling. For example, I'm experiencing sadness, boredom, anger, and so on. Name it to tame it. Then let it go. Research has shown that this easy technique is enough to interrupt the emotional brain to get your thinking brain to catch up.[7]

With enough mindfulness practice, you'll notice an important shift in understanding that emotions are what you feel. They are not who you are. And they can be changed.

When you start to recognize emotions as physiological experiences in the body, you can move from feeling, "I am angry" to the understanding that "I am experiencing anger in my body."

This shift opens up the possibility to master your emotions. Said another way, if I am my emotions, then there's nothing I can do about it. But if I recognize that emotions are experiences in my body, then I can influence them.

An injured muscle sends you valuable information telling you to slow down, recover, and modify your training routine. Emotions can do the same. Consider them a radar system in your body, constantly sending you signals to pay attention. Once you tune in and label the emotion, thought, or sensation, you can defuse the charge. You can then act on it instead of being trapped by the feeling. More importantly, emotions that are negative often lead us to the source of unresolved friction. Oftentimes, we'll find there's another person on the other side of those feelings. If so, they're likely experiencing similar emotions. Wouldn't it be nice to more quickly get to the heart of your conflict so you can resolve it?

We live in the age of data-driven everything. As leaders, we take in information, analyze it, and then take action constantly. We can do the same with our emotions. There's a tremendous freedom when you hone the ability to catch yourself when you're experiencing unhelpful emotions and then skillfully change course. Use the data. Be like Yoda. Don't be like the Hulk. Hulk mad.

Body Scan

I'd like to go deeper on the body scan practice we tried earlier to help improve your sleep. This is a foundational mindfulness practice that can be done anytime. I must admit, the first time I heard "body scan," it prompted an immediate eye roll. It's a terrible name. It sounds like it came right out of a 1950s sci-fi movie ... "and then Ming the Merciless did a body scan to imprison Flash Gordon's inner spirit."

Now that I know what it is, the name kind of says it all. We do a mindfulness meditation practice to scan the body to check in with how our body is feeling and to get a better sense of our emotions. While research of the brain as a whole is in its infancy stages, a part of the brain called the insula plays a key role in a number of important functions including self-awareness, perception, and cognition. The insula receives sensory information from the body and integrates it with the cognitive PFC for an appropriate response to that sensory information.

The insula is key for processing information about the internal state of our body. The body scan trains the insula to better process this information. It's like a workout for the insula. Studies have even shown the insula to be thicker in long-term mindfulness meditators.[8] We actually grow gray matter by practicing. Practice makes your body better at surfacing emotions and the thinking brain better at coming online to help you manage emotions before they manage you.

Learning to listen to the body for emotions and access them more readily through practice is an important skill for leaders. While we may not be taken over and controlled by aliens, the average person is regularly abducted by their emotions. The body scan helps to surface emotions so that you can stop, think about what's going on, and then choose how to manage them more skillfully.

Body Scan

Here's a five-minute practice from the Whil training library to experience bringing awareness to your body.

Start by settling your attention (one minute).

Begin by sitting in a way that feels comfortable, alert, and relaxed. You may close your eyes or soften your gaze.

Take five full, deep breaths in, and a long breath out. Allow your breath to find its natural rhythm. Notice whatever emotions you are feeling. Label them and let them pass.

Body Scan (four minutes)

Now, bring your attention to the very top of your head. Notice any sensation or lack of sensation.

Move your awareness slowly down to your face, your forehead, the muscles around the eyes, your cheeks, jaw, and mouth, softening your face.

And now moving down to the neck, bring attention to the front of your neck. Notice any sensations in your throat as you breathe in and breathe out.

Allow attention to flow down to your shoulders. With kind awareness, what sensations can you notice in the shoulders? Allow any tension to release.

Continue to cycle through your body, becoming aware of the upper arms, the lower arms, and your hands.

Now moving awareness to your upper back. Notice your shoulder blades and your lower back. Sensing your chest, notice any movement as you breathe. Notice your heart beating.

Becoming aware of your stomach. If you are able, even inviting awareness of the internal organs of your body.

Move down through the lower part of your body to your thighs, down to your knees, your shins, your calves and farther down to your ankles, the tops of your feet, the bottoms of your feet, and your toes.

Complete the practice by expanding your awareness to include your whole body. Notice your body breathing in and breathing out.

Allow yourself to bring attention back to different areas of your body and see if you notice anything new or different. Bring the practice to a close by offering appreciation to your body. You rely on it for so much. Developing a deeper awareness of how it feels can help you in many aspects of your life.

Pro Tip: When teaching a live training, I like to share an Open Awareness exercise. Try a 10-minute practice, moving your point of focus inside and outside of your body. Start by focusing on your breath (inside). Then pick an object to focus your sight (outside). Back to your head and neck (inside). Then to listening (outside), and so on. It's like CrossFit to heighten your internal and external awareness.

CHAPTER 15

Improving Self-Regulation

> Lord, please give me patience. If you give me
> strength, I may need bail money.
> —My sister Sherry

Have you ever gotten so mad that you just blew up? You didn't even think about it. It just came out. Ever eaten something when you weren't hungry? Even though you knew it was bad for you? Have you ever checked Facebook or Twitter 50 times a day? These actions are called compulsions. We get stuck in routines where we're compelled to act without really thinking.

The same thing happens when we get triggered. We can be compelled to act or make decisions without really thinking. When emotions are high, things can get ugly.

Self-regulation is the process of managing your internal states to perform optimally. This includes your impulses, resources, and especially your triggers. Self-regulation builds upon self-awareness skills. Once you're more aware of the quality and intensity of emotions as they occur, you can begin to identify, recognize, and work with your emotional "triggers" and the circumstances that cause them to arise.

Self-regulation isn't just stopping yourself from getting angry or yelling. It includes other important leadership qualities like being flexible, adaptable, resilient, and optimistic.

Most importantly, the practice of self-regulation helps take us out of automaton mode where it's easy to be driven by our emotions. We get better at the things we practice. When leaders practice being angry, distracted, or short-fused, they get better at it. With the help of positive neuroplasticity training, we can reach the point at which we are actually compelled to act a certain way. Here's an example:

When I worked in advertising, I managed the global relationship for our top client, a Fortune 30 technology company. The client's global marketing organization, starting with the CMO, was toxic. She had an enforcer who managed the $1.5 billion-dollar annual advertising budget that was spent through our agency. Let's call him Mick. Twenty years earlier, Mick had been a mid-level employee at a small West Coast office in our company. Like many folks who move client side, Mick had grown stale in a rapidly evolving digital landscape. Nonetheless, his favorite phrase was "I know that. I worked at your agency." He used it to intimidate our team and have them back off of informed strategies if they didn't support his own ideas. The client's stock had been on a rocket ship for years and there were no PC police in his company. To our staff's thinking, Mick had some $50 million reasons to be a jerk and confirming he was great at his job.

By the time I arrived, Mick was already legendary for his anger management issues. He had an advanced way of attacking people. When triggered, he'd make cutting analogies that reduced his staff to tears. In one negotiation, a manager on Mick's team wasn't fully prepared. Mick began aggressively pushing the manager to share his research, proving the agency should do more work and cut its pricing. It was obvious to the folks in the room that the manager didn't have the information. He couldn't make the case.

Working with Mick was like watching a volcano preparing to erupt. It kept everyone on edge. I can feel it in my body as I retell the story. In this case, the volcano erupted. Mick raised his voice, stood, and leaned across the conference room table and began banging his fist at his direct report. "You're like my frickin' five-year-old. I tell him to take a shower and he comes back stinking. He goes through the motions, but he doesn't do the job. That's you. You're a five-year-old pretending you did what you were told. Get out!" The manager exited without a word. Mick then turned to me, "This meeting is over. The next time we meet, he'd better come with the right information. And you guys better come prepared to cut your fees." I've negotiated over five billion dollars in agency contracts over the years. I've gotten used to bravado and faux anger. Mick's wasn't faux. He was triggered regularly by things big and small. He was prone to yelling. He was actually compelled to be that way.

I'd like to say this was the most uncomfortable of our meetings, but that wouldn't be true. The client's culture didn't just tolerate Mick's behavior. It celebrated it. Their macho, hero culture embraced the lack of self-control. That encouraged others to adopt similar behaviors. When fighting it head on didn't produce results, we raised our global fees by 15% to accommodate the ongoing inefficiency, wasted time, and abusive nature of the relationship. As Sun Tzu wrote in *The Art of War*, "The greatest victory is that which requires no battle."[1]

For leaders, there's always a cost to not being in control of your emotions. You will rarely be aware of the full cost. Employees will leave. Clients will change vendors. Vendors will increase their prices to adjust for the cost of doing business with an a-hole. Developing EQ skills helps you take an active self interest in not being a Jerk. Don't be a Mick.

Recognize Your Triggers

Every leader can name a few people who trigger them. The employee who talks too much or the person who always misses deadlines. Without realizing it, we're compelled to see them in a certain way. They become personified triggers for us. It's easy to put them into boxes and label them a moron, clown, troublemaker, and so forth. It's easy to slip into an unintentional style of managing these folks. We can become short, sarcastic, or dismissive without even realizing it. When this happens, others come to know who your favorites are, and that creates a domino effect for a team's culture.

With practice, you can recognize your triggers as they occur. Triggers can take any form. In the body, you might experience shallow breathing, a rapid heartbeat or feeling sick in your stomach. In your emotions, you might experience a flight-or-fight response, an emotional outburst, the desire to do harm, or the feeling that you have been harmed. In your thoughts, you might slip into blame, being judgmental, feeling like a victim, or go right to conspiracy theories about what is happening and why. Get used to witnessing them to take back control.

Triggers can also take the form of the neighbor's barking dog, meatloaf three days in a row, and even our kids. The environment we find ourselves in (intentionally or not) can present a continuous source of micro traumas or external triggers. Mindfulness helps you recognize them as they occur. Once you're aware, you can bring control and self-regulation to your response. Dr. Rick Hanson uses the double arrow metaphor. When we're triggered, we can't always help getting hit by the first arrow, but we can learn to stop giving ourselves the second or third arrows (through revisiting the triggers over time).

Being Hijacked by Your Emotions. Mick's example is only extreme in his meanness. Over the course of ongoing disruption and change, it's ordinary to be worn down and to act out of compulsion. When our actions are taken over and we're driven by our emotions, brain researchers call this an "amygdala hijack."

Remember, the thinking brain involves more neural circuitry, so its response time is slower than the emotional brain. The more we're led by our emotions, the more we can get hijacked by them. Over time, we can become experts at jumping to conclusions, assuming the worst, and flying off the handle. That affects how we make decisions and how we treat others. Sound familiar? We all have a colleague who occasionally flips his or her lid. And the more they do, the more likely they'll do it again. Sooner or later, some people walk around with their lids flipped all the time. We all know co-workers who are always looking for a fight, assuming the worst, and spinning up conspiracy theories at the drop of a hat. They've gotten good at being hijacked by their emotions because they practice like it they're training for the next Olympics.

Self-regulation helps you move from compulsion to choice. Studies have even shown that people with more meditation practice had less activity in the amygdala (the brain's fight-or-flight mechanism) when triggered by negative distractions. The more hours of training, the lower the likelihood to be triggered.[2]

To be clear, self-regulation is not about avoiding, denying, or suppressing feelings. As leaders, it's certainly not about hiding from what triggers us. It's about *fluency*, and being able to more comfortably translate emotion signals into conscious (kind) responses. It's about moving away from "shooting from the hip" and moving towards a more connected human response to management.

Practice Choice

A leading researcher in self-regulation was the Austrian neurologist, psychiatrist, and Holocaust survivor, Viktor Frankl. Frankl died in 1997 at the age of 92. Much of his work centered around the notion that we have power over our own feelings. In his book, *Man's Search for Meaning*, he explored the importance of finding meaning in all forms of existence, even the most brutal ones, so there's a reason to continue living.[3] Perhaps Frankl's best-known quote is, "Between stimulus and response, there is a space. In that space lies our freedom and our power to choose our response. In our response lies our growth and our happiness." In mindfulness and EQ training, this has come to be known as the "sacred pause."

As a leader, wouldn't it be nice to pause time for a few seconds to be one or two steps ahead of everyone else? Just enough time to collect your thoughts and then respond in a calm, cool, and collected fashion. Well, with a little practice, this superpower will be yours. As ABC News Correspondent, Dan Harris put it, "This respond, not react thing is a game changer. And this is why you see all these incredible people, these really successful athletes and business folks and entertainers doing this thing (mindfulness). The Superpower of not being yanked around by the voice in your head is immeasurably valuable."[4]

EQ Goes Way, Way Back

The notion that we can be compelled by our emotions is not new. The Roman emperor, Marcus Aurelius, wrote about it in his famous writings *Meditations* back in the year 170, "If you are distressed by anything external (or internal), the pain is not due to the thing itself, but to your estimate of it; and this you have the power to revoke at any moment."[5] For anyone still thinking this meditation stuff is too woo-woo, Marcus wasn't just an emperor and a leader. Dude was a warrior, too.

Pro Tip: Another warrior, Bruce Lee, was also an avid writer and philosopher, writing, "Realizing that my emotions are both *positive* and negative, I will form daily *habits* that will encourage the development of the *positive emotions*, and aid me in converting the negative emotions into some form of useful action."[6] His mindset allowed him to overcome a long-standing racial bias to become one of the biggest stars in Hollywood. What daily habits will you commit to?

Make Equanimity a Habit

Meditations is still revered as a literary tribute to service and duty. In it, Aurelius describes how to find and preserve equanimity. Equanimity is another foundational element of mindfulness and describes a state of mental stability and composure in the midst of conflict. Think of it as taking things just as they are without adding or taking away from them. Picking up my prior example—Mick was a client who wanted us to cut our fees. Nothing more. Nothing less. However, the mind's normal tendency is to make things worse than they are. In this case, our agency employees could add stories about how important the client is, Mick is evil, what if we lose the global business, he doesn't like me, what if I lose my job, and so on. In doing so, we would make the situation worse for all concerned. Maintaining a sense of equanimity (balanced reality) helps you to keep your emotions in check. There is usually a big difference between what is actually happening and how our egos, emotions and the stories we tend to add to our circumstances make it all seem worse. It's compounded when we share that worse view of events with our colleagues who're dealing with their own interpretations, assumptions, and stories. The stories in all of our heads make business harder than it needs to be. Developing a sense of equanimity allows you to stick to what is actually happening.

Practice Working with Triggers

Leaders are kind of like air traffic controllers for triggered employees. If you accept this as part of the job description, you will have removed a very common trigger for leaders - employees. You can also practice managing other triggers in the moment, any time. For now, let's explore this with something that's already happened.

Bring to mind a time when you were recently triggered. Pick something meaty enough to explore, but not too traumatic. For example, a work situation that left you feeling exposed and vulnerable. Something that includes a reaction that you later regretted.

Try to recapture the moment. You were triggered. What were you feeling in your body? What emotions were you experiencing? Did the flight-or-fight response kick in? Did you feel a sense of righteousness? What thoughts went through your head? What was your actual response? How did you feel about your response afterward? There's a good chance the situation is still impacting you right now. That's normal. Over time, it may have even become worse in your recollection than it really was. That's also normal, just the storytelling brain doing what it does so naturally. Is there anything you can do now to alleviate this trigger or any recurring ruminations? If so, take that action.

STOP, IN THE NAME OF LOVE

Now, let's check in on one of most powerful mindfulness techniques for self-regulation, SBNRR. This acronym stands for Stop-Breathe-Notice-Reflect-Respond. This is a potent tool to interrupt the wandering mind and bring yourself back to a point of calm and focus. It is especially powerful when you've been triggered. Let's explore each part of the acronym. You can also use the example you just brought to mind if you like.

SBNRR Practice

Stop. Whenever you feel triggered, stop and catch yourself. Don't react. Give yourself a few moments with the sacred pause. You might even give yourself a catchphrase. In my case, I find that things like "Don't react" or "Stop and think, Joe." This simple act will engage your thinking brain and give it time to catch up to the emotional brain.

Breathe. Bring your attention to your breath to relax yourself. This reinforces the sacred pause and injects calm. You are back in control.

Notice. Get a clearer experience of your emotions by bringing attention to your body. What does it feel like in your face, neck, shoulders, chest, abdomen, and back? Even notice changes in tension or temperature without judging it. Be curious. This helps you move from the existential experience of "I am angry" or "I feel ashamed" to the physiological experience of "I am experiencing anger (or shame) in my body."

Reflect. What's causing the emotion? Where are your reactions coming from? Is there some history that's impacting this moment? Is your ego getting involved? Is there a self-perceived inadequacy at work? Is this story you're telling yourself true? What's the evidence? Is there another way to look at this? Without judging it as right or wrong, bring more perspective to it.

If it involves another person (and it usually does), consider an empathic viewpoint. Put yourself in their shoes. Remind yourself this person wants to be happy, just like you. What is causing them to act this way and can you be compassionate?

Respond. Consider how to respond to create a more positive outcome. Ask yourself: How can I bring kindness to this moment? Then respond.

This is a deep dive into the SBNRR practice. In real time, you don't need more than a few seconds to catch yourself to create a more positive outcome. The most important step is to create enough space to move from being compelled to respond out of emotion versus choosing to respond. Or not.

You May Not Even Have to Respond

Oftentimes, leaders are invited into drama without warning. This can happen when an employee gets fired up and want you to take sides. Taking the bait can reinforce the wrong behaviors and it can be divisive. Try, instead, listening with your full attention as if hearing it for the first time. Witness what's happening. Ask a few questions and let the person know you'll thoughtfully consider it for a later discussion. This also gives you the opportunity not only to think, but to allow emotions to dissipate, as well as allow you to speak to others involved. Instead of being triggered, you can be the calm in the storm—the coach with helpful advice.

Now, let's revisit how your example situation could have been better using the SBNRR technique. Based on the feelings in your body, the emotions felt, and the thoughts going through your head, how could SBNRR have helped? Would your response be different? Would you even have responded in that moment?

Even a few seconds of the SBNRR technique creates enough of a pause and reflection to explore different choices, ask a few questions, and connect with the person, or interrupt yourself when you get stuck in unhelpful ruminations. Set an intention to try the SBNRR practice once a day this week.

Recognize and Change

Use this reflection and planning journaling exercise from the Whil library to periodically explore and alleviate triggers. Give yourself five minutes, split evenly between the two prompts.

(continued)

(continued)

Your first prompt is: Something that triggered me recently was ...

Your second prompt is: My response could have been different if ...

Each time you journal, it's an opportunity to reflect, plan, and take action to improve your situation. A big part of mindfulness is personal accountability.

USE MUSIC AS A PRACTICE

You can use any single point of focus, including music, as an opportunity to train your attention and increase positive emotions.[7] Use the lyrics as your point of focus. When you notice you're distracted, come back to them. Singing with others has also been shown to improve positive emotions, no matter what your musical ability is.[8] I even find both practices help me to more deeply appreciate the message of the music and find inspiration for my own life.

During our *CML Workshop*, I play the a capella version of the song *Under Pressure* by David Bowie and Freddie Mercury for an attention training exercise. You can find it on YouTube.[9] It's become one of my favorite songs. Bowie and Mercury cover the full range of human emotions from crushing despair through incredible hope. One of the last lines in the song dares us to change our way of caring about ourselves.

I get mixed reactions from audiences during this practice. A good 75% of participants enjoy it. They realize that, although they've loved the song (sometimes for decades), they've never really listened to the words. The song's emotional highs and lows are intense. The hints at losing friends to suicide are crushing. The message of hope and love and giving yourself another chance are powerful and uplifting. Most people miss all of it. They never focus on the words, the emotions, and what's at risk. This can also be true in our daily relationships. Too much of what's going on is background music to our own stories and dramas playing out in our minds. With focus, we can explore, appreciate, and be inspired by the day-to-day norms, events, and relationships in our lives.

The remaining 25% of participants have a visceral negative reaction. They actually get triggered by the song. One leader shared he couldn't take the song being out of key. Huh? Others felt like Bowie and Mercury were yelling at them. Some find the lyrics too depressing. This is intentional. And magical when you have a hundred driven leaders in one room.

Don't Worry, We're All Under Pressure

The other reason I love this song is that it relates to business. Being a leader means dealing with challenges like ambiguity, conflict, and influencing others. It can be easy to feel like we're constantly under pressure. That can be offset by the satisfaction of closing a big deal or the adrenaline rush from the pace of business. Our physical, mental, and emotional health are all intertwined. Using music, art, and other hobbies to practice attention training can make the experiences even more enjoyable and simultaneously give you the benefits of a meditation practice. Two for the price of one.

Moreover, this attention training can unwittingly inspire both confidence and kindness. Yes, that's right. When you're under pressure, you can be vulnerable to irritability, impatience, and meanness. Mindfulness practice can help avoid the modern business "trifecta" mentioned earlier: unmanaged stress, mood disorders, and substance abuse.[10] This always makes things worse.

Some leaders worry that mindfulness can dull the desire to win. CEOs, leaders, and warriors throughout history have found the opposite to be true. We're practicing mental strategies for being cool, focused, and confident under pressure. That's not woo-woo. It's a competitive advantage.

WELLBEING PERFORMANCE CAREER

CHAPTER 16

Boosting Motivation

I get to do what I like to do every single day of the
year. I tap dance to work, and when I get there,
I think I'm supposed to lie on my back and paint
the ceiling. It's tremendous fun.

—Warren Buffett

I once had the pleasure of having dinner with Warren Buffett. He spoke to some 500 leaders at a Harvard Business School executive program. At dinner, he spent an hour talking and taking pictures pretending to whisper stock advice or holding his wallet out to offer people money. His passion for his craft and for humanity fit perfectly with his keynote remarks on the importance of enjoying your work.

As we continue to climb up the ladder in training EQ skills, the next step is understanding your motivation. Or as we say at Whil, "Where are you going and what will you create?"

If you're a fan of the movie classic, *Office Space*, the lead character, Peter, played by Jon Livingston, had a great quote. "It's not that I'm lazy. It's that I just don't care." While the movie hilariously shared the downside of corporate life, the Gallup polls I shared earlier remind us that most professionals actually do go through life without a connection to the type of work they are doing, the company they're with, or why they are there.

A major benefit of developing EQ skills is living life with more intention. This helps us enjoy each moment and to be more aware of how we spend those moments. Jack London once said, "You can't wait for inspiration. You have to go after it with a club." In the absence of being intentional and aware, many professionals fall into coincidental career and life paths they may have never wanted. In my experience, living with intention creates calm and focus. Living by coincidence creates anxiety and regret.

How Much of Your Stressed-Out Life Is Coincidental?

When I look back on my own career, I appreciate three themes. I was making more money than I ever thought possible. I was miserable. And most of my stressed-out life was self-inflicted or coincidental.

We're all born into families and surroundings that are the luck of the draw. Some are coincidentally born into the top 1%. The rest of us are coincidentally born into the other 99%. For me, it was a lower-middle class family in Pittsburgh, Pennsylvania. I was coincidentally the youngest of six and a twin. Our father was coincidentally an unemployable alcoholic. My mother was a stay-at-home mom and suffered from a walking disability caused by muscular dystrophy.

We coincidentally lived in a poor area. Growing up, I got my brother's hand-me-downs, including his chores, snow shoveling and paper routes. We attended public schools that were close enough to walk to. I got my first real job at Sears because it was across the street from our high school. My accounting teacher referred me because I was good at math and she knew I could use the money.

I dated the first woman to show interest in me. For eight years. Gulp. To be fair, I had zero rap. I didn't know how to speak to women. I wasn't clever or charming and had never heard of mindfulness. Just like EQ, it didn't occur to me that these were learnable skills.

I was the first person in my family to go to college. I didn't know much, but I knew I had to be a commuter and I had to keep my job at Sears. Mom started charging us rent when we turned 15, so I needed the money. Seems funny to say that now, "I had to keep my minimum wage job at Sears." $3.65/hr. back in the day.

you do, but you definitely value its impact. While purpose is a [powe]rful driver for performance, it's one step removed from the work [...] which generally makes it a less powerful motive than play.

[Pr]o Tip: A global study by LinkedIn showed that the percent[ag]e of Millennials driven by purpose (30%) was lower than [th]at of Gen Xers (38%) and Boomers (48%).[4] Erik Erikson, [a] German psychoanalyst, theorizes that Millennials are more [in]terested in cultivating relationships as a key part of their [id]entity. Only when they reach middle age do they shift toward [a] identity that involves contributing more to society.[5] With [M]illennials now making up the majority of the workforce, [he]lping them instill a sense of purpose earlier in their career [sh]ould be a priority for leaders – and for yourself if you happen [to] be one.

Potential: The potential motive occurs when you take part in an [endea]vor because it will eventually lead to something you believe is [impor]tant. An example would be a stepping-stone job to get a promo[tion.] The potential motive is not as powerful as play or purpose—it's [two s]teps removed from the work (play) itself.

Together, play, purpose, and potential are known as direct motives [becau]se they're most directly linked to the work itself. A culture that [inspir]es employees to bring play, purpose, and potential to their jobs [creat]es the opportunity for high and sustainable performance and [bett]er work cultures.

[D]oshi and McGregor also cover three indirect motives, including [emot]ional pressure (guilt or shame), economic pressure (get a reward [or avo]id punishment), and inertia, where employees do what they do [b]ecause they can't think of a good reason to leave. When your [reaso]ns to work are due to indirect motives, your performance tends [to suf]fer.

I studied business at Duquesne University (just below Ivy League) because they provided the best scholarship. I studied accounting because I was good at math. It wasn't a passion. Then, I took a job at Price Waterhouse in Pittsburgh because they offered $29,000 instead of the $27,000 offered by the other Big 8 audit firms. I needed the extra $2k and I had to stay in town to help with family.

Soon, I was assigned to the audit group and then to accounts I had no say in. I worked on steel, oil, and coal companies, which, coincidentally were clients of PW's Pittsburgh office at the time.

My Career Unfolded on a Similar Coincidental Path from There. Transferring where the company needed me. Tackling the big projects that needed the most help. Lucking into some amazing experiences. Tolerating some crap experiences. Step by step, it all kind of just happened. At no point did I afford myself the luxury of asking, "What's my motivation? Am I doing what I want to do with my life?" In hindsight, my thinking was probably limited to "I'll do anything to create a better life for me and my family."

Ultimately, it all led to my first global COO role. Twelve-to-14 hour days. 70% travel. I ran and flew to where I was needed. And the market shifted. Coincidentally, I spent less time working with CMOs and launching new capabilities and global offices and more time working with procurement professionals. This was my first experience with "faster, cheaper" as the new norm.

DO YOU HAVE A PLAN?

Sure, I worked hard to manifest success in whatever I was doing, but it all happened without much of a plan. A tremendous amount of hard work led to increasingly big titles, responsibility, stress, and unhappiness.

By the time I got married, I had developed enough rap, game, and charm to land the woman of my dreams. Because of Sarah, the conversation in my life changed. At 40, I started to realize that most of my life was coincidental. Sure, I'd (mostly) chosen wisely from the options that were in front of me. And I've always been grateful for the opportunities in my life. But I didn't plan for what I wanted out of life or a career. To be honest, it hadn't even occurred to me that creating my own path was an option. Looking back, I'd made coincidental choices with the women I dated, where I lived, the schools I attended, the area in which I focused my studies, and every job that I'd ever had. The one exception was choosing my spouse and having her choose me.

Don't get me wrong. I've been incredibly fortunate in my life. I've had opportunities I would never have imagined growing up, like working in over 50 countries. But I became so addicted to chasing rewards and recognition that I never really enjoyed the journey.

Realizing that many of your life choices are coincidental can instill an undercurrent of regret, anxiety, and resentment. I wasn't able to label these emotions until I started mindfulness training. Ultimately, I stepped away from running global advertising agencies to focus on building Whil. Changing the direction of my career was the first time I had a plan and the intentions to set my own life path. It was terrifying. Turns out, building a stress resilience company has been incredibly stressful. And wonderful. It's made all the difference in my life.

Three things provided a wake-up call to my coincidental life: increasing unhappiness, failing health, and a spouse who cared more deeply about both than I did myself. Training EQ skills on a foundation of mindfulness was the rocket fuel that allowed me to live life with intention.

In the coming pages, we'll explore your own motivation. Let's try another planning and reflection exercise to explore what has been coincidental in your own life.

Live with Greater Intention

Here's a five-minute Whil journaling practice to help explore where coincidental stress may be impacting your life. Do the first prompt for 2½ minutes. Then move on to the second prompt at the midpoint.

Your first prompt is: The things in my career and life that are coincidental include …

Your second prompt is: If I were leading v
tion, I would …

Following this exercise, commit to make
choices that will make you happier in you
career. Make journaling a practice to explore
address them.

Why You Work Affects How Well You

A lot of research has been done confirming that
(self-worth, personal growth, passion, satisfaction
meaning, making a difference, and so on) are n
extrinsic motivators (social status, money, power
ning, public recognition, and so on). This may exp
to Deloitte, only 13% of employees report bein
their work.[1]

In their 2015 book, *Primed to Perform*, consulta
Lindsay McGregor share research and case studies
high-performing cultures based on three direct mc

Play: You're most likely to succeed when y
when you engage simply because you enjoy it. Mi
curiosity, being open, nonjudgmental, and experin
heart of play. People intrinsically enjoy learning an
the play motive is created by the work itself, it's t
most powerful driver of high performance. Plato v
cover more about a person in an hour of play than in
tion." Numerous studies support that play is impor
vitality, cultivating empathy, collaboration, and cre
me years to stop being the grumpy "get back to w
stand this. I still have to wrestle that guy to the
How much do you play at work? Do you truly kno

Purpose: The purpose motive happens wher
because you value the outcome. You may or may n

In their estimation, the motivators you focus on determine which one of the four kinds of leaders you are.

1. **Quid Pro Quo Leaders:** This leader believes in something for something. They give rewards for good behavior and punishments or threat to try to control bad behavior. They produce high levels of indirect motives in their employees.

2. **Hands-Off Leaders:** This leader uses neither direct nor indirect motivators. They get involved only when there's a problem. They generally have good intentions, believing their teams want lots of space. But they're wrong. Teams perform best when the leader is involved.

3. **Enthusiast:** This leader tries everything, direct and indirect, but has a tendency to cancel out the direct motives through lack of focus.

4. **Fire Starter:** This leader uses direct motivators and do whatever they can to eliminate the indirect motivators. They play.

Most of us fluctuate between these kinds of leaders over time and generally without specific intention. These days, I make it a practice to be a Fire Starter. I'm not great at it yet, but practicing makes every week fun.

Other authors have explored similar themes.

• In *Drive*, best-selling author Daniel Pink used 50 years of research in behavioral science to argue that external motivators (or pleasure rewards) like promotions and money are not the best drivers of high performance.[6] Instead, his research found the best motivators to be "intrinsic motivators" like the mastery of work, having a higher purpose, and autonomy—the desire to direct our own lives.

• In *Why We Work*, Barry Schwartz shared, "Satisfied people do their work because they feel that they are in charge. Their workday offers them a measure of autonomy and discretion. And they use that autonomy and discretion to achieve a level of mastery or expertise. They learn new things developing both as workers and as people."[7]

- In *Delivering Happiness*, Tony Hsieh shared how Zappos created a corporate culture based on pleasure, passion, and higher purpose. Happy employees provide the level of service that makes for happy customers who then spend more money. Hsieh has since launched a consulting company by the same name with his co-founder, Jenn Lim. Today, Delivering Happiness inspires passion and purpose in the workplace.[8] I'm proud to say they are a partner of Whil's. Mindfulness and culture go hand in hand.

Don't Chase the Wrong Things

Instinctively, most of us chase after pleasure and indirect motivators. Over time, we may find that monetary rewards and promotions are not the source of sustainable happiness. What if you flipped your personal model on its head to pursue direct motivators? How would that change your motivations as a leader and how you manage teams?

Looking back, I pursued mastery and autonomy intuitively at the earliest stage in my career. Purpose, not so much. That approach delivered results for me. And a commanding style of leadership, when stressed, likely caused me to withhold the same opportunities for my direct reports to find their own direct motivators. Command and control worked for many decades in business. Now it doesn't.

Connect Your Life and Work

So much of motivation has to do with being engaged in work that aligns with your own personal purpose. Here's a short Whil exercise to check in on the degree to which your personal motivation and purpose are aligned with your company. Draw two large circles that overlap by about one third in the middle. In the left circle, write five to 10 key values

I studied business at Duquesne University (just below Ivy League) because they provided the best scholarship. I studied accounting because I was good at math. It wasn't a passion. Then, I took a job at Price Waterhouse in Pittsburgh because they offered $29,000 instead of the $27,000 offered by the other Big 8 audit firms. I needed the extra $2k and I had to stay in town to help with family.

Soon, I was assigned to the audit group and then to accounts I had no say in. I worked on steel, oil, and coal companies, which, coincidentally were clients of PW's Pittsburgh office at the time.

My Career Unfolded on a Similar Coincidental Path from There. Transferring where the company needed me. Tackling the big projects that needed the most help. Lucking into some amazing experiences. Tolerating some crap experiences. Step by step, it all kind of just happened. At no point did I afford myself the luxury of asking, "What's my motivation? Am I doing what I want to do with my life?" In hindsight, my thinking was probably limited to "I'll do anything to create a better life for me and my family."

Ultimately, it all led to my first global COO role. Twelve-to-14 hour days. 70% travel. I ran and flew to where I was needed. And the market shifted. Coincidentally, I spent less time working with CMOs and launching new capabilities and global offices and more time working with procurement professionals. This was my first experience with "faster, cheaper" as the new norm.

Do You Have a Plan?

Sure, I worked hard to manifest success in whatever I was doing, but it all happened without much of a plan. A tremendous amount of hard work led to increasingly big titles, responsibility, stress, and unhappiness.

By the time I got married, I had developed enough rap, game, and charm to land the woman of my dreams. Because of Sarah, the conversation in my life changed. At 40, I started to realize that most of my life was coincidental. Sure, I'd (mostly) chosen wisely from the options that were in front of me. And I've always been grateful for the opportunities in my life. But I didn't plan for what I wanted out of life or a career. To be honest, it hadn't even occurred to me that creating my own path was an option. Looking back, I'd made coincidental choices with the women I dated, where I lived, the schools I attended, the area in which I focused my studies, and every job that I'd ever had. The one exception was choosing my spouse and having her choose me.

Don't get me wrong. I've been incredibly fortunate in my life. I've had opportunities I would never have imagined growing up, like working in over 50 countries. But I became so addicted to chasing rewards and recognition that I never really enjoyed the journey.

Realizing that many of your life choices are coincidental can instill an undercurrent of regret, anxiety, and resentment. I wasn't able to label these emotions until I started mindfulness training. Ultimately, I stepped away from running global advertising agencies to focus on building Whil. Changing the direction of my career was the first time I had a plan and the intentions to set my own life path. It was terrifying. Turns out, building a stress resilience company has been incredibly stressful. And wonderful. It's made all the difference in my life.

Three things provided a wake-up call to my coincidental life: increasing unhappiness, failing health, and a spouse who cared more deeply about both than I did myself. Training EQ skills on a foundation of mindfulness was the rocket fuel that allowed me to live life with intention.

In the coming pages, we'll explore your own motivation. Let's try another planning and reflection exercise to explore what has been coincidental in your own life.

Live with Greater Intention

Here's a five-minute Whil journaling practice to help explore where coincidental stress may be impacting your life. Do the first prompt for 2½ minutes. Then move on to the second prompt at the midpoint.

Your first prompt is: The things in my career and life that are coincidental include…

> Your second prompt is: If I were leading with more intention, I would …
>
> Following this exercise, commit to make more intentional choices that will make you happier in your life and your career. Make journaling a practice to explore issues and then address them.

Why You Work Affects How Well You Work

A lot of research has been done confirming that intrinsic motivators (self-worth, personal growth, passion, satisfaction, fun, purpose and meaning, making a difference, and so on) are more powerful than extrinsic motivators (social status, money, power, titles, perks, winning, public recognition, and so on). This may explain why, according to Deloitte, only 13% of employees report being passionate about their work.[1]

In their 2015 book, *Primed to Perform*, consultants Neel Doshi and Lindsay McGregor share research and case studies of leaders creating high-performing cultures based on three direct motives for work.

Play: You're most likely to succeed when your motive is play; when you engage simply because you enjoy it. Mindful elements like curiosity, being open, nonjudgmental, and experimentation are at the heart of play. People intrinsically enjoy learning and adapting. Because the play motive is created by the work itself, it's the most direct and most powerful driver of high performance. Plato wrote, "You can discover more about a person in an hour of play than in a year of conversation." Numerous studies support that play is important to our survival, vitality, cultivating empathy, collaboration, and creativity.[2–3] It's taken me years to stop being the grumpy "get back to work" guy to understand this. I still have to wrestle that guy to the ground sometimes. How much do you play at work? Do you truly know your co-workers?

Purpose: The purpose motive happens when you do something because you value the outcome. You may or may not enjoy the kind of work you do, but you definitely value its impact. While purpose is a powerful driver for performance, it's one step removed from the work itself, which generally makes it a less powerful motive than play.

> Pro Tip: A global study by LinkedIn showed that the percentage of Millennials driven by purpose (30%) was lower than that of Gen Xers (38%) and Boomers (48%).[4] Erik Erikson, a German psychoanalyst, theorizes that Millennials are more interested in cultivating relationships as a key part of their identity. Only when they reach middle age do they shift toward an identity that involves contributing more to society.[5] With Millennials now making up the majority of the workforce, helping them instill a sense of purpose earlier in their career should be a priority for leaders – and for yourself if you happen to be one.

Potential: The potential motive occurs when you take part in an endeavor because it will eventually lead to something you believe is important. An example would be a stepping-stone job to get a promotion. The potential motive is not as powerful as play or purpose—it's two steps removed from the work (play) itself.

Together, play, purpose, and potential are known as direct motives because they're most directly linked to the work itself. A culture that inspires employees to bring play, purpose, and potential to their jobs creates the opportunity for high and sustainable performance and happier work cultures.

Doshi and McGregor also cover three indirect motives, including emotional pressure (guilt or shame), economic pressure (get a reward or avoid punishment), and inertia, where employees do what they do just because they can't think of a good reason to leave. When your reasons to work are due to indirect motives, your performance tends to suffer.

In their estimation, the motivators you focus on determine which one of the four kinds of leaders you are.

1. **Quid Pro Quo Leaders:** This leader believes in something for something. They give rewards for good behavior and punishments or threat to try to control bad behavior. They produce high levels of indirect motives in their employees.

2. **Hands-Off Leaders:** This leader uses neither direct nor indirect motivators. They get involved only when there's a problem. They generally have good intentions, believing their teams want lots of space. But they're wrong. Teams perform best when the leader is involved.

3. **Enthusiast:** This leader tries everything, direct and indirect, but has a tendency to cancel out the direct motives through lack of focus.

4. **Fire Starter:** This leader uses direct motivators and do whatever they can to eliminate the indirect motivators. They play.

Most of us fluctuate between these kinds of leaders over time and generally without specific intention. These days, I make it a practice to be a Fire Starter. I'm not great at it yet, but practicing makes every week fun.

Other authors have explored similar themes.

- In *Drive*, best-selling author Daniel Pink used 50 years of research in behavioral science to argue that external motivators (or pleasure rewards) like promotions and money are not the best drivers of high performance.[6] Instead, his research found the best motivators to be "intrinsic motivators" like the mastery of work, having a higher purpose, and autonomy—the desire to direct our own lives.

- In *Why We Work*, Barry Schwartz shared, "Satisfied people do their work because they feel that they are in charge. Their workday offers them a measure of autonomy and discretion. And they use that autonomy and discretion to achieve a level of mastery or expertise. They learn new things developing both as workers and as people."[7]

- In *Delivering Happiness*, Tony Hsieh shared how Zappos created a corporate culture based on pleasure, passion, and higher purpose. Happy employees provide the level of service that makes for happy customers who then spend more money. Hsieh has since launched a consulting company by the same name with his co-founder, Jenn Lim. Today, Delivering Happiness inspires passion and purpose in the workplace.[8] I'm proud to say they are a partner of Whil's. Mindfulness and culture go hand in hand.

Don't Chase the Wrong Things

Instinctively, most of us chase after pleasure and indirect motivators. Over time, we may find that monetary rewards and promotions are not the source of sustainable happiness. What if you flipped your personal model on its head to pursue direct motivators? How would that change your motivations as a leader and how you manage teams?

Looking back, I pursued mastery and autonomy intuitively at the earliest stage in my career. Purpose, not so much. That approach delivered results for me. And a commanding style of leadership, when stressed, likely caused me to withhold the same opportunities for my direct reports to find their own direct motivators. Command and control worked for many decades in business. Now it doesn't.

Connect Your Life and Work

So much of motivation has to do with being engaged in work that aligns with your own personal purpose. Here's a short Whil exercise to check in on the degree to which your personal motivation and purpose are aligned with your company. Draw two large circles that overlap by about one third in the middle. In the left circle, write five to 10 key values for your company. In the right circle, do the same for yourself. In the middle, write down the values that connect. How can you bring more into the middle? Alternatively, you may find that two cannot be aligned. How does this impact your motivation and performance?

Get to Know Your Team

When we think about motivation, there are two key questions to ask yourself. First, do I really have a good understanding of my own goals, plans, and motivations? You need a touchstone for success and something to measure yourself against. Second, do my co-workers have a good understanding of what motivates me? This is equally important. As leaders, we enroll teammates into missions and we expect them to deliver. If they feel the only mission is making money, or worse, making my manager look good, then it's difficult to establish the bonds important for sustainable success.

Really Introduce Yourself. Every time you introduce yourself is an opportunity to share what motivates you as a leader. Instead, most of us use our canned 10-second elevator pitch. For me, it might be something like, "Hi. I'm Joe Burton. I own the leading digital training platform for employee wellbeing. I started it four years ago and now we have clients around the world." Blah, blah, blah. These short intros usually don't convey much. Too many of us treat them as opportunities to try to look good. Whenever a sales friend of mine makes an intro, he ends with "Are we done lying to each other yet?" The point is, most intros don't allow you to get to know much about the other person.

The same is true for people who you may work with for years. You spend eight hours a day in nearby cubes or offices, countless meetings, trainings, and so forth. But do you really know what drives them?

I'm reminded of my friend, John Eaton. We worked together for a year in a startup turnaround situation. I knew John as an entrepreneur and a brilliant social media strategist. I also knew he had been in the music business earlier in his career. We worked together for an entire year before I learned that he was also a Grammy Award–winning producer. Initially, I was shocked. I joked that if I had won a Grammy, I'd be wearing it around my neck on a big gold chain on top of my "Ask me about my Grammy" T-shirt. In time, I found that John was also a great father, husband, and someone who cares deeply about others, society at large, and our planet. We had a wide array of common interests that connected us. If we knew that earlier on, managing the difficulties of a startup turnaround would have come more easily.

The same is true for any team. A small amount of openness and vulnerability goes a long way to creating the ties that bind. Since we spend more time with work colleagues than we do with our families, it makes sense to move beyond the surface-level "I'm good at my job" chatter to find out what really inspires and motivates them. Then you can determine if the right motivations are at play to help them and your company succeed.

Be Like Inigo Montoya

When is the last time you shared what motivates you with someone else? What if that became part of your conversation with colleagues and new people who you meet regularly?

In the movie, *The Princess Bride*, Mandy Patinkin plays the character Inigo Montoya. As a child, the villainous "six-fingered man" kills Inigo's father in a swordfight. The young boy dedicates his life to avenging his father's death. During the film, he keeps practicing how he will introduce himself once he finally finds the six-fingered man. "Hello, my name is Inigo Montoya. You killed my father. Prepare to die." Near the end of the movie, he finally meets the villain. During their sword fight, he keeps repeating this mantra. It's a powerful scene. There's no doubt what motivates him. Here's someone who dedicated his life to becoming an expert swordfighter. He has a purpose and a mission. "Hello, my name is Inigo Montoya. You killed my father. Prepare to die." I'm not suggesting that you go out and kill someone. But what if your co-workers really know what you stand for?

The following is a short exercise you can do with anyone. In our *CML Workshop*, attendees find this exercise to be transformational. They move from trying to look good in surface level conversations to truly connecting. They move from concern about being judged to experiencing the power of being open and authentic. If you're married, I especially recommend doing this with your partner. The short exercise quite often ends with a hug from attendees who were complete strangers a few minutes earlier. That's the power of authentic connection.

Allow Myself to Introduce Myself

It's good to share all that you are with the people in your life. Walt Whitman wrote, "I am larger, better than I thought. I did not know I held so much goodness."

Here's a Whil exercise to better get to know yourself and your colleagues better. First, do a standard 10-second introduction to one another. What is your normal generic way of meeting someone new?

Next, take three minutes to introduce yourself using the phrase, "If you really knew me, you'd know ... " Just like Inigo Montoya, keep repeating it time and again while you fill in the blank. An example for me might be, "Hello. I'm Joe Burton. If you really knew me, you'd know my life is dedicated to my wife and two sons. Family means everything to me. If you really knew me, you'd know I started a business to help people. I suffered from stress, chronic back pain, and insomnia for years. I harmed my health and wellbeing. If you really knew me, you'd know I'd do anything for my team. My success is due to them. If you really knew me, you'd know my biggest fear is failure. If you really knew you me, you'd know I grew up on welfare with a lot of shame at a young age. Learning mindfulness put that in my past." And so on.

Treat this an opportunity to be authentic. In my experience, you'll find the other person will do the same. We all crave true human connection. And when leaders truly connect with their team, the impact can be transformative.

What's Your Best Possible Future?

Most of us tend to predict futures that are consistent with our past. We manifest what we expect to happen.

We all know people who get locked into a way of being based on their past. For some, that turns into the Debbie Downer syndrome in which they feel nothing ever goes their way, they never get a break, and everything is stacked against them. Over time, this becomes part of their subconscious. We get locked into negative thoughts without realizing it. (For you folks named Debbie, my apologies. If it helps any, my name is Joe. As in the "Average Joe." I feel your pain.) Debbie Downer folks tend to expect the worst and then the worst happens. Conversely, we all know people who look at the sunny side of life. They believe that the universe conspires in their favor and they tend to work toward the good results that they expect. What approach do you feed?

When it comes to motivation, envisioning is a powerful tool to think about the future, commit to goals, and then make them happen. One of my favorite people is Chris Bertish. I met Chris a while back on the speaking circuit. He's a high-energy speaker and shares the story of training for the 2010 Mavericks, the top surfing competition in the world. The Mavericks are announced based on weather patterns for the most favorable waves, giving the 24 athletes who qualify only 48 hours to get there. Chris shares a powerful story of envisioning the impossible. As an unranked surfer with no sponsors, he trained and committed himself to winning the event inside of 10 years.

When the call finally came, he was trained and mentally prepared (Chris learned attention training from his father as a young performance athlete). But he wasn't ready. He was living in South Africa, had $40 to his name and 48 hours to get to the event in Half Moon Bay, California. He borrowed enough money to fly coach, got a total of six hours sleep in two days and landed with just four hours to make the event. But his equipment didn't arrive. He had to compete on borrowed equipment. Imagine Andre Agassi without his racket! Sorry, my analogies are all from the 1980s. Chris competed to the final heat, nursing a rib he feared had been broken on his first run. On the final wave of the final heat, having traveled across the world in 48 hours on six hours of sleep and on borrowed equipment, he won the Mavericks in front of 50,000 spectators. His adventure would later be showcased in Ocean Driven an award-winning documentary and a best-selling book, *Stoked!*.[9]

What's Next? In 2016, Chris set another goal for himself. He committed to raising funds for children in Africa by SUPing across the Atlantic. SUP stands for stand-up paddle boarding. His website described it as "paddling a marathon every day for 93 days, over 4,500 miles to show the world what's possible, one stroke at a time." Two months before his trip, Chris visited Whil to share his plans with our team. We were inspired—and concerned for his life.

He had a special craft built. The trip started on the northwest coast of Africa, in Morocco. He battled the currents, storms, sharks, exhaustion, and the loneliness of being at sea without another soul for months. He started and ended each day with breathing and focus practices. By the fourth week, his craft had flipped dozens of times, electrical systems failed, the craft sprung a leak, two great whites threatened attacks, a safety harness got trapped on a giant squid, and a storm blew him 200 miles off track. But he never lost sight of his goal. After 93 days of paddling, he arrived in Florida. Chris credits his higher purpose and ability to remain alert and focused in getting him through. Beyond breaking multiple world records, he raised over six times his goal – enough to build a school, provide one million meals, and over 1,000 life-changing surgeries for children in Africa.

Chris's story is not unlike my own (kidding). Most of us can't relate to that kind of potential danger. However, as leaders, we can all relate to the constant challenge of feeling alone in the face of ongoing change, risk, and uncertainty.

Setting goals and envisioning the outcomes you want in your life are important tools for focus, drive, and achievement. In the absence of creating space to chase goals, we can end up chasing our own tales. The numbers and business results matter, but so do personal goals. Pick ones that make you want to jump out of bed in the morning.

Plan for the Future

Helen Keller once said, "The only thing worse than being blind is having sight and no vision." I shared Chris's story to inspire you. You don't need to break world records, but envisioning helps you to set a plan and touchstones to make progress against. Here's a 10-minute Whil journaling exercise to explore this for yourself.

Your prompt is: If your dreams come true, describe all aspects of your life 10 years from now. How will others describe you? Is your life on track for this legacy to manifest itself? Where are you going and what will you create?

CHAPTER **17**

Getting Positive – Don't Call it a Comeback

> I never lose. I either win or I learn.
> —Nelson Mandela

One of the keys to maintaining positivity and bringing what you envision into the world is resilience. Webster defines resilience as "the ability to recover from or adjust easily to misfortune or change."[1]

Over the past few years, "resilience" has become the preferred term for the skill to adapt and thrive. Employers want employees to be resilient in the face of ongoing change and disruption. For many employers, resilience sounds more relatable than "mindfulness" or "emotional intelligence." Resilience has an edge to it—a feeling of accomplishment. It also sounds better than "suck it up," a sentiment that old-school leaders should drop. Yesterday.

Our emotions, actions, and performance are all interconnected. When it comes to being a motivated and high-performing professional, strong mental resilience (a positive way to think, perceive, and remember information) leads to inner calm. This, in turn, leads to higher emotional resilience (our ability to roll with the punches, adapt, and move forward).

The opposite is also true. Limited mental resilience (a negative mindset) leads to inner turmoil in which stress and anxiety are fed by ongoing negative thoughts and perceptions. This, in turn, leads to a

Figure 17.1   The resilience cycle

reduced ability to manage our emotions. As leaders, we are practicing one cycle or the other (Figure 17.1). The question is, are you being intentional about it?

DEVELOP A GROWTH MINDSET TO INCREASE RESILIENCE

Research shows that when leaders have a fixed mindset about whether or not we can do something or learn something, we're more susceptible to a loss of confidence or giving up when we encounter challenges. A fixed mindset is the belief that one's intelligence is static.[2] That can lead to being disengaged, which contributes to stress and burnout.

When we have a growth mindset, we're more willing to try new things, and persist when facing obstacles. We're also more reflective and open to feedback. We can cultivate being more positive, curious, and nonjudgmental. In one study, university students who believe intelligence is malleable had a greater appreciation for academics, were more motivated to do well, were able to improve performance after failures and setbacks, and had a better GPA than students who believed that intelligence is fixed.[3] Being a lifelong student is important for all leaders when managing change, challenges and setbacks is the norm. A growth mindset is particularly important as we age. Technology is changing the world rapidly. We need to evolve to stay relevant.

Microsoft and other leading companies have evoked the same need to evolve in recently placing a growth mindset at the core of their corporate culture.[4]

Pro Tip: Talk yourself up. A "growth mindset" relies on self-talk that is positive and encouraging. Practice becoming aware of the messages you give yourself when you are feeling stuck or challenged. As you start your day tomorrow, choose self-talk that is kind, compassionate, and empathetic. Look for multiple opportunities to give yourself positive and uplifting messages throughout your day. Do this in between meetings, at lunch, and even during your commute home. Ongoing pep talks also helps drown out your inner critic, that noisy board of directors you can do without.

YOUR EXPLANATORY STYLE IMPACTS YOUR RESILIENCE

There's a growing body of research on negativity bias; the notion that unpleasant thoughts, emotions, and events have a greater effect on our psychological state and wellbeing than do positive or neutral feelings. The human brain is actually hardwired to remember painful or negative experiences better than we remember positive experiences. That means even the most wonderful positive experiences do not hang around in our minds to the same degree as negative experiences that aren't on the same level as moderate negative experiences. This is not a new notion. Author Henry James (William's brother) wrote, "Be not afraid of life. Believe that life is worth living, and your belief will help create the fact."

Cultivating this positivity is critical. The average person has 60,000 to 70,000 thoughts a day. According to Stanford researcher Fred Luskin, 90% of them are the same thoughts that we recycle constantly.[5] The majority of those thoughts are inaccurate and negative.

Psychologist Rick Hanson explains the negativity bias his book, *Hardwiring Happiness.*[6] With the pace of modern living, it's easy for

Figure 17.2 Keep it positive

negativity to become our default way of being. Worse, we tend to relive those negative events over and over again. As Hanson states, "Staying with a negative experience past the point that's useful is like running laps in hell: You dig the track a little deeper in your brain each time you go around it." We get better at the thoughts we practice most. Attention training helps you to be careful in choosing your thoughts wisely.

Getting stuck in negative ruminations happens when we feel like we've been wronged, when a project that we care about fails, or we're at risk of losing our job or financial security. It's also normal for our minds to swing from past regrets to future worries. In fact, most of us practice that all the time. Neuroscientists call this negative rumination the "Default Mode Network" of the brain.[7] It's a powerful habit in which we get lost in unhelpful, stressful thoughts—practices that actually strengthen our negativity bias.

BIAS AND DECISION-MAKING

Negativity bias doesn't just relate to the lingering psychological impact on memory. For leaders, it's also been found to impact how we form impressions and evaluate others, how we make unconscious decisions to pay attention and learn (or not), and how we analyze risk and make decisions.

Over time, leaders tend to develop outlooks that are either optimistic or pessimistic. This happens unconsciously and we get better at the outlook we practice most.

Winston Churchill once said, "Success is stumbling from failure to failure without losing enthusiasm." Failure is a common experience for any leader, especially when it comes to driving innovation. We start with betas. We learn from failure. We optimize and, if we move quickly, we develop some competitive advantage generally for a short period of time. Rinse and repeat.

Here are a few EQ tips to help you be more optimistic, curious, and nonjudgmental.

Practice Being Open. There are two sides to every coin. Bring employees to the table to increase your understanding of what's on their minds. When we really listen, we learn to differentiate the emotional issues that grab employees' attention (gossip, rumors, us against them, and so on) and the real issues (concerns over jobs, resources, disruption, and stress).

Make Friends with Your Mind. EQ gives us greater control over our emotions, and increases our capacity to think clearly and act with purpose. We all have implicit biases we're unaware of. There are 188 known confirmation biases.[8] It's helpful to understand how the brain works so that you can correct for its powerful natural tendencies. Following are ten of the most common cognitive biases:

- Confirmation Bias: being drawn to details that confirm our beliefs
- Negativity Bias: recalling events as worse than they were
- Self-Serving Bias: taking more responsibility for success than failure
- Status Quo Bias: avoiding irreversible decisions to avert mistakes
- Projection Bias: projecting our current mindset onto the past / future

- Stereotyping: filling in characteristics from generalities
- Halo Effect: imagining people we're fond of to be "better"
- Gambler's Fallacy: projecting patterns from sparse data
- Sunk Cost Fallacy: investing in what we've started to "get it done"
- Naive Cynicism: noticing flaws in others more easily than ourselves

---

Listen More. Try to be more accepting of others as they are. A lot of times you won't see eye to eye with your employees. Trying to get them to understand your point of view might feel like you're beating a dead horse. Sometimes, it's better to just listen. Acceptance can go a long way in opening up to others—and having them open up to hear you. It's also key to breaking through the attention-grabbing headlines in your company, real and imagined, to get to what actually matters to the individual.

Pro Tip: This week's challenge is to be as kind, open, and trusting to your neighbor, family, and coworkers as you are to strangers you believe to be important (potential clients, investors, and so on). It might actually be this life's challenge.

LANGUAGE MATTERS

In their book, *The Three Laws of Performance*, Steve Zaffron and Dave Logan refer to the power of language and how things "occur" to us impacts our performance. Their three laws include:[9]

1. How people perform correlates to how situations occur to them.

2. How a situation occurs arises in language.

3. Future-based language transforms how situations occur to people.

How we think and talk to ourselves makes all the difference in performance. When you set a goal, do you say, "We will grow revenue by 20%" or "We might grow revenue 20%"? The former is a commitment that moves teams to action. The later sounds like it would be cool if it happened. Your words matter. Do you create clarity and commitment or confusion and chaos?

MINDSET DETERMINES PERFORMANCE

This difference between the two mindsets determines whether a leader can be resilient through disruption or someone who gives up when the going gets tough. Spoiler alert. In today's fast-paced world, the going is always tough.

In his 2006 book, *Learned Optimism*, Martin Seligman calls this phenomenon our "explanatory style."[10] People with an optimistic explanatory style react to perceived setbacks from a position of personal power; setbacks are temporary circumstances and will be overcome by effort, confidence, and ability. People with a pessimistic explanatory style react to perceived setbacks from a position of personal helplessness; setbacks are more permanent, and because of personal inadequacies, are viewed as harder to overcome.

As an example, early in my career, I worked for the CBS Television Network. We went through rapid multibillion-dollar acquisitions, including the $3.9 billion acquisition of Infinity Broadcasting. At the time, Mel Karmazin was Infinity's hard-driving CEO and a Wall Street darling. Following the acquisition, all of CBS's previously owned and operated radio stations were consolidated under Mel. He drove such good results that, within a short time, the CBS-owned-and-operated TV stations were also consolidated under him.

Internally, there were hurt feelings and concern. What could a radio guy know about TV stations? Worse, Mel was known as a relentless salesman and cost-cutter. As tensions rose, Mel called all of the 14 TV stations' sales teams to New York. To boost sales, he announced the company would be cutting salaries and increasing commissions. The room was stunned. They were coming off a 4% sales increase year and expected a celebration of sorts. Instead, they learned that significantly more of their compensation would be at risk.

Questions came rapid-fire from the audience of 40 sales leaders. Two concerns mattered most:

1. "Are you prepared if we all leave?" Mel had a one-word answer, "Yes."

2. "If we beat our numbers, a lot of the people in this room could double our compensation. Are you prepared for that?"

Mel had a longer answer, "If you guys double your compensation on commissions, what do you think that means for the company? I hope you triple your compensation. That's up to you."

The GM who asked the first question was a negative force in the company. He complained to Michael Jordan, our CEO, and to everyone who would listen. His team adopted his style. His station was one of three that drove 3% to 4% growth in the following year. Mel laughed at 3%, "That's called inflation. We don't need salespeople to get inflation. It happens on its own." The GM and his entire team were replaced.

The GM who asked the second question was a cheerleader for the new approach. He set goals for his team to beat expectations. He talked to anyone who would listen about how great this opportunity would be. That year, he more than doubled his compensation in 12 months and so did most of the sales leads across the TV stations. His was one of seven TV stations that grew revenue 20%-plus in a year the market forecasted 3% growth.

In this case, the optimists outsold the pessimists by 17 points (and seven times the market growth). Moreover, the trend continued in the following year. In his book, Seligman shares a similar experiment with MetLife, where job applicants who scored low on knowledge and talent, but high on optimism significantly outsold their more qualified, but more pessimistic counterparts.[10] For anyone who works in sales, this will hit home. You have to be resilient and optimistic to be successful. Eighty percent of sales don't occur until after the fifth call. And 90% of salespeople give up after the third call.[11]

Practice a Positive and Optimistic Outlook. Benjamin Franklin said, "The constitution only guarantees the American people the right to 'pursue' happiness. You have to catch it yourself." When it comes to pursuing happiness, EQ helps us improve awareness regarding our moods, tendencies, and biases toward certain behavior. By being in the present moment, we can see our thoughts more clearly and not get lost in them. This awareness can help you cultivate a more positive mindset. You then have a better starting point from which to take corrective action as negative tendencies arise. Over time, this will help you to feel more clear, engaged, and positive on a regular basis.

Understanding how the brain's natural negativity bias works is also the first step in addressing it as it occurs. We all spend a lot of time reinforcing a negativity bias. As leaders, having that awareness can motivate us to make the time and commitment to rewire the brain for a positivity bias. With practice, a positive attitude can become your new default way of being. And when that happens, it's transformative for your health, your performance, and your relationships. Literally, everyone in your life will benefit, including you. It's contagious.

POSITIVITY PAYS OFF

Happiness is the new rich. Health is the new wealth. Here are nine scientifically backed benefits of cultivating a positive outlook and nine on the cost of developing a negative outlook.

9 Benefits of a Positive Outlook

1. Positive leaders exhibit better decision making under pressure.[12]

2. 94% reported that Calm, Happy and Energized are the three "leadership states of mind" that drive the greatest levels of effectiveness and performance.[13]

3. Positive people live longer.[14]

4. Positive, optimistic salespeople sell more than pessimistic salespeople.[15]

5. Marriages are much more likely to succeed when the couple experiences a five-to-one ratio of positive to negative interactions. When the ratio approaches one-to-one, couples are more likely to divorce.[16]

6. Positive people can see the big picture to identify solutions. Negative people maintain a narrower perspective and tend to focus on problems.[17]

7. Positive emotions including gratitude and appreciation help athletes perform at a higher level.[18]

8. Positive people have more friends; a key factor of happiness and longevity.[19]

9. Positive work environments outperform negative work environments.[20]

9 Costs of a Negative Outlook

1. Too many negative work interactions compared to positive ones can decrease a team's productivity.[21]

2. Non-cheerful people are more likely to develop coronary heart disease.[22]

3. One negative person can create a miserable office environment for the entire office.[23]

4. Research at the University of Virginia found that 90% of work anxiety is created by 5% of an employee's network; the naysayers who drain others' energy.[24]

5. Men who are pessimistic are three times more likely to develop high blood pressure compared to their optimistic counterparts.[25]

6. Negative employees can permanently scare off every customer they speak with.[26]

7. Negative emotions increase the risk of heart attack and stroke.[27]

8. Negativity is associated with greater stress, less energy, and more chronic pain.[28]

9. According to the CDC, 90% of doctor visits are stress related.[29]

PERFORMANCE   RELATIONSHIPS   CAREER

CHAPTER 18

Building EQ Skills for Others: Sharing a Better You

> Before you are a leader, success is all about growing yourself. When you become a leader, success is all about growing others.
> —Jack Welch

To this point, the steps we've covered on our way up the EQ stairs will have the greatest impact on us as individuals. Mindfulness practice leads to self-awareness, which leads to improved self-regulation, which opens us up to better understand our motivations and to live a life with greater intention. The next few steps will surely benefit you as a leader, but will also have a tremendous impact on those around you.

EMPATHY

Empathy is the ability to understand another person's feelings and perspectives. Compassion goes one step further by adding the desire to help the other person.

Effective empathy is understanding others' feelings while maintaining your own feelings and perspectives. When tough situations

Figure 18.1   How well do you relate to others?

arise, we human beings tend to operate in packs. We want to enroll
support and especially when it helps us prove we're right and someone
else is wrong. As leaders, it's easy to get drawn into the chaos and
to take a side early on. It's a far better approach to be empathetic
while remaining open and curious about the facts and what is actually
happening. By the time most issues get to a leader, emotions have
gotten involved. When you take a perceived problem and mix in
emotions, you often end up with a growing set of stories that gets
worse with age. When several employees are involved, you can also
get a multiplier effect.

Early research suggested that humans are wired to be empathetic
through mirror neurons.[1] That research has increasingly been set aside
because of the simplicity of the methods and analysis applied.[2] Empathy is a complex process involving complicated neural pathways which
are influenced by our unique human interactions as well as environ-
mental conditions. What allows us to mirror each other's emotions,
feel empathy, and show compassion are as much about innate instincts
as they are about honing our emotional intelligence skills. Social scientists agree that empathy, compassion, caring, and kindness have been

critical to the survival of our species. We are wired to care. We tend to pick up what's going on with other human beings. We have an innate ability to reflect that response through emotional contagion—the idea that we pick up and adopt other people's emotions.[3] The idea of contagion goes beyond the mimicking suggested in early mirror neuron research and feels more intuitive to me.

Humans Are Social Beings, Wired to Connect

When a leader walks into a room, their mood tends to infect others. If you're in a great and playful mood, others join along. If you're in a serious and angry mood, people tend to offer the same. You get what you give. Over time, employees tend to expect a certain mood in their leaders and they plan for it.

When I was the CFO of a media agency, we placed about $5 billion annually in media. Our president of National Broadcast was a high energy, upbeat guy and a legend in the industry. He loved the media business and was a great storyteller. He had a team of 100 employees in our New York headquarters. They modeled his behavior. When he walked into our board meetings, we also adopted his behavior: happy, curious, open, empathetic, and fun. I was disappointed if he didn't make a meeting. When he retired, he gave our management team clocks with the inscription, "Enjoy your time. I sure did" that we all displayed in our offices.

Unfortunately, his replacement had the opposite approach. He was too serious, overly direct, and made it clear he cared more about his bonus than relationships. Within a few months, his team adopted his behavior. The joy and compassion that had emanated from his team turned to suspicion and a "we're in it for us" vibe in a few short months. Same team, different leader. Within 12 months, we had a dysfunctional organization in which one team believed they were more important than the others. Our New York HQ turnover jumped from 15% to 30% in one year. The advertising industry benchmark was 20% at the time, so we moved from having a competitive advantage to a disadvantage with that one hire. When the new guy walked into our board meetings, the board adopted his behavior: serious, defensive, positioning for self-preservation, and strength.

Years later, I was reminiscing about this with one of our former colleagues. She shared that she removed the beautiful clock from her desk because the new president was a painful reminder of what we used to have. I'm not sure if clock-neurons are a thing, but I had done the same.

Just Like Me + Kindness = More Happiness

As leaders, empathy is a skill worth developing to connect with, motivate, inspire, and encourage others to be resilient through change. There are two foundational practices to develop this skill. The first is a "Just Like Me" practice to open up an understanding of what another person may be going through. No matter what your differences are, we tend to have more in common than we know. Making it a habit to recognize those similarities opens up the opportunity to be empathetic, compassionate, and even accept others as they are.

The second is "Loving Kindness" to wish others well. The act of thinking about and wishing other people well (even your enemies) can actually transform your relationships. When they are present, it's also easier to be nice and connect with someone you've been pulling for.

Pro Tip: Dr. Richie Davidson at the Center for Healthy Minds is a leading expert in scientifically testing the power of mindfulness and compassion, noting even small doses matter. "We conducted a simple experiment where we trained people over the course of two weeks in a simple compassion practice. We can see measurable changes in the brain that are detectable with functional MRI (magnetic resonance imaging) after just two weeks of this simple compassion practice. And what we see is a strengthening in the connection between the prefrontal cortex and a region of the brain that we know to be involved in positive emotions including kindness, empathy and compassion." Even a little practice goes a long way.

Mo Empathy. Mo Cheeks. EQ and human connection go hand in hand. Being in the moment allows leaders to actively apply their skills as coaches to understand others' feelings and perspectives and offer help in real time. One of my favorite examples comes from the retired All-Star basketball player-turned-coach, Maurice "Mo" Cheeks. In April 2003, a 13-year-old named Natalie Gilbert won the chance to sing the National Anthem before a Portland Trail Blazers playoff game against the Dallas Mavericks. Gilbert had been suffering from the flu. She started the first line of the anthem just fine, but then quickly stumbled with the words in front of 20,000 fans. She stalled, laughed nervously, and then looked to her father in the stands for help. Within a few seconds, Mo Cheeks (then the Trail Blazers' head coach) came to her rescue. It was captured on live TV for millions of viewers. It's an amazingly touching moment.

If you search "Mo Cheeks and Natalie Gilbert anthem" on YouTube, here's what you'll find.[4] Cheeks arrives in the blink of an eye. He immediately puts his arm around Natalie (I'm here for you) and begins to sing too (we're in this together). On several occasions, Natalie lowers the microphone to give up. Mo keeps gently pulling it back up (you can do this). He then begins to wave his free hand to bring the crowd into it (we're *all* in this together). And they begin singing, too. Young Gilbert rebounds and finishes strong. She then melts into Mo's arms. What could have been the worst day of a 13-year-old's life turned into a triumph for everyone watching. There are a few other things you'll notice if you watch. First, Mo isn't a very good singer. He barely knew the words himself. He put himself out there without worrying about anything except Gilbert. Second, as the camera follows him back to the bench, you realize that he had walked about 50 feet, half the distance of the court to get to her. This was a coach doing what coaches do: helping someone feel supported, focus, and perform under pressure.

During his storied 15-year career, Mo Cheeks won an NBA championship, was on the All-Star team four times and made the All-Defensive squad four straight years. At the time of his retirement, he was ranked first in steals and fifth in all-time in assists. But no victory or statistic will live up to what he did in one moment to show empathy and compassion for a 13-year-old girl.

Pro Tip: To learn more about empathy, I recommend Dr. Tara Cousineau's book, *The Kindness Cure: How the Science of Compassion Can Heal Your Heart and Your World.*[5]

SOCIAL SKILLS

The preceding EQ skills add up to being calm and present on a more regular basis, which leads to better social skills, the ability to understand, lead, connect with, inspire, and motivate others.

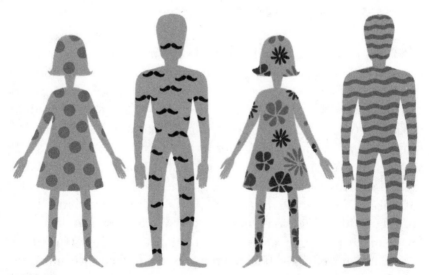

Figure 18.2   Modern business requires openness, curiosity, and team ball.

Leaders slip all the time. We're like everyone else. Our brains have been trained to be distracted. Distraction leads to behaviors that don't always suit us. In the same way that mindfulness helps us notice distraction, and come back to a point of focus, we need the tools to check in on our own management styles. This realization lead me to creating our *How to Be Mindful, Not Mindless* tool (Figures 18.3 and 18.4). I'm including it here as an easy way to check in with yourself. Visit it periodically and circle all the ones that apply to your behavior over the last two weeks. Early on, you may find that you slip a lot. That's fine. In fact, it's normal. Don't be too hard on yourself.

The goal is to be present to what's going on with your thoughts, beliefs, and actions as a leader more regularly. Once you are, you can catch yourself when you're in automaton mode, bring yourself back to being present and make things right when you've done harm.

Years ago, I interviewed with a public ad agency holding company. I had little interest in going back into the business, but after five rounds of calls enticing me to just meet the CEO and "a package that will make it well worth your while", I relented. Prior to the interview, the global HR lead spent 30 minutes cautioning me that the CEO was prone to responding to email and taking calls during interviews. "Oh, and he often asks people to talk faster," she said. My response was, "please tell me you're joking." She was not. The CEO performed as promised. Fifteen minutes, two phone calls and many emails into an hour-long meeting, I politely ended the interview, sharing that I didn't feel our working styles were a good fit. He didn't bother to look up from his Blackberry, saying "your loss." The HR lead then asked me for another 30 minute debrief, ending with "I can't take this." She left the company a few months later. In the coming years, five c-level colleagues had similar experiences, all passing on high paying jobs with the company. Social skills matter and being mindless has a cost. How you treat people, even in small increments, matters. The CEO resigned a few years later amidst an SEC ethics investigation requiring him to pay back over $20 million in questionable expenses and other payments.[6]

Develop Quality Relationships

Studies have shown that mindfulness practitioners develop deeper, more authentic relationships. Practitioners have even experienced an

MINDFUL

☁ Things I Believe	⏱ Things I Do	✎ Things I Say
Everything's gonna be alright.	A feeling of abundance/openness.	"We got this." "We're a team."
I'd rather learn than be right.	Mindful breathing.	"I appreciate you for..."
Being transparent/vulnerable creates connection and puts people at ease.	Be authentic; Share life stories.	"Here's what I learned from this..."
I don't have all the answers. There are always more than two possibilities.	Mindful listening; Make others feel heard and appreciated.	"Why is the opposite just as true?"
Everything and everyone is my ally.	Take responsibility; Speak openly.	"I take responsibility for..."
It's good to question my thoughts, beliefs, and assumptions.	Body scan; Label my emotions.	"I feel..." "I'm experiencing..."
The only validation I need comes from myself.	Mindful conversation; Create win/win solutions.	"What I heard you say is..." "What I heard you feel is..."
I don't take things too seriously.	Create fun for myself and others.	"Let's find the fun in this."
There is a difference between what actually happened and "stories."	Separate facts from emotions.	"What happened, without adding to it or taking away from it?"
Jumping into arguments or chaos isn't for me.	Stop-Breathe-Notice-Reflect-Respond (SBNRR).	"I understand your perspective." "How can I help?"

whil.

Figure 18.3 Practice being mindful

198

MINDLESS   whl.

🗨 Things I Believe	⊗ Things I Do	📣 Things I Say
• Being right is most important.	Cling to power and opinions.	"I have to..."
• I'm threatened.	Find fault; Place blame.	"It's not possible."
• People and/or circumstances are working against me.	Gossip and tell stories.	"This is/They are a joke."
• I suffer from scarcity. There's never enough.	Get overwhelmed.	"It's not my fault." "I'm overwhelmed."
• I don't have control.	Justify; Rationalize.	"I'm trying to..." "The fact is..."
• There is a right way and a wrong way.	Protect my ego/identity.	"You don't understand..."
• My perspective is the right one.	Ensure others lose; Gather support.	"Whose side are you on?"
• I don't have a choice.	Avoid conflict.	"I'm sorry, but..."
• I'm not committed.	Check out; Take advantage; Get mine.	"I could do better."
• I'm better/worse than...	Argue; Compare.	"Why am I treated this way?"

Figure 18.4   Avoid being mindless

199

increase in size and activation of the prefrontal cortex (PFC).[7] The thinking part of the brain plays an important role in regulating the "emotional" part of the brain. Training the connection between the two allows for less reactivity and more stable emotional relationships.

Pro Tip: Maintaining an active social life with friends and family is also critical to cognitive health. Cognitive decline was reduced by an average of 70% in people who were frequently socially active compared to those who were not.[8]

Take Things Less Personally

EQ can help you not take your successes and failures so personally. Research has shown practitioners were able to shift from overreliance on their internal narratives about success and failure to view life experiences with more objectivity.[7]

Imagine moving from "My performance means (insert list of self-defeating beliefs) about my worth" to a deeper understanding that success and failure are experiences not linked to your underlying worth.

Slow Down and Listen Better

Another way our brains work against us is they're too darn fast. In his book, *Thinking, Fast and Slow*, Nobel Prize–winner Daniel Kahneman describes that the brain has two thinking systems:[9]

- "System 1" for fast thinking, like recognizing faces or making assumptions. It's the automatic, always-on system that leverages past experiences. It creates and uses mental shortcuts and is, therefore, prone to our cognitive biases.

- "System 2" is for slow or careful thinking, like solving complex math problems. The two systems work independently.

Not surprisingly, the brain prefers to think fast. It's a machine. Accordingly, the brain tends to engage System 1, especially when the context is not clear or we can simply infer context. Kahneman's research shows that our current thoughts rely heavily on prior thoughts (consistent with the many cognitive biases I shared earlier). Humans also prefer simple answers; generally, those based on prior thoughts. So when we think fast, we tend to make assumptions without regard for data or fully understanding the context. Then we make mistakes.

Most people speak at 125 to 150 words per minute, but the brain can process thoughts at 1,000 to 3,000 per minute.[10] Consider this with Kahneman's research and it's no wonder the brain tends to wander when listening to others speak. It's bored. Using the brain just to listen is like using an airline carrier to step across a stream. There's too much capacity. This can cause leaders to hurry others to get to the point, or to zone out because we feel we already know the answer. Both can leave the speaker feeling disrespected. Both create risk when we make decisions based on historical emotional associations versus data and the probability of success—again, one of the 188 confirmation biases we covered earlier.

Various studies stress the importance of listening as a key skill for leaders. According to the University of Missouri, we spend 70% to 80% of our waking hours in some form of communication. On average, we spend about 9% writing, 16% reading, 30% speaking, and 45% listening. Spoiler Alert: Studies also confirm that, wait for it ... the average human is not a good or efficient listener.[11]

Mindful Listening

Richard Branson once said, "Courage is what it takes to stand up and speak; courage is also what it takes to sit down and listen." Here's a five-minute "Mindful Listening" exercise to make another person's words the focus of your attention.

(continued)

(continued)

Do the exercise with a colleague or friend. Ask two questions and let them speak without interrupting. Make them the complete focus of your attention. Each time the mind wanders, gently bring it back to their words.

Your prompts: What causes you stress in life? What brings you joy in life?

When it's your turn, you may find that this exercise to be a surreal experience. Because of System 1 behavior, no one ever lets you speak without interrupting, let alone for two to three full minutes. Try mindful listening throughout your week and see how it transforms your conversations and relationships.

WHO ARE YOU? AND WHAT HAVE YOU BECOME?

If you're like most professionals, ten to twenty years in a challenging career can slowly change you into someone else without you ever realizing it. Ongoing stress and change management can cause you to lose sight of the bigger mission, your team, and even yourself. In his book, *Discover Your True North*, Bill George describes the difference between "I Leaders" and "We Leaders" (Figure 18.5).[12]

In the same way that stress causes us to slip into being commanding, we can slip into being the "I Leader" or even the worst version of ourselves.

I recently had dinner with a global chief human resources officer friend in advertising. Let's call her Diva. During dinner, her energy went from bad to worse. She was complaining about clients, her staff, colleagues, 24/7 expectations, wearing multiple hats in a public company, you name it. It was all "killing" her. I've had similar conversations with friends in Silicon Valley, Wall Street, travel, healthcare, you name it. We're all "crazy-busy."

I versus **We** Leaders

I Leaders	We Leaders
• Leaders attain power and position	• Leaders serve others
• Self-interest drives decision making	• Purpose drives decision making
• "I can do it on my own"	• "It takes a team with complementary strengths"
• Pace setter: "I'll be out front; follow me"	• Empower: "Work together to fulfill mission"
• Ask for compliance with rules	• Seek alignment through values
• Arrogant	• Humble
• Leaders direct others	• Leaders coach and mentor others
• Focus on near-term results	• Focus on serving customers and employees
• Fire in their eye-extreme conviction	• Inspire and uplift
• Develop loyal followers	• Empower people to lead
• Leaders get credit	• Team gets the credit

Figure 18.5   I versus We leaders

Diva is usually one of the most fun people I know. Smart, energetic, and a natural leader. Historically, things don't get her down. She was thrown when I pointed out that she was showing up as pure anger. This was not easy to say, but we've known each other for a long time and, for me, her behavior that day felt like she was losing the essence of who she is. She became seriously pissed (Exhibit A, your honor) until she realized it was true.

Share Tough Advice to Be a Good Friend

I was on the receiving end of a similar conversation in my early 40s. I was going full steam in a similar b*tch session (we all do it sooner or later) and my friend Karl Haller cut me short. "Please stop. You're one of my closest friends. You used to be the most fun person I know. I always looked forward to spending time with you. Now you're usually in a dark place. Nothing is good enough. You're obsessed with your public company crap and it's getting harder to hang out with you." Ouch. That was a brick to the head. It was also a much-needed wake-up call.

When you're building a career, it's easy to get caught up in the corporate game. Each industry and company has its own version and they usually align around a few key themes like:

1. Always win (even better when someone else has to lose)

2. Never show weakness

3. Make sure you get credit (or as Tupac put it, "I gotta get mine. You gotta get yours.")

It's exhausting and it distracts us from taking care of the relationships that are most important in our lives and careers.

Find Inspiration Where You Can. I discovered two things that helped me. The first was Johnny Cash's 2002 cover of the Nine Inch Nails song, *Hurt*. He released it the year before his death at age 71. The song laments aging, turning into someone else and wishing he could start over.[13] Over the years, I've seen too many executives change before my eyes. We start out standing for a few things. And we lose our way. We turn into something else. We can get so caught up in the pace of business that we lose who we are. The song is a touching and haunting poem to change, regret, and life. Johnny Cash's body, ravaged by time and hard living, made it even more so.

Make Practicing a Habit. The second thing that helped me was an easy practice to stay grounded. I shared it with Diva and it goes like this. First, pick three words that define who you are; I mean at your core. What drives you and how do you want to show up consistently in your life? The words don't have to relate solely to business. They can relate to anything.

For me those three words are: fun, encouraging, leader. That's how I want to show up for my colleagues, friends, and family. I use it as a reflection when I drive to work every morning.

Who Have You Become?

After my chat with Karl (go ahead, call it an intervention), I started to notice that friends were no longer using the word "fun" to describe me. In fact, when I asked close friends and colleagues the three words they would use to describe me, they centered around "serious," "driven," and "direct." I guess that's better than "pr*ck," but it didn't align with who I want to be.

Worse yet, when I was honest with myself, the three words that really best described me at that time in my life were "impatient," "angry," and "competitive." That's a far cry from "fun," "encouraging," and "leader." And it certainly didn't scream "mindful."

Unless you have some touchstone to measure yourself against, it's hard to compare who you want to be to the person you've become. The migration to a foreign, angrier Joe wasn't evident to me. On the contrary, I had tremendous success while being impatient, angry, and competitive. I was like the grumpy lead doctor on the old TV show *House*—in pain, limping around, and snarkily thinking I had all the answers and annoyed that everyone else didn't too. Not a good look for a leader, but my show got renewed season after season—racking up promotions, stock, bonuses, and plenty of congratulatory steak dinners.

Recognize When Winning Is Losing. So long as you're winning, the corporate world generally offers great reinforcement for leaders no matter how they show up. I had countless confirmations that being impatient, angry, and competitive was a great way to get rewarded. But it always catches up to you. When you start to wear it, it's time to take a different approach.

Pro Tip: Leaders spend countless hours putting complex measurement and data feedback loops in place. How much time do you spend creating data checkpoints for yourself? What's your personal optimization plan?

Create a Powerful Trigger. Am I showing up as the person that I want to be? Start your day with it. You can use the three words to check in with yourself during a meeting, employee review, or dinner with your honey. At Whil, we even incorporated "Three Words" into our onboarding process for new hires. It's created an invitation for team members to both be themselves and to be direct, but supportive with other team members when someone veers out of bounds. And we all do.

As a self-reporting perfectionist, I'm always looking to get sh*t done. I can't help myself. I struggle with my anchors constantly, especially the "encouraging" part. That's why they call it practice. But I've found this small practice helps me continue to drive events while striving to be happier, more connected, and more collaborative.

Create Your Three-Word Anchor

If you have a friend who's moving right into the anger zone (queue the *Top Gun* theme song), they may need your help. Ask them two simple questions: What three words define the leader you want to be? What three words describe the person you've actually become? When it comes to being present, focused, and kind, we all slip sometimes. We could all use a touchstone to measure against how we think we show up as leaders versus how we're really showing up. Sometimes, there's a chasm between the two. How about for you?

Consistency Matters. Leaving Ogilvy & Mather was the hardest decision of my career. I'd been with our parent company, WPP, for 10 years, running three of their global agencies. I loved the company and provided two months' notice while I continued working my normal 12-hour days. During my last week, I had my final meeting with Shelly Lazarus, Ogilvy's legendary CEO. Shelly was gracious, encouraging, and thanked me, saying, "The doors of Ogilvy will forever be open to you." I was in the presence of greatness. It was a touching moment that I will never forget. The identical words came in meetings with the now current CEO, John Seifert, and each of our board members and division CEOs. Honoring people is part of Ogilvy's DNA.

The only exception came from the (now former) CEO of one division. The day after my departure, in a meeting with about 200 staff, he shared that he considered my leaving to join a competitor to be a personal betrayal. "As far as I'm concerned, the doors of Ogilvy will forever be closed to Joe Burton." Several board members called me to apologize. It didn't fit the culture. It didn't fit my track record. I forgave the misstep immediately. I loved the company. But it sent a powerful conflicting message to the organization. Core values, consistency, and social skills matter. And for leaders, even small slips in your emotions can have a lasting impact.

WELLBEING   PERFORMANCE   RELATIONSHIPS

CHAPTER 19

Applying EQ Skills at Home (Parenting)

> The only time you truly become an adult is when you finally forgive your parents for being just as flawed as everyone else.
> —Douglas Kennedy

Happiness begins at home. And so does stress. Parenting is one of our greatest leadership challenges, but only one-third of us believe we're doing a good job of managing our stress.[1] This isn't surprising. We have to keep on top of our career, finances, school schedules, homework, and the extended family. That stress increased in 2016 when the number of young adults 18 to 34 living at home in the United States jumped to a 75-year high.[2] It's pretty common to feel like you don't have any more to give. In fact, one in four parents feel they don't get enough emotional support.[3]

There are two things we're never taught in school. One is how to be parents. The other is how to manage our emotions. In both cases, we let folks bump into each other and hope it turns out for the best. Not a great strategy. It's easy to bring your stressed-out, distracted mind home and share it with your family. The gift that keeps on giving.

A "commanding" culture is hard to deal with in a work setting. At home, it can permanently alter your relationships with the people you love the most while setting your kids on a path to inherit some of your worst traits.

As more of us become dual-income households, mindful parenting has more to do with a positive relationship with your child, opening up communication, and setting boundaries, than it does with bringing your child up "perfectly." That ain't possible. A more practical approach is simply to stay present and connected. Modeling the emotionally intelligent behavior I've shared in this book is important. Research links mindfulness training for children to less anxiety, depression, and acting out.[4]

Just a few years ago, I was the "always on" father who treated our home like just another place to work. I'd arrive home and spend 30 to 60 minutes finishing my last conference call of the day. I had just one hour a day to see the kids before bedtime. I wasted much of that precious time responding to email.

One of the biggest benefits of developing mindfulness and EQ skills is the ability to recognize when I'm not actually present with my family so that I can change course. It's been transformational. Studies have even shown we can significantly increase parenting quality by improving our self-efficacy and self-confidence, even for those of us who experienced high levels of childhood trauma.[5]

START SMALL

Mindfulness and EQ are lifelong skills for both you and your children's wellbeing. In my experience, the best way to bring these leadership techniques into parenting is to disrupt unhealthy norms that are not serving your family and to recognize when the things you love most have slipped into autopilot mode. Start now. The next generation, Gen Z, is already reporting the highest levels of stress. Your kids will need these skills in school, college, and life.

Try picking one easy and recurring routine for your family to be more connected and start there. Then you can create more positive new habits, routines, and traditions. Here are a few that I've found to work wonders.

Involve Your Kids. Our sons were introduced to mindfulness at school, in martial arts, and even in sports (coaches looking for the

Figure 19.1   Taking care of mini-me

edge). A few years ago, we started doing five-minute sits together as a family on the weekend. It's helped us to educate our kids on how the brain works, change the tone and language of the family, and catch one another when we slip into bad routines,

Practice Gratitude at Dinner. One of my favorite daily family practices with younger children is the "rose, bud, thorn" conversation at dinnertime. Each member shares the best thing about his or her day (the rose), the worst thing about the day (the thorn), and one thing he or she is looking forward to the most (the bud). It spurs conversation and helps us notice and appreciate what's good in our lives, even when things are difficult. It's also a great way to practice saying what we feel out loud, like "Thank you," "I love you," and "I'm proud of you." Research has shown that even small gratitude practices can transform your mindset for positivity.[6]

Make Family Night Special. One of the Burton family's favorite traditions is Friday "Movie Night." For too many families, it's an evening of autopilot, catching up on emails, or cleaning the house while the kids watch TV. We now treat it as a special time to connect with intention. Discussing each movie allows the family to get into a conversation around what they liked, didn't like, and why. It creates an atmosphere of healthy debate where your kids can understand that their opinions matter and they can represent them with confidence, while also respecting that others may feel differently.

Create Opportunities to Let Go. When you have a Type A personality, it's easy to be a wet blanket when you're looking for the perfect hike, restaurant, or vacation. It can stifle the family. A few years ago, I started a new tradition. I let the kids plan my birthday. I took the day off from work. I'd never done that in 30 years of working. It sent the right message to the family. I got exactly what you'd expect. The kids planned miniature golf, pizza for lunch, a video arcade, and then we built my gift—an architectural Lego set of the Trevi Fountain. Letting go with young kids was amazing!

Pro Tip: Set a time limit for younger children to use their electronic devices. Consider having them earn the time. Our kids get 20 minutes of iPad time on weekends for 20 minutes of learning on Khan Academy. Gotta put in the work to reap the rewards.

Practice Self-Compassion. Give yourself some "alone time." Getting more sleep, exercising, or just hanging out with your own friends are all forms of self-care. Children watch what you do more than they listen to what you say. It's good for them to see you taking care of yourself.

Appreciate Your Partner. Studies have shown mindfulness to be positively associated with relationship satisfaction. Furthermore, high levels of mindfulness reduced the impact of attachment anxiety, thereby reducing the risk of breakup.[7] What's good for you is good for the whole family.

Gratitude Practice

It's easy to slip into taking your partner for granted. Here's a one-minute gratitude practice from the Whil library to show appreciation to your partner.

Find a relaxed and alert position, close your eyes, and imagine that your partner is there with you. Visualize your partner. How he or she looks and feels. Bring a sense of appreciation into your heart to recognize him or her for all they are as a person and everything they do in raising your family. Notice any images that come to you and extend this heartfelt appreciation toward him or her. Notice how you feel when you do this. As you close the practice, thank them inwardly for being in your life. When you see him or her next, take that gratitude into your interactions let them know you were thinking about them.

Help Them Sleep. Try introducing a two-to-three-minute mindfulness practice when your kids lie down to help calm anxiety and ease them into sleep. It's a great routine to teach them that "being in the now" means learning to let go of what is not happening. If that doesn't work, consider Adam Mansbach's 2011 best-selling book, *Go the F**k to Sleep.*[8] Or maybe not.

Figure 19.2   Modern teens especially need the help

Share Generational Stories. Bruce Feiler, author of *The Secrets of Happy Families*, wrote that sharing intergenerational stories is one of the best ways of learning because you learn the struggles and triumphs of people like you.[9] This helps kids understand that life is full of ups and downs and that we don't have to take it so seriously.

Focus on Intrinsic Rewards. A growing body of research dating back to the early 1970s shows that we can undermine children's intrinsic interest by focusing on extrinsic rewards.[10] Bribes make for unmotivated children.

Research has shown that successful kids have a number of things in common including lower stress, responsibility at a young age, social skills, healthy relationships with their parents, and growth mindsets.[11] Bringing EQ and mindful leadership techniques into your parenting offers a way to be present rather than reactive, intentional rather than impatient, and understanding rather than assumptive. These skills enable you to see and listen to your child with an attitude of calm, curiosity, and wonder. They can also affect your physiology, nudging brain chemistry away from stress and toward wellbeing; something every family could use.

Manage Parenting Triggers

Children have a way of doing things repetitively that may not bother them, but can cause parents to snap. When it happens enough, it becomes the norm. Either the child learns to ignore the parent snapping or they become afraid of it. Left unchecked, a set of unhealthy recurring triggers and responses can become the family's culture. Here's a five-minute Whil journaling practice to help explore and alleviate those triggers. Do the first prompt for 2½ minutes, then move on to the second prompt at the midpoint.

Your first prompt is: Things my children do that upset me include …

Your second prompt is: I can handle these better if I ...

Following this exercise, and set an intention to deal with your triggers in real time using the S.T.O.P or SBNRR techniques that we covered earlier.

Explore Similarities and Differences. One of the greatest joys of parenting is watching a child become their own person. As they develop their own personalities, senses of humor, and tastes in clothing and food, it's a wonder to behold. And sometimes parents fall into autopilot and forget their young children are unique human beings. When this happens, you may find yourself encouraging your child to be just like you—to an unhealthy degree.

Pro Tip: Dr. Tara Cousineau recommends speaking with your child about similarities and differences between you and them, such as likes and dislikes, why and why nots, and pros and cons. This creates the opportunity for openness and to celebrate common ground and core values in the family as a whole. You can celebrate how each of you is completely unique, amazing, and quirky.

ROLE MODEL RESILIENCE

It's helpful to share what it was like when you were their age or how you overcame adversity or what your proudest moments were. What it felt like to be sad, disappointed, angry, hurt and confused, or elated, inspired, and happy. How normal it all is. That it's okay to experience physical and emotional pain and suffering. How sometimes it takes guts to say, "I'm sorry" or "I love you." And how everyone wants to be safe, healthy, happy, and loved. These are all human experiences that can help a child feel okay, just as they are, as they deal with the normal challenges of just becoming themselves. Be mindful about what you share and take into account your child's developmental stage and the purpose of your story or the teachable moment. Remember, too, of course, that some stories (for example, drinking, drugs, vandalism, and teen sex) are best not shared.

Change Your Routines and Change Your World. Mindful parenting and mindful leadership invite in more play, joy, and appreciation in all aspects of life. It also helps you to be young at heart. Practice in plain sight and it will be contagious for the people in your life.

> Pro Tip: If you're having issues connecting with a teenager, I highly recommend reading *Brainstorm: The Power and Purpose of the Teenage Brain* from our brilliant friend, Dr. Dan Siegel.[12]

CHAPTER **20**

Do or Die: It's Called Practice For a Reason

> I've got to keep breathing. It'll be my worst
> business mistake if I don't.
> —Steve Martin

I've made the case for mindfulness and EQ to help your own well-being as a leader, but also as a tool to transform employee performance and your company culture. In 2018, half of the Fortune 500 will have formal mindfulness programs to help their employees reduce stress and improve performance, productivity, and safety. Companies like Google, GE, SAP, PWC, Aetna, Ford, Apple, Kaiser Permanente, Target, and Salesforce have all made mindfulness and resilience training part of their work culture to improve both employee health and business outcomes.

Thousands of studies share the health and performance benefits of mindfulness training including reducing stress, increasing resilience and improving your sleep. And businesses benefit by improving their culture and increasing productivity while decreasing absenteeism, reducing turnover, and healthcare costs. You now have a bevy of science supporting the return on investment (ROI) for yourself and your company.

Committing to the mindfulness and EQ training, including the practices I've shared in this book, has been transformational in my

Figure 20.1   Success begins with self-care

life. Mindfulness and meditation practices aren't about navel gazing. As a leader, you push your brain constantly. Giving your brain time to recover and repair is necessary for your mental and emotional wellbeing, performance, relationships, and sleep. Being a leader has to start with self-care.

Mindfulness also isn't just about the 5 to 10 minutes of meditation practice each day. It's about a way of life. It's about changing the negative and unhealthy routines that create the disease states and career states that erode your happiness and performance that can take years off of your life. It's about changing the conversation with your inner critics—that pushy board of directors in your mind.

There are two times in my life when events changed the conversation in my own mind. The first was when I was a nine-year-old kid growing up on welfare in Pittsburgh, Pennsylvania. The Boys and Girls Clubs of America (BGCA) got a hold of me and didn't let go. They changed the conversation in my head from shame, anxiety, and fear to hope, confidence, and possibility. Having lost two sisters along the way, I can say without hesitation that the BGCA saved my life.

The second was when I turned 40. These mindfulness practices changed the conversation in my mind from being angry, impatient, and frustrated to creating a life experience with more intention, purpose, and compassion. In hindsight, I've had an amazing career—including my roles as a global CFO and COO. What I did not have was the right training, tools, or mindset to skillfully manage my own mental and emotional wellbeing in the face of ongoing change and disruption. In the absence of the right skills, I trained my brain to focus on the negative and worry about things that weren't happening in the moment. I fell into the normal traps of the mind without even realizing it to the point of destroying my own health. I now know it's the human condition. Mindfulness and emotional intelligence training has given me a new start on life.

In the face of ongoing change, we learn to mistrust our colleagues. We learn to hate our clients. We learn to ignore our employees and family members. We become addicted to our phones. We become experts at insomnia. We increase chronic pain through constant unhealthy rumination. These are all trained behaviors. We get better at what we practice most.

In the same way, you can now train yourself to be more focused and present. You can establish optimism and trust and patience as your default mode. You can learn to be happier, healthier, and more engaged. But you have to practice. The average person takes about 21,600 breaths each day. Each is an opportunity to bring attention to the moment to help focus your mind, relax your nervous system, and be the leader you are meant to be.

That creates the competitive advantage of being calm under pressure, which allows you to pause and reflect before you react. We get better at the things we practice most. I encourage you to practice gratitude, compassion, acceptance, purpose, and forgiveness. Each can transform your mindset for a healthier and more positive existence. Practice creates possibilities. Learning to catch yourself when you're distracted and coming back to a point of focus may be the single most important life skill for modern living. As Charles Darwin wrote, "It is not the strongest of the species that survive, nor the most intelligent, but the one most responsive to change." Well, the times they are a changin' - and with a quickness.

Les Brown said, "You must be willing to do the things today others don't do in order to have the things tomorrow others won't have."[1] Everyone dreams of success, but you have to be awake, present, and engaged to achieve it. There is no pill form of mindfulness. There's a reason it's called *practice*.

This book is a call to action. Use mindfulness to train your attention and awareness. Commit to five minutes of practice every day. Use what you learn to live a more mindful lifestyle. Integrate the emotional intelligence skills here to bring greater self-awareness, self-regulation, intention, purpose, and compassion into all you do. You can form a new default way of being - calm, curious, nonjudgmental, focused, present, and aware. Learn to reset, restart, and refocus as many times as you need to each day. Let mindfulness saturate your wellbeing in all aspects of your life experience. Then reap the rewards. Become the person, partner and leader you are meant to be.

Abraham Lincoln once wrote, "Folks are usually about as happy as they make their minds up to be." Learning these EQ and mindfulness practices helped me realize that I'd been working under the wrong frame of mind for far too many years. Using the practices in *Creating Mindful Leaders* in a few short months, I transformed my life to get back to being the person I want to be. May you do the same.

You're training your brain all the time. You get better at the things you practice most. Why not be intentional about it? You owe it to yourself, your family, and your colleagues. Keep it going.

And so, I ask you: Where are you going and what will you create?

One Last Pro Tip: Life can be hard. Don't take it all too seriously or too personally. The truth is, you're perfect the way you are. And you could be a little better.

FREE WHIL RESOURCES

If you're interested in additional resources, please visit whil.com for dozens of free articles, eBooks, best practice guides, and monthly webcasts offering continuing education (CE) credits for HR, L&D and employee benefits professionals.

Our digital wellbeing training programs provide professionals with access to over 250 science-based programs supported by over 1,500 video and audio training sessions on resilience, mindfulness, emotional intelligence, yoga, and sleep. Whil is a SaaS business, with employee subscriptions costing (plus or minus) $15 per year, per employee for large employers. Whil integrates into all major wellness and learning management systems.

For more information on offering our *Creating Mindful Leaders Workshop*, certification programs, keynotes, books or digital training to transform your employee wellbeing and company culture, please contact us at info@whil.com.

You can find the author on LinkedIn and follow him on Twitter at @joeWburton.

About the Author

Joe Burton is the founder and CEO of Whil Concepts, Inc. (Whil), the world's leading digital wellbeing training platform helping professionals reduce stress, increase resilience, and improve their sleep and performance. He's an entrepreneur in scientific wellbeing, former president of Headspace, and spent 15 years as a global COO in public companies. Joe is an alumnus of Harvard Business School and a regular contributor to *Forbes, Entrepreneur, Business Insider,* the *Observer,* 24 Hour Fitness, and *HuffPost.* He's worked in over 50 countries and travels the world speaking on topics including disruption, corporate culture, emotional intelligence skills, situational awareness, and mindfulness as competitive advantage. Joe is also a certified Search Inside Yourself instructor. He discovered mindfulness as a super-stressed-out executive after dismissing it as "definitely not for me" and it changed his life.

Joe has been featured on dozens of webcasts and podcasts and as a keynote speaker at events around the world, including Fitbit Captivate, Stanford Medicine X, HR Tech Fest, HERO Forum, Virgin Pulse Thrive Summit, 4A's Talent 2030, the Connected Health Symposium, Mainstream, Globoforce WorkHuman, National Business Group on Health, and the Brain Futures Conference.

He's spoken to audiences as large as 5,000. Known for his off-the-cuff humor and a casual, relatable speaking style, Joe shares a moving experience in dealing with stress, disruption, and in running high-performance organizations. He boils complex topics down into easy-to-understand language, supported by the latest research. As Whil's CEO, he's modernized brain training techniques for professionals, by professionals ... creating mindfulness for the rest of us.

Joe has consulted for over 30 technology startups, including being a board advisor and investor in Headspace, Lantern, Refresh Body, and Open Hour. He's a former board member of the Social Media Advertising Consortium. He is the coauthor of *The Mindful Business Conference*

White Paper: A Roadmap for High Performance, Leadership and Culture in the Age of Disruption (2016). He is the author of *The Value of the Power Middle in Social Marketing* (2013) and *Understanding the Economics of Digital Compared to Traditional Advertising and Media Services* (2009), a white paper for the American Association of Advertising Agencies. In 2010, he was inducted into the Boys and Girls Clubs Alumni Hall of Fame for creating the "Be Great" campaign, which continues to run today. Joe is a nonpracticing CPA and CMA, maintaining his license for the cheap insurance (accountants get the lowest rates). He asks that you not tell anyone.

ENDNOTES

INTRODUCTION: BEING A LEADER IS AMAZING. AND IT KINDA SUCKS.

1. Kozlowski, Lori. "Getting America To Check In With Itself." *Forbes*, Forbes Magazine, 28 Jan. 2013, www.forbes.com/sites/lorikozlowski/2013/01/28/getting-america-to-check-in-with-it self/#748cc4ffa7a8.
2. "Workplace Stress," The American Institute of Stress, March 14, 2017. https://www.stress .org/workplace-stress/.
3. Christina Congleton, Britta K. Hölzel, and Sara W. Lazar. "Mindfulness Can Literally Change Your Brain." *Harvard Business Review*, 8 Jan. 2015, hbr.org/2015/01/mindfulness-can-literally-change-your-brain.
4. "Seventy-Five Percent of U.S. Employers Say Stress Is Their Number One Workplace Health Concern." Willis Towers Watson. https://www.willistowerswatson.com/en/press/ 2016/06/75-percent-of-us-employers-say-stress-is-top-health-concern (accessed October 30, 2017).

CHAPTER 1: WHAT IS MINDFULNESS AND WHY SHOULD I CARE?

1. Santiago Ramón y Cajal and Larry W. Swanson, "Advice for a Young Investigator," translated by Neely Swanson. *The Quarterly Review of Biology* 75, no. 1 (2000): 25.
2. D. O. Hebb, *Organization of Behavior: A Neuropsychological Theory* (Mahwah, NJ: Lawrence Erlbaum Associates, 2002).
3. Bill D. Moyers, *Healing and the Mind* (New York: Doubleday, 1993).
4. Rick Hanson, *Hardwiring Happiness: The New Brain Science of Contentment, Calm, and Confidence* (New York: Harmony Books, 2016).
5. Brain Futures Conference, September 7, 2017, Washington, DC. https://www.brainfutures .org/conference/.
6. *Attention spans*, 2015. https://advertising.microsoft.com/en/WWDocs/User/display/cl/ researchreport/31966/en/microsoft-attention-spans-research-report.pdf.
7. "Multitasking Undermines Our Efficiency, Study Suggests." *Monitor on Psychology* 32, no. 9 (2001): 13, http://www.apa.org/monitor/oct01/multitask.aspx.
8. "Multitasking: Switching costs." 2017. *American Psychological Association*. American Psychological Association. Accessed October 28. http://www.apa.org/research/action/multitask .aspx.
9. Mark, Gloria, Shamsi T. Iqbal, Mary Czerwinski, Paul Johns, and Akane Sano. 2016. "Neurotics Cant Focus." *Proceedings of the 2016 CHI Conference on Human Factors in Computing Systems - CHI 16*. doi:10.1145/2858036.2858202.
10. Steve Bradt, "Wandering Mind Not a Happy Mind," *Harvard Gazette*, November 11, 2010, https://news.harvard.edu/gazette/story/2010/11/wandering-mind-not-a-happy-mind/.
11. Shimoff, Marci, and Carol Kline. *Happy for no reason: 7 steps to being happy from the inside out*. New York: Atria Paperback, 2013, 83.

12. "Tiny Habits," *Tiny Habits w/Dr. B. J. Fogg—Behavior Change*, http://tinyhabits.com/ (accessed August 5, 2017).

13. "Many Americans Stressed about Future of Our Nation, New APA Stress in America™ Survey Reveals." American Psychological Association. Accessed July 17, 2017. http://www.apa.org/news/press/releases/2017/02/stressed-nation.aspx.

14. Jacqueline Andriakos, "Meditation Made Mobile: On-the-Go Apps," *TIME Special Edition*, February 3, 2014.

15. Tim Ryan, *A Mindful Nation: How a Simple Practice Can Help Us Reduce Stress, Improve Performance, and Recapture the American Spirit* (Carlsbad, CA: Hay House, 2013).

16. Dreyfus, Rebecca, director. *On Meditation*. Snapdragon Films, 2016.

17. "Home." American Mindfulness Research Association, https://goamra.org/ (accessed October 31, 2017).

18. David M. Levy, Jacob O. Wobbrock, Alfred W. Kaszniak, and Marilyn Ostergren, "The Effects of Mindfulness Meditation Training on Multitasking in a High-Stress Information Environment." *GI '12 Proceedings of Graphics Interface*, 2012, 45–52, https://faculty.washington.edu/wobbrock/pubs/gi-12.02.pdf.

19. Julie A. Brefczynski-Lewis, A. Lutz, H. S. Schaefer, D. B. Levinson, and R. J. Davidson, "Neural Correlates of Attentional Expertise in Long-Term Meditation Practitioners," *Proceedings of the National Academy of Sciences, USA*, 104, no. 27 (2007): 11483–21488. doi:10.1073/pnas.0606552104.

20. David J. Kearney, Carol A. Malte, Carolyn McManus, Michelle E. Martinez, Ben Felleman, and Tracy L. Simpson, "Loving-Kindness Meditation for Posttraumatic Stress Disorder: A Pilot Study," *Journal of Traumatic Stress* 26, no. 4 (2013): 426–434.

21. Fadel Zeidan, Nakia S. Gordon, Junaid Merchant, and Paula Goolkasian, "The Effects of Brief Mindfulness Meditation Training on Experimentally Induced Pain," *Journal of Pain* 11, no. 3 (2010): 199–209. doi:10.1016/j.jpain.2009.07.015.

22. Richard J. Davidson, Jon Kabat-Zinn, Jessica Schumacher, Melissa Rosenkranz, Daniel Muller, Saki F. Santorelli, Ferris Urbanowski, Anne Harrington, Katherine Bonus, and John F. Sheridan, "Alterations in Brain and Immune Function Produced by Mindfulness Meditation," *Psychosomatic Medicine* 65, no. 4 (2003): 564–570. doi:10.1097/01.psy.0000077505.67574.e3.

23. B. Barrett et al., "P02.36. Meditation or Exercise for Preventing Acute Respiratory Infection: A Randomized Controlled Trial," *BMC Complementary and Alternative Medicine* 12, Suppl 1 (2012). doi:10.1186/1472-6882-12-s1-p92.

24. Joel W. Hughes, David M. Fresco, Rodney Myerscough, Manfred H. M. Van Dulmen, Linda E. Carlson, and Richard Josephson, "Randomized Controlled Trial of Mindfulness-Based Stress Reduction for Prehypertension," *Psychosomatic Medicine* 75, no. 8 (2013): 721–728. doi:10.1097/psy.0b013e3182a3e4e5.

25. Marci Shimoff and Carol Kline, *Happy for No Reason: 7 Steps to Being Happy from the Inside Out* (New York: Atria Paperback, 2013), 83.

26. Loucks, Eric B., Willoughby B. Britton, Chanelle J. Howe, Charles B. Eaton, and Stephen L. Buka, "Positive Associations of Dispositional Mindfulness with Cardiovascular Health: The New England Family Study," *International Journal of Behavioral Medicine* 22, no. 4 (2014): 540–550. doi:10.1007/s12529-014-9448-9.

27. Ute R. Hülsheger, Alina Feinholdt, and Annika Nübold, "A Low-Dose Mindfulness Intervention and Recovery from Work: Effects on Psychological Detachment, Sleep Quality, and Sleep Duration," *Journal of Occupational and Organizational Psychology* 88, no. 3 (2015): 464–489.

28. Heleen Slagter, Antoine Lutz, Lawrence L. Greischar, Andrew D. Francis, Sander Nieuwenhuis, James M. Davis, and Richard J. Davidson, "Mental Training Affects Distribution of Limited Brain Resources," *PLoS Biology* 5, no. 6 (2007). doi:10.1371/journal.pbio.0050138.

29. Taylor, Tess. "22% of companies now offering mindfulness training." HR Dive. August 16, 2016. Accessed August 5, 2017. http://www.hrdive.com/news/22-of-companies-now-offering-mindfulness-training/424530/.

Chapter 2: What's Stressing People Out?

1. Abstract, *The Outsourcing Revolution*, 2004, https://pdfs.semanticscholar.org/61ca/86672 db149bc4bb9981b287b328ba7bf1dec.pdf.

2. *Deloitte's 2016 Global Outsourcing Survey*, May 2016, https://www2.deloitte.com/content/dam/ Deloitte/nl/Documents/operations/deloitte-nl-s&o-global-outsourcing-survey.pdf.

3. Associated Press, "Japan's Robot Hotel: A Dinosaur at Reception, a Machine for Room Service," *The Guardian*, July 15, 2015, https://www.theguardian.com/world/2015/jul/16/ japans-robot-hotel-a-dinosaur-at-reception-a-machine-for-room-service.

4. Oliver Cann, "Five Million Jobs by 2020: The Real Challenge of the Fourth Industrial Revolution," World Economic Forum, January 18, 2016, https://www.weforum.org/press/2016/ 01/five-million-jobs-by-2020-the-real-challenge-of-the-fourth-industrial-revolution/.

5. Lesley Stahl, "The Great Brain Robbery," *CBS News*, January 25, 2016, https://www.cbsnews .com/news/60-minutes-great-brain-robbery-china-cyber-espionage/.

6. Alison DeNisco Rayome, "Report: US Tech Jobs Hit Nearly 7 Million Workers, Up 3% from Year Before," *TechRepublic*, April 3, 2017, https://www.techrepublic.com/article/report-us-tech-jobs-hit-nearly-7-million-workers-up-3-from-year-before/.

7. Gary Hamel, *What Matters Now: How to Win in a World of Relentless Change, Ferocious Competition, and Unstoppable Innovation* (San Francisco, CA: Jossey-Bass, 2012).

8. Christine Comaford, "63% of Employees Don't Trust Their Leader—Here's What You Can Do to Change That," *Forbes*, January 30, 2017, https://www.forbes.com/sites/ christinecomaford/2017/01/28/63-of-employees-dont-trust-their-leader-heres-what-you-can-do-to-change-that/2/#42a8eb21a430.

Chapter 3: The $500 Billion Dollar Slow Leak

1. "Workplace Stress," The American Institute of Stress, March 14, 2017, https://www.stress .org/workplace-stress/.

2. Kathy Flora, "There's a Workplace Trust Gap. How Can Leaders Close It?" *Leadership Topics*, A. J. O'Connor Associates HR Consulting, July 7, 2016, http://www.ajoconnor.com/blog/ close-leader-trust-gap.

3. Carolyn Gregoire, "Work Stress on the Rise: 8 in 10 Americans Are Stressed About Their Jobs, Survey Finds," *Huffington Post*, April 10, 2013, https://www.huffingtonpost.com/2013/ 04/10/work-stress-jobs-americans_n_3053428.html.

4. "Financial Cost of Job Stress: How Costly Is Job Stress?" Report, *Financial Cost of Job Stress: How Costly Is Job Stress?* University of Massachusetts Lowell, 2017, accessed July 2, 2017, https://www.uml.edu/Research/CPH-NEW/stress-at-work/financial-costs.aspx#costly.

5. Harvey R. Colten and Bruce M. Altevogt, *Sleep Disorders and Sleep Deprivation: An Unmet Public Health Problem* (Washington, DC: Institute of Medicine, 2006), https://www.ncbi.nlm .nih.gov/books/NBK19960/.

6. "2015 Work and Well-Being Survey," —American Psychological Center for Organizational Excellence," 2015, http://www.bing.com/cr?IG=72E3C72D5C14499EBA1988F990BFF1 AE&CID=06937A7456A96B2126B2715857AF6AB3&rd=1&h=mgRlE14SBF-Wmis2oaZ9 ab0GvAbjeShS561rF7Yd5jE&v=1&r=http%3a%2f%2fwww.apaexcellence.org%2fassets %2fgeneral%2f2015-work-and-wellbeing-survey-results.pdf&p=DevEx,5063.1.

7. Anthony Bleetman, Seliat Sanusi, Trevor Dale, and Samantha Brace, "Human Factors and Error Prevention in Emergency Medicine," *Emergency Medicine Journal* 29, no. 5 (2011): 389–393. doi:10.1136/emj.2010.107698.

8. "2016 Turnover Rates by Industry," 2017. *Compensation Force*, http://www.compensationforce .com/2017/04/2016-turnover-rates-by-industry.html (accessed October 31, 2017).

9. Kathryn Dill, "Survey: 42% of Employees Have Changed Jobs due to Stress," *Forbes*, April 18, 2014, https://www.forbes.com/sites/kathryndill/2014/04/18/survey-42-of-employees-have-changed-jobs-due-to-stress/#635796053380.

10. Gallup, Inc., "State of the American Workplace," Gallup.com, http://news.gallup.com/reports/178514/state-american-workplace.aspx?g_source=position1&g_medium=related&g_campaign=tiles (accessed September 6, 2017).

11. "2015 Work and Well-Being Survey," American Psychological Association, http://www.apa excellence.org/assets/general/2015-work-and-wellbeing-survey-results.pdf?_ga=1.101252289 .1351206308.1462281864.

12. Gallup, Inc., "Unhealthy, Stressed Employees Are Hurting Your Business," Gallup.com, May 22, 2012, http://news.gallup.com/businessjournal/154643/unhealthy-stressed-employees-hurting-business.aspx.13. "Research and Advisory Services in Enterprise Learning and Talent Management," Bersin by Deloitte, http://marketing.bersin.com/predictions-for-2017.html (accessed August 31, 2017).

13. Bersin, Josh. *Bersin by Deloitte 2017 Predictions Everything is Digital*. January 2017. Http://www.bersin.com/uploadedFiles/011817_PPT_BersinbyDeloitte2017PredictionsEverything isDigital_JB_Final.pdf.

14. Saul McLeod, "Maslow's Hierarchy of Needs," *Simply Psychology*, February 4, 2016, https://www.simplypsychology.org/maslow.html.

15. David DeSteno, David. 2017. "The Simplest Way to Build Trust." *Harvard Business Review*. September 22. https://hbr.org/2014/06/the-simplest-way-to-build-trust.

16. Rhonda Magee, "How Mindfulness Can Defeat Racial Bias," *Greater Good Science Center*, May 14, 2015, https://greatergood.berkeley.edu/article/item/how_mindfulness_can_defeat_racial_bias.

17. Bruce Feiler, *The Secrets of Happy Families: Improve Your Mornings, Tell Your Family History, Fight Smarter, Go Out and Play, and Much More* (New York: HarperCollins, 2013).

18. Amy Adkins, "Majority of U.S. Employees Not Engaged Despite Gains in 2014," *Gallup News*, January 28, 2015, http://news.gallup.com/poll/181289/majority-employees-not-engaged-despite-gains-2014.aspx.

19. Barry Schwartz, "The Paradox of Choice," *TED Talk*, https://www.ted.com/talks/barry_schwartz_on_the_paradox_of_choice/transcript (accessed October 30, 2017).

20. "Consumer Health Mindset Study 2016," Report, Aon Hewitt, http://www.aon.com/attachments/human-capital-consulting/2016-Consumer-Health-Mindset.pdf.

21. Rich Bellis, "Why It's So Hard to Pay Attention, Explained by Science," *Fast Company*, September 25, 2015, https://www.fastcompany.com/3051417/why-its-so-hard-to-pay-attention-explained-by-science26.

22. "Email Statistics Report, 2015–2019," The Radicati Group, Inc., March 2015, https://www.radicati.com/wp/wp-content/uploads/2015/02/Email-Statistics-Report-2015-2019-Executive-Summary.pdf.

23. "How Many Ads Do You See in One Day? Get Your Advertising Campaigns Heard," Red Crow Marketing, August 3, 2017, http://www.redcrowmarketing.com/2015/09/10/many-ads-see-one-day/.

24. Sarah Perez, "U.S. Consumers Now Spend 5 Hours per Day on Mobile Devices," *TechCrunch*, March 3, 2017, https://techcrunch.com/2017/03/03/u-s-consumers-now-spend-5-hours-per-day-on-mobile-devices/.

25. Jason Karaian, "We Now Spend More than Eight Hours a Day Consuming Media," *Quartz*, June 1, 2015, https://qz.com/416416/we-now-spend-more-than-eight-hours-a-day-consuming-media/.

26. Satoshi Kanazawa, "We Haven't Evolved in Over 10,000 Years—Video," *Big Think*, April 12, 2010, http://bigthink.com/videos/we-havent-evolved-in-over-10000-years.

27. "Holmes-Rahe Stress Inventory," The American Institute of Stress, August 15, 2017, https://www.stress.org/holmes-rahe-stress-inventory/.

28. Melanie Greenberg, "Find Relief from the Stress of Life's Daily Hassles," *Psychology Today*, October 15, 2014, https://www.psychologytoday.com/blog/the-mindful-self-express/201410/find-relief-the-stress-lifes-daily-hassles.

29. Allen D. Kanner, James C. Coyne, Catherine Schaefer, and Richard S. Lazarus, "Comparison of Two Modes of Stress Measurement: Daily Hassles and Uplifts versus Major Life Events," *Journal of Behavioral Medicine* 4, no. 1 (1981): 1–39. doi:10.1007/bf00844845.

30. "Research and Advisory Services in Enterprise Learning and Talent Management," Bersin by Deloitte, accessed August 31, 2017, http://marketing.bersin.com/predictions-for-2017.html.

31. "2015 Stress in America: The Impact of Discrimination," n.d. PsycEXTRA Dataset. doi:10.1037/e503172016-001.

32. Dreyfus, Rebecca, director. *On Meditation*. Snapdragon Films, 2016.

Chapter 4: Are You Increasing Your Resilience or Decreasing It?

1. "Elizabeth Stanley," *School of Foreign Service—Georgetown University*, accessed October 31, 2017, https://sfs.georgetown.edu/faculty-bio/elizabeth-stanley/.

2. Elizabeth A. Stanley, "War Duration and the Micro-dynamics of Decision Making Under Stress," Polity, vol. 50, no. 2 (April 2018).

3. Tom Vanden Brook, "Suicide Kills More U.S. Troops than ISIL in Middle East," *USA Today*, Gannett Satellite Information Network, December 29, 2016, https://www.usatoday.com/story/news/nation/2016/12/29/suicide-kills-more-us-troops-than-isil-middle-east/95961038/.

4. Elizabeth A. Stanley, Widen the Window: Training Your Brain and Body to Thrive during Stress, Uncertainty, and Change (New York: Avery Books, forthcoming in 2019).

5. Elizabeth A. Stanley, "Optimizing the Caveman within Us," TEDx Georgetown, October 2013. At https://www.youtube.com/watch?v=e0AMlf-mwY4.

6. Gillespie, Patrick. "The opioid crisis is draining America of workers." CNNMoney. Accessed August 4, 2017.

7. George Guerin, "Turning Up the Energy for Corporate Professionals—The J&J Human Performance Institute," NJ.com, January 13, 2016, http://www.nj.com/healthfit/fitness/index.ssf/2016/01/post_90.html.

8. Martin P. Paulus et al., "Subjecting Elite Athletes to Inspiratory Breathing Load Reveals Behavioral and Neural Signatures of Optimal Performers in Extreme Environments," *PLoS ONE* 7, no. 1 (January 19, 2012). doi:10.1371/journal.pone.0029394.

9. "HEROForum," in Phoenix, accessed September 12, 2017, http://hero-health.org/.

10. W. Atkinson, "Stress: Risk Management's Most Serious Challenge?" *Risk Management*, 51, no. 6 (2004).

11. C. Hammem, "Stress and Depression," *Clinical Psychology*, vol. 1 (April 27, 2005): 293–319, doi:10.1036/1097-8542.yb071370.

12. K. Goodkin and A. P. Visser, eds., *Psychoneuroimmunology: Stress, Mental Disorders, and Health* (Washington, DC: American Psychiatric Press, 2000).

13. Bruce S. McEwen and Teresa Seeman, "Protective and Damaging Effects of Mediators of Stress: Elaborating and Testing the Concepts of Allostasis and Allostatic Load," *Annals of the New York Academy of Sciences* 896, no. 1 (1999): 30–47, doi:10.1111/j.1749-6632.1999.tb08103.x.

14. Robert M. Sapolsky, "Stress, Glucocorticoids, and Damage to the Nervous System: The Current State of Confusion," *Stress* 1, no. 1 (1996): 1–19, doi:10.3109/10253899609001092.

15. N. Schneiderman, G. Ironson, and S. D. Siegal, "Stress and Health: Psychological, Behavioral, and Biological Determinants," *Annual Review of Clinical Psychology* 1, no. 1 (2005): 607–628.

16. Lars Schwabe and Oliver T. Wolf, "Learning Under Stress Impairs Memory Formation," *Neurobiology of Learning and Memory* 93, no. 2 (2010): 183–188, doi:10.1016/j.nlm .2009.09.009.

17. Richard A. Dienstbier, "Arousal and Physiological Toughness: Implications for Mental and Physical Health," *Psychological Review* 96, no. 1 (1989): 84–100. doi:10.1037//0033-295x .96.1.84.

18. Elissa S. Epel, Bruce S. McEwen, and Jeannette R. Ickovics, "Embodying Psychological Thriving: Physical Thriving in Response to Stress," *Journal of Social Issues* 54, no. 2 (1998): 301–322. doi:10.1111/0022-4537.671998067.

19. P. A. Hancock and J. L. Weaver, "On Time Distortion Under Stress," *Theoretical Issues in Ergonomics Science* 6, no. 2 (2005): 193–211. doi:10.1080/14639220512331325747.

20. Crystal L. Park and Vicki S. Helgeson, "Introduction to the Special Section: Growth Following Highly Stressful Life Events—Current Status and Future Directions," *Journal of Consulting and Clinical Psychology* 74, no. 5 (2006): 791–796. doi:10.1037/0022-006x.74.5.791.

21. Richard G. Tedeschi and Lawrence G. Calhoun, "Posttraumatic Growth: Conceptual Foundations and Empirical Evidence," *Psychological Inquiry* 15, no. 1 (2004): 1–18. doi:10.1207/ s15327965pli1501_01.

22. L. Cahill "Enhanced Human Memory Consolidation with Post-Learning Stress: Interaction with the Degree of Arousal at Encoding," *Learning and Memory* 10, no. 4 (2003): 270–274. doi:10.1101/lm.62403.

23. Alia J. Crum, Peter Salovey, and Shawn Achor, "Rethinking Stress: The Role of Mindsets in Determining the Stress Response." *Journal of Personality and Social Psychology* 104, no. 4 (2013): 716–733. doi:10.1037/a0031201.

24. Alia J. Crum, Modupe Akinola, Ashley Martin, and Sean Fath, "The Role of Stress Mindset in Shaping Cognitive, Emotional, and Physiological Responses to Challenging and Threatening Stress," *Anxiety, Stress, and Coping* 30, no. 4 (2017): 379–395. doi:10.1080/ 10615806.2016.1275585.

CHAPTER 5: WHAT DOES "PERFORMANCE" MEAN TO YOU?

1. *Stress in America: Our Health at Risk*, American Psychological Association, January 11, 2012, https://www.apa.org/news/press/releases/stress/2011/final-2011.pdf.

2. Alex Gray, "5 million jobs to be lost by 2020," *World Economic Forum*, accessed July 1, 2017, https://www.weforum.org/agenda/2016/01/5-million-jobs-to-be-lost-by-2020.

3. Tiffany McDowell, Dimple Agarwal, Don Miller, Tsutomu Okamoto, and Trevor Page, "Organizational Design," *Deloitte Insights*, February 29, 2016, https://dupress.deloitte.com/ dup-us-en/focus/human-capital-trends/2016/organizational-models-network-of-teams .html.

4. "New Study Suggests We Remember the Bad Times Better than the Good," *Association for Psychological Science*, accessed August 4, 2017, http://www.psychologicalscience.org/news/ releases/new-study-suggests-we-remember-the-bad-times-better-than-the-good.html#, WFl0l6IrLUI.

5. "United States Department of Labor," Occupational Safety and Health Administration, accessed July 2, 2017, https://www.osha.gov/SLTC/healthcarefcilities/index.html.

CHAPTER 6: YOU VERSUS TECHNOLOGY

1. "Global Mobile Consumer Survey: U.S. edition," Deloitte U.S. October 24, 2017, https:// www2.deloitte.com/us/en/pages/technology-media-and-telecommunications/articles/ global-mobile-consumer-survey-us-edition.html.

2. John Brandon, John, "The Surprising Reason Millennials Check Their Phones 150 Times a Day," Inc.com., April 17, 2017, https://www.inc.com/john-brandon/science-says-this-is-the-reason-millennials-check-their-phones-150-times-per-day.html.

3. Jacqueline Howard, "Americans at More than 10 Hours a Day on Screens," CNN, July 29, 2016, http://www.cnn.com/2016/06/30/health/americans-screen-time-nielsen/.

4. Nadia Whitehead, "People Would Rather Be Electrically Shocked than Left Alone with Their Thoughts," *Science AAAS*, July 26, 2017, http://www.sciencemag.org/news/2014/07/people-would-rather-be-electrically-shocked-left-alone-their-thoughts.

CHAPTER 7: INVEST FIVE MINUTES A DAY TO SAVE YOUR LIFE

1. The NPD Group, "The NPD Group Reports 34 Million Core Gamers Spend an Average of 22 Hours per Week Playing Video Games," NPD Group, May 13, 2014, https://www.npd.com/wps/portal/npd/us/news/press-releases/the-npd-group-reports-34-million-core-gamers-spend-an-average-of-22-hours-per-week-playing-video-games/.

2. Jane McGonigal, "Create the Building Blocks of Lasting Resilience: The Power of a Gameful Mindset." Lecture presented at the 2017 Resilience and Well-Being Conference, October 5, 2017.

3. Peter Kafka, "You Are Still Watching a Staggering Amount of TV Every Day," *Recode*, June 27, 2016, http://www.recode.net/2016/6/27/12041028/tv-hours-per-week-nielsen.

4. Joe Flint, "TV Networks Load Up on Commercials," *Los Angeles Times*, May 12, 2014, http://www.latimes.com/entertainment/envelope/cotown/la-et-ct-nielsen-advertising-study-20140510-story.html.

5. Shea Bennett, "This Is How Much Time We Spend on Social Networks Every Day," *Adweek*, November 18, 2014, http://www.adweek.com/digital/social-media-minutes-day/.

6. Larry Copeland, "Americans' Commutes Aren't Getting Longer," *USA Today*, March 5, 2013, https://www.usatoday.com/story/news/nation/2013/03/05/americans-commutes-not-getting-longer/1963409/.

7. Stacey Vanek Smith, "Why We Sign Up for Gym Memberships But Never Go to the Gym," NPR, December 30, 2014, http://www.npr.org/sections/money/2014/12/30/373996649/why-we-sign-up-for-gym-memberships-but-don-t-go-to-the-gym.

8. *Mindfulness Goes Mainstream*. Performed by Jewel, Eileen Fischer and Jon Kabat-Zinn. http://www.pbs.org/video/mindfulness-goes-mainstream-jjfwvu/.

9. "PositivityRatio.com—Home," *PositivityRatio*, accessed October 1, 2017, http://www.positivityratio.com/.

CHAPTER 8: IT'S NOT A RELIGION. IT'S A LIFESTYLE.

1. "Stress in America: Paying with Our Health," *PsycEXTRA Dataset*, February 2015. doi:10.1037/e513292015-001.

2. Richard Fry, "Millennials Surpass Gen Xers as the Largest Generation in U.S. Labor Force," Pew Research Center, May 11, 2015, http://www.pewresearch.org/fact-tank/2015/05/11/millennials-surpass-gen-xers-as-the-largest-generation-in-u-s-labor-force/.

3. Thomas H. Holmes and Richard H. Rahe, "The Social Readjustment Rating Scale," *Journal of Psychosomatic Research* 11, no. 2 (1967): 213–218. doi:10.1016/0022-3999(67)90010-4.

4. "Happy People Don't Need to Feel Superior," *Greater Good*, accessed November 1, 2017, https://greatergood.berkeley.edu/article/item/happy_people_dont_need_to_feel_superior.

5. "New Research Reveals the Secret to Making a Good First Impression," University of Glasgow, March 13, 2014, https://www.gla.ac.uk/news/archiveofnews/2014/march/headline_312691_en.html.

6. Douglas Stone, *Difficult Conversations: How to Discuss What Matters Most* (London: Penguin, 2011).

7. "Daring Greatly Engaged Feedback Checklist—Brené Brown," 2017, accessed August 29, http://buhx139thfh1fcf2n21cd78o.wpengine.netdna-cdn.com/wp-content/uploads/2017/10/Engaged-Feedback-Checklist-Download.pdf.

8. Michael Landers, *Culture Crossing: Discover the Key to Making Successful Connections in the New Global Era* (Oakland, CA: Berrett-Koehler, 2017).

9. Jean L. Kristeller and Ruth Q. Wolever, "Mindfulness-Based Eating Awareness Training for Treating Binge Eating Disorder: The Conceptual Foundation," *Eating Disorders* 19, no. 1 (2010): 49–61. doi:10.1080/10640266.2011.533605.

10. Stephen G. Post, *Giving, Happiness, and Health*, accessed August 24, 2017, http://www.stephengpost.com/.

11. John Medina, "Essay," in *Brain Rules: 12 Principles for Surviving and Thriving at Work, Home, and School* (Seattle, WA: Pear Press, 2008).

12. Bridget Murray, "Writing to Heal," *Monitor on Psychology*, 33, no. 6 (2002), http://www.apa.org/monitor/jun02/writing.aspx.

13. K. A. Baikie and Kay Wilhelm, "Emotional and Physical Health Benefits of Expressive Writing," *Advances in Psychiatric Treatment* 11, no. 5 (2005): 338–346. doi:10.1192/apt.11.5.338.

14. Linda Wasmer Andrews, "How Gratitude Helps You Sleep at Night," *Psychology Today*, November 9, 2011, https://www.psychologytoday.com/blog/minding-the-body/201111/how-gratitude-helps-you-sleep-night.

15. SIYLI, "Mindfulness-Based Emotional Intelligence for Leaders," March 2015, http://www.swissnexsanfrancisco.org/wp-content/uploads/sites/6/2015/04/SIY-at-Swissnex-March-2015.pdf.

16. IU Bloomington Newsroom , "Not-So-Guilty Pleasure: Viewing Cat Videos Boosts Energy and Positive Emotions, IU Study Finds," *IU Bloomington Newsroom*, June 16, 2015, http://archive.news.indiana.edu/releases/iu/2015/06/internet-cat-video-research.shtml.

17. Christine Carter, "The Three Parts of an Effective Apology," *Greater Good Science Center*, accessed October 2, 2017, https://greatergood.berkeley.edu/article/item/the_three_parts_of_an_effective_apology.

18. Fredrickson, Barbara L., Michael A. Cohn, Kimberly A. Coffey, Jolynn Pek, and Sandra M. Finkel, "Open Hearts Build Lives: Positive Emotions, Induced Through Loving-Kindness Meditation, Build Consequential Personal Resources," *Journal of Personality and Social Psychology* 95, no. 5 (2008): 1045–1062. doi:10.1037/a0013262.

Chapter 9: Reality Check: How Toxic Is Your Work Culture?

1. Michael D. Watkins, "What Is Organizational Culture? And Why Should We Care?" *Harvard Business Review*, August 7, 2014, https://hbr.org/2013/05/what-is-organizational-culture.

2. John A. Bargh, John A. and Tanya L. Chartrand, "The Unbearable Automaticity of Being," *American Psychologist* 54, no. 7 (1999): 462–479. doi:10.1037//0003-066x.54.7.462.

3. Sigal Barsade, Sigal and Olivia A. O'Neill, "Manage Your Emotional Culture," *Harvard Business Review*, November 17, 2016, https://hbr.org/2016/01/manage-your-emotional-culture.

4. Daniel Goleman, *Emotional Intelligence* (London: Bantam Books, 2006).

5. Joel Goh, Jeffrey Pfeffer, and Stefanos A Zenios, "The Relationship Between Workplace Stressors and Mortality and Health Costs in the United States," Submitted to *Management Science*, manuscript MS-12-01264.R3.

6. YouTube, June 30, 2007, accessed July 4, 2017, https://www.youtube.com/watch?v=Sv5iEK-IEzw.

7. Gallup, Inc., "Why Your Workplace Wellness Program Isn't Working," *Gallup.com*. May 13, 2014, http://news.gallup.com/businessjournal/168995/why-workplace-wellness-program-isn-working.aspx.

8. Rajendra Sisodia, David B. Wolfe, and Jagdish N. Sheth, *Firms of Endearment: How World-Class Companies Profit from Passion and Purpose* (Upper Saddle River, NJ: Pearson Education), 2014, 3.

9. "Mental and Substance Use Disorders," *SAMHSA*, September 20, 2017, https://www.samhsa.gov/disorders.

CHAPTER 10: SLEEPLESS NIGHTS AND THE WALKING DEAD

1. "1 in 3 Adults Don't Get Enough Sleep," Centers for Disease Control and Prevention, accessed October 2, 2017, https://www.cdc.gov/media/releases/2016/p0215-enough-sleep.html.

2. "Sleep and Sleep Disorders," Centers for Disease Control and Prevention, May 2, 2017, https://www.cdc.gov/sleep/data_statistics.html.

3. "Division for Heart Disease and Stroke Prevention." Centers for Disease Control and Prevention. May 12, 2017. Accessed January 05, 2018. https://www.cdc.gov/dhdsp/maps/national_maps/hd_all.htm.

4. "CDC Mental Illness Surveillance," Centers for Disease Control and Prevention, accessed November 1, 2017. https://www.cdc.gov/mentalhealthsurveillance/fact_sheet.html.

5. Robin S. Haight and Paul Saskin, "Getting a Good Night's Sleep," American Psychological Association, accessed October 11, 2017, http://www.apa.org/helpcenter/sleep-disorders.aspx.

6. "Sleep Deprivation Can Slow Reaction Time, National Sleep Foundation, accessed October 1, 2017, https://sleepfoundation.org/sleep-news/sleep-deprivation-can-slow-reaction-time.

7. Sandee LaMotte, "Sacrificing Sleep? Here's What It Will Do to Your Health," *CNN*, September 27, 2017, http://www.cnn.com/2017/07/19/health/dangers-of-sleep-deprivation/index.html.

8. Steven Zeitchik and James Queally, "Walmart Driver Charged in Tracy Morgan Crash; Report Cites .,'" *Los Angeles Times*, June 7, 2014, http://www.latimes.com/entertainment/tv/showtracker/la-et-st-tracy-morgan-car-crash-charges-wal-mart-20140607-story.html.

9. Brian Christopher Tefft, "Prevalence of Motor Vehicle Crashes Involving Drowsy Drivers, United States, 2009–2013," November 2014. doi:10.1016/j.aap.2011.05.028.

10. Prashant Kaul, Jason Passafiume, Craig R. Sargent, and Bruce F. O'Hara, "Meditation Acutely Improves Psychomotor Vigilance, and May Decrease Sleep Need," *Behavioral and Brain Functions* 6, no. 47 (2010), https://www.ncbi.nlm.nih.gov/pubmed/20670413.

11. Sheila Garland, Linda Carlson, Michael Antle, Charles Samuels, and Tavis Campbell, "I Can Sleep: Rationale and Design of a Non-Inferiority RCT of Mindfulness-Based Stress Reduction and Cognitive Behavioral Therapy for the Treatment of Insomnia in Cancer Survivors," *Contemporary Clinical Trials* 32, no. 5 (2011): 747–754, https://www.ncbi.nlm.nih.gov/pubmed/21658476.

12. "How Long Should It Take to Fall Asleep?" Sleep.Org, accessed October 19, 2017, https://sleep.org/articles/how-long-to-fall-asleep/.

13. Ute R. Hülsheger, Alina Feinholdt, and Annika Nübold, "A Low-Dose Mindfulness Intervention and Recovery from Work: Effects on Psychological Detachment, Sleep Quality, and Sleep Duration," *Journal of Occupational and Organizational Psychology* 88, no. 3 (2015): 464–489 doi:10.1111/joop.12115.

14. Amit Sood "To Improve Your Health, Practice Gratitude," Mayo Clinic, Mayo Foundation for Medical Education and Research, November 29, 2016, https://www.mayoclinic.org/healthy-lifestyle/adult-health/in-depth/improve-health-practice-gratitude/art-20270841

CHAPTER 11: LOOK, A SQUIRREL! DISTRACTION AND THE GROWING SAFETY CRISIS

1. Nationalsafety, "The OSHA Fatal Four," Nationalsafety's Weblog, January 4, 2012, https://nationalsafetyinc.org/2012/01/05/the-osha-fatal-four/.
2. Praveen Garg, ed., "Human Factors versus Accident Causation," September 2010, http://www.hrdp-idrm.in/e5783/e17327/e28899/e28897/Theme-7CDR-11-11-fb.pdf.
3. Monika Goretzki and Ania Zysk, "Using Mindfulness Techniques to Improve Student Well-being and Academic Performance for University Students: A Pilot Study," April 2017.
4. "OS TB 10/27/2016 Table 1: Incidence Rates—Detailed Industry Level—2015" 2016, Report , OSHA, https://www.bls.gov/iif/oshwc/osh/os/ostb4732.pdf.
5. "Business Case for Safety and Health," Occupational Safety and Health Administration, United States Department of Labor, accessed November 1, 2017, https://www.osha.gov/dcsp/products/topics/businesscase/costs.html.
6. "2015 Stress in America Snapshot," American Psychological Association, accessed September 28, 2017, http://www.apa.org/news/press/releases/stress/2015/snapshot.aspx.
7. "2015 Stress in America: The Impact of Discrimination," *PsycEXTRA Dataset*, March 2016. doi:10.1037/e503172016-001.
8. Melissa Dittmann, Melissa, "Anger Across the Gender Divide," *Monitor on Psychology* 34, no. 3 (March 2003), http://www.apa.org/monitor/mar03/angeracross.aspx.
9. "Brief Training in Meditation May Help Manage Pain, Study Shows," *ScienceDaily*, November 9, 2010, https://www.sciencedaily.com/releases/2009/11/091110065909.htm.

CHAPTER 12: TURN DEPRESSING DATA INTO HEALTHY EMPLOYEES

1. davidsteele1975, "IDC Predicts Huge Growth in Wearable Technology Sales," Android-Headlines.com, *Android News*, June 18, 2015, https://www.androidheadlines.com/2015/06/idc-predicts-huge-growth-wearable-technology-sales.html.
2. "The Largest Connected Health Ecosystem," *Validic*, accessed October 30, 2017, https://validic.com/ecosystem/.
3. Edward L. Deci, *Intrinsic Motivation* (New York: Plenum Press, 1975).
4. Edward L. Deci and Richard M. Ryan, *Intrinsic Motivation and Self-Determination in Human Behavior* (New York: Plenum Press, 1985).
5. Mark Lepper and David Greene, *The Hidden Costs of Reward* (Hillsdale, NJ: Erlbaum, 1978).
6. Gianluigi Cuccureddu, "Gallup: There's No One-Size-Fits-All Employee Engagement Strategy," *Damarque*, July 23, 2013, http://www.damarque.com/blog/gianluigi-cuccureddu/gallup-theres-no-one-size-fits-all-employee-engagement-strategy.
7. "Predictions for 2017—Everything Is Becoming Digital," 2016, Report, Bersin by Deloitte, https://www2.deloitte.com/content/dam/Deloitte/at/Documents/about-deloitte/predictions-for-2017-final.pdf.
8. Theresa Boyce, "A CT Exclusive Event—Google's Most Popular Program for Executives and Engineers," *CEO Trust*, March 11, 2016, https://ceotrust.org/breaking-news/3875821.
9. Eric B. Loucks, Willoughby B. Britton, Chanelle J. Howe, Charles B. Eaton, and Stephen L. Buka, "Positive Associations of Dispositional Mindfulness with Cardiovascular Health: The New England Family Study," *International Journal of Behavioral Medicine* 22, no. 4 (2014): 540–550. doi:10.1007/s12529-014-9448-9.
10. B. Barrett et al., "P02.36, Meditation or Exercise for Preventing Acute Respiratory Infection: A Randomized Controlled Trial" *BMC Complementary and Alternative Medicine* 12, Suppl 1 (2012). doi:10.1186/1472-6882-12-s1-p92.
11. Epel, Elissa, Jennifer Daubenmier, Judith Tedlie Moskowitz, Susan Folkman, and Elizabeth Blackburn. "Can Meditation Slow Rate of Cellular Aging? Cognitive Stress, Mindfulness, and

Telomeres." *Annals of the New York Academy of Sciences* 1172, no. 1 (2009): 34-53. doi:10.1111/j.1749-6632.2009.04414.x.

12. Mindful Staff, "How the Most Successful People Avoid Burnout," *Mindful*, February 12, 2016, https://www.mindful.org/how-the-most-successful-people-avoid-burnout/.

13. "Mindful Leadership Research Results," Institute for Mindful Leadership, accessed September 4, 2017, https://instituteformindfulleadership.org/research/.

14. "New Study Shows We Work Harder When We Are Happy," accessed September 26, 2017, https://www2.warwick.ac.uk/newsandevents/pressreleases/new_study_shows/.

15. "8.0% of U.S. Adults (18 million) Used Meditation," *National Center for Complementary and Integrative Health*, U.S. Department of Health and Human Services, September 24, 2017, https://nccih.nih.gov/research/statistics/NHIS/2012/mind-body/meditation.

CHAPTER 13: BUILDING EMOTIONAL INTELLIGENCE (EQ) SKILLS FOR YOURSELF

1. Harvey Deutschendorf, "7 Reasons Why Emotional Intelligence Is One of the Fastest-Growing Jobs," *Fast Company*, May 6, 2016, https://www.fastcompany.com/3059481/7-reasons-why-emotional-intelligence-is-one-of-the-fastest-growing-job-skills.

2. Alex Gray, "The 10 Skills You Need to Thrive in the Fourth Industrial Revolution," World Economic Forum, January 19, 2016, https://www.weforum.org/agenda/2016/01/the-10-skills-you-need-to-thrive-in-the-fourth-industrial-revolution/.

3. "A Brief History of EQ—Practical EQ," *Emotional Intelligence*, accessed August 26, 2017, http://www.emotionalintelligencecourse.com/eq-history.

4. Goleman, Daniel, *Emotional Intelligence* (London: Bantam Books, 2006).

5. Bliss, Samuel E., "The Affect of Emotional Intelligence on a Modern Organizational Leader's Ability to Make Effective Decisions," *Steve Hein's EQI.Org*, n.d., http://eqi.org/mgtpaper.htm.

6. "FAQ: The 16 Competencies: Defining Behaviors," Zenger and Folkman, n.d., http://zengerfolkman.com/wp-content/uploads/2013/12/FAQ-16-Competencies-Defining-Behaviors.pdf.

7. Michael A. Trabun, "The Relationship Between Emotional Intelligence and Leader Performance" (Thesis, Naval Postgraduate School, March 2002), https://calhoun.nps.edu/bitstream/handle/10945/6007/02Mar_Trabun.pdf?sequence=1.

8. "Old Man's Advice to Youth: 'Never Lose a Holy Curiosity,'" *LIFE* (May 2, 1955), 64.

9. Lane Beckes and James A. Coan, "Social Baseline Theory: The Role of Social Proximity in Emotion and Economy of Action," *Social and Personality Psychology Compass* 5, no. 12 (2011): 976–988. doi:10.1111/j.1751-9004.2011.00400.x.

10. Maria Popova "William James on Attention, Multitasking, and the Habit of Mind that Sets Geniuses Apart," *Brain Pickings*, August 28, 2016, https://www.brainpickings.org/2016/03/25/william-james-attention/.

11. "Daniel Goleman's Five Components of Emotional Intelligence," *Goleman's ET*, accessed September 29, 2017, https://web.sonoma.edu/users/s/swijtink/teaching/philosophy_101/paper1/goleman.htm.

CHAPTER 14: INCREASING SELF-AWARENESS

1. Daniel Goleman, *Working with Emotional Intelligence* (London: Bloomsbury, 1998).

2. Daniel Goleman, "How Emotionally Intelligent Are You?," April 21, 2015, http://www.danielgoleman.info/daniel-goleman-how-emotionally-intelligent-are-you/.

3. Mindfulness Goes Mainstream. Performed by Jewel, Eileen Fischer and Jon Kabat-Zinn. http://www.pbs.org/video/mindfulness-goes-mainstream-jjfwvu/.

4. Britta K. Hölzel, James Carmody, Karleyton C. Evans, Elizabeth A. Hoge, Jeffery A. Dusek, Lucas Morgan, Roger K. Pitman, and Sara W. Lazar, "Stress Reduction Correlates with Structural Changes in the Amygdala," *Social Cognitive and Affective Neuroscience* 5, no.) (2009): 11–17. doi:10.1093/scan/nsp034.

5. "News: Finnish Research Team Reveals How Emotions Are Mapped in the Body," Aalto University, December 30, 2013, http://www.aalto.fi/en/current/news/view/2013-12-31/.

6. Malcolm Gladwell, *Blink: The Power of Thinking Without Thinking* (New York: Back Bay Books, 2013).

7. Matthew Lieberman, "Putting Feelings into Words: The Neural Basis of Unintentional Emotion Regulation," *PsycEXTRA Dataset*, 2007. doi:10.1037/e634112013-130.

8. Davide Laneri, Verena Schuster, Bruno Dietsche, Andreas Jansen, Ulrich Ott, and Jens Sommer, "Effects of Long-Term Mindfulness Meditation on Brain's White Matter Microstructure and Its Aging," *Frontiers in Aging Neuroscience* 7 (2016). doi:10.3389/fnagi.2015.00254.

CHAPTER 15: IMPROVING SELF-REGULATION

1. Sun Tzu, *The Art of War* (New York: Oxford University Press, 1971).

2. J. A. Brefczynski-Lewis, JA. Lutz, H. S. Schaefer, D. B. Levinson, and R. J. Davidson, "Neural Correlates of Attentional Expertise in Long-Term Meditation Practitioners," *Proceedings of the National Academy of Sciences* 104, no. 27 (2007): 11483–11488. doi:10.1073/pnas.0606552104.

3. Viktor Emil Frankl, *Man's Search for Meaning: An Introduction to Logotherapy* (Boston: Beacon Press, 1992).

4. *Mindfulness Goes Mainstream*. Performed by Jewel, Eileen Fischer and Jon Kabat-Zinn. http://www.pbs.org/video/mindfulness-goes-mainstream-jjfwvu/.

5. Marcus Aurelius, , *Meditations*, n.d.

6. Maria Popova, "Bruce Lee's Never-Before-Seen Writings on Willpower, Emotion, Reason, Memory, Imagination, and Confidence," Brain Pickings, August 9, 2016, https://www.brainpickings.org/2016/08/01/bruce-lee-notebook/.

7. Dr. Daniel J. Levitin, RSS, "This Is Your Brain on Music," http://daniellevitin.com/publicpage/books/this-is-your-brain-on-music/ (accessed October 4, 2017).

8. "'Imperfect Harmony': How Singing with Others Changes Your Life," *NPR*, June 3, 2013, http://www.npr.org/2013/06/03/188355968/imperfect-harmony-how-chorale-singing-changes-lives.

9. DolceCamy87, YouTube, November 30, 2011, https://www.youtube.com/watch?v=1PbHX MJJ-dY.

10. "How the Prescription Drug Crisis Is Impacting American Employers," National Safety Council, 2017, http://www.nsc.org/NewsDocuments/2017/Media-Briefing-National-Employer-Drug-Survey-Results.pdf.

CHAPTER 16: BOOSTING MOTIVATION

1. John Hagel, "If You Love Them, Set Them Free," *Deloitte Insights*, https://dupress.deloitte.com/dup-us-en/topics/talent/future-workforce-engagement-in-the-workplace.html (accessed August 3, 2017).

2. Stuart Brown, "Play Is More than Just Fun," *TED Talk*, https://www.ted.com/talks/stuart_brown_says_play_is_more_than_fun_it_s_vital (accessed November 1, 2017).

3. "Press Play," Audio blog, *TED Radio Hour Podcast*, NPR, n.d., http://www.podcasts.com/npr_ted_radio_hour_podcast/episode/press-play.

4. Abbot, Lydia, "New Insights that May Make You Rethink How You Recruit Millennials," *LinkedIn Talent Blog*, https://business.linkedin.com/talent-solutions/blog/hiring-

millennials/2016/new-insights-that-may-make-you-rethink-how-you-recruit-millennials (accessed November 1, 2017).

5. Brad White, "Millennials or Boomers: Who Is More Purpose Driven?" *BrightHouse, Home of Purpose*, July 5, 2017, http://thinkbrighthouse.com/millennials-or-boomers-who-is-more-purpose-driven/.

6. Daniel H. Pink, *Drive: The Surprising Truth About What Motivates Us* (New York: Riverhead Books, 2012).

7. Barry Schwartz, *Why We Work* (New York: TED Books, Simon and Schuster, 2015), 1–3.

8. "What Is Delivering Happiness?" *Delivering Happiness*, http://deliveringhappiness.com/company/ (accessed October 13, 2017).

9. Adrian Charles, Nadia Tarlow, and Chris Bertish, dirs., *Ocean Driven*, n.d., http://www.oceandrivenfilm.com/.

CHAPTER 17: GETTING POSITIVE – DON'T CALL IT A COMEBACK

1. "Resilience," *Merriam-Webster*, n.d., https://www.merriam-webster.com/dictionary/resilience#medicalDictionary.

2. Maria Popova "Fixed versus Growth: The Two Basic Mindsets that Shape Our Lives," *Brain Pickings*, September 18, 2015, https://www.brainpickings.org/2014/01/29/carol-dweck-mindset/.

3. Carol S. Dweck, "Mindsets and Math/Science Achievement," Carnegie-IAS Commission on Mathematics and Science Education, 2008, https://www.nd.gov/dpi/uploads/1381/Dweck2008MindsetsandMathScienceAchievemented.pdf.

4. Carol Dweck and Kathleen Hogan, "How Microsoft Uses a Growth Mindset to Develop Leaders," *Harvard Business Review*, April 21, 2017, https://hbr.org/2016/10/how-microsoft-uses-a-growth-mindset-to-develop-leaders.

5. Christine Comaford-Lynch, *SmartTribes: How Teams Become Brilliant Together* (New York: Portfolio/Penguin, 2013), https://books.google.com/books?id=UNhOa4zLfCsC&pg=PT256&lpg=PT256&dq=fred luskin research 90%25 thoughts&source=bl&ots=pzdHm0nLCn&sig=oMOLgf3nyvuxf13ywhrnkTZ2nSE&hl=en&sa=X&ved=0ahUKEwji35b1nevVAhVX42MKHfJ6Bn4Q6AEIPTAE#v=onepage&q=fred%20luskin%20research%2090%25%20thoughts&f=false.

6. Rick Hanson, *Hardwiring Happiness: The New Brain Science of Contentment, Calm, and Confidence* (New York: Harmony Books, 2016).

7. "Neuroscience of Mindfulness: Default Mode Network, Meditation, and Mindfulness," *Mindfulness, MD*, June 17, 2017, https://www.mindfulnessmd.com/2014/07/08/neuroscience-of-mindfulness-default-mode-network-meditation-mindfulness/.

8. Malcolm Gladwell, *Blink: The Power of Thinking Without Thinking* (New York: Back Bay Books, 2013).

9. Steve Zaffron, and Dave Logan, *Three Laws of Performance: Rewriting the Future of Your Organization and Your Life* (San Francisco: Jossey-Bass, 2009).

10. Martin E. P. Seligman, *Learned Optimism* (North Sydney, N.S.W.: William Heinemann Australia, 2011).

11. "Don't Give Up: Why Sales Persistence Pays Off (Op-Ed)," *Business News Daily*, October 31, 2013, http://www.businessnewsdaily.com/5389-in-sales-persistence-pays-off.html.

12. Jon Gordon, *The Positive Dog: A Story About the Power of Positivity* (Hoboken, NJ: John Wiley & Sons, 2012).

13. Alexander Caillet, Jeremy Hirshberg, and Stefano Petti, "How Your State of Mind Affects Your Performance," *Business Insider*, May 13, 2015, http://www.businessinsider.com/how-state-of-mind-affects-performance-2015-5.

14. Deborah D. Danner, David A. Snowdon, and Wallace V. Friesen, "Positive Emotions in Early Life and Longevity: Findings from the Nun Study," *Journal of Personality and Social Psychology* 80, no. 5 (2001): 804–813. doi:10.1037/0022-3514.80.5.804.

15. Jim Keenan, "The Proven Predictor of Sales Success Few Are Using," *Forbes*, December 5, 2015, https://www.forbes.com/sites/jimkeenan/2015/12/05/the-proven-predictor-of-sales-success-few-are-using/#255565a74ede.

16. Ellie Lisitsa "The Positive Perspective: More on the 5:1 Ratio," The Gottman Institute, March 13, 2017, https://www.gottman.com/blog/the-positive-perspective-more-on-the-51-ratio/.

17. Alok Chakrawal and Pratibha Goyal, *Stress Management*(Delhi, India: Studera Press), 312.

18. "What Is Gratitude and What Is Its Role in Positive Psychology?" *Positive Psychology Program—Your One-Stop PP Resource!* April 28, 2017, https://positivepsychologyprogram .com/gratitude-appreciation/.

19. R. D. Putnam, *Bowling Alone: The Collapse and Revival of American Community* (New York: Simon and Schuster, 2000).

20. Daniel Goleman, *Leadership: The Power of Emotional Intelligence* (Florence, MA: More than Sound, 2011).

21. B. L. Fredrickson and M. F. Losada, "Positive Affect and the Complex Dynamics of Human Flourishing," *American Psychologist* 60, no. 7 (2005): 678–686.

22. Harvard Health Publications, "Optimism and Your Health," May 1, 2008, http://www .health.harvard.edu/newsletters/Harvard_Mens_Health_Watch/2008/Mayoptimism-and-your-health.

23. "Group Affect," *Group Affect: Annual Review of Organizational Psychology and Organizational Behavior,* November 1. http://www.annualreviews.org/doi/abs/10.1146/annurev-orgpsych-032414-111316?journalCode=orgpsych (accessed November 1, 2017).

24. Rob Thomas and Robert J. Cross, "Managing Yourself: A Smarter Way to Network," *Harvard Business Review*, July–August, 2014, https://hbr.org/2011/07/managing-yourself-a-smarter-way-to-network.

25. Sheldon Cohen, Cuneyt M. Alper, William J. Doyle, John J. Treanor, and Ronald B. Turner, "Positive Emotional Style Predicts Resistance to Illness After Experimental Exposure to Rhinovirus or Influenza A Virus," *Psychosomatic Medicine* 68, no. 6 (2006): 809–815. doi:10.1097/01.psy.0000245867.92364.3c.

26. T. Rath and D. O. Clifton, *How Full Is Your Bucket? Positive Strategies for Work and Life* (New York: Gallup, 2004).

27. Christopher Bergland, "Negative Emotions Can Increase the Risk of Heart Disease," *Psychology Today*, May 6, 2014, https://www.psychologytoday.com/blog/the-athletes-way/201405/negative-emotions-can-increase-the-risk-heart-disease.

28. Mary C. Davis, Alex J. Zautra, and Bruce W. Smith, "Chronic Pain, Stress, and the Dynamics of Affective Differentiation," *Journal of Personality* 72, no. 6 (2004): 1133–1160. doi:10.1111/ j.1467-6494.2004 .00293.x.

29. J. L. Boone and J. P. Anthony, "Evaluating the Impact of Stress on Systemic Disease: The MOST Protocol in Primary Care," *Journal of the American Osteopathic Association* 103, no. 5 (200): 239–246, https://www.ncbi.nlm.nih.gov/pubmed/12776765.

CHAPTER 18: BUILDING EQ SKILLS FOR OTHERS: SHARING A BETTER YOU

1. Fariss Samarrai, "Human Brains Are Hardwired for Empathy, Friendship, Study Shows," *UVA Today*, August 21, 2013, https://news.virginia.edu/content/human-brains-are-hardwired-empathy-friendship-study-shows.

2. "Mirror Neurons After a Quarter Century: New Light, New Cracks," *Science in the News*, August 15, 2016, http://sitn.hms.harvard.edu/flash/2016/mirror-neurons-quarter-century-new-light-new-cracks/.

3. John Mark Taylor, "Mirror Neurons After a Quarter Century: New Light, New Cracks," *Science in the News*, August 15, 2016, http://sitn.hms.harvard.edu/flash/2016/mirror-neurons-quarter-century-new-light-new-cracks/.

4. jayshox, *YouTube*, January 7, 2013, https://www.youtube.com/watch?v=Sin9M9boANo.

5. Cousineau, T. (2018). The Kindness Cure: How the Science of Compassion Can Heal Your Heart and Your World (Oakland, CA: New Harbinger Publications)

6. Flavelle, Dana. "MDC's Miles Nadal resigns, agrees to pay $12.5M in SEC probe." Thestar.com. July 21, 2015. Accessed January 05, 2018. https://www.thestar.com/business/2015/07/21/mdcs-miles-nadal-resigns-agrees-to-pay-125m-in-sec-probe.html.

7. Norman A. S. Farb, Zindel V. Segal, Helen Mayberg, Jim Bean, Deborah McKeon, Zainab Fatima, and Adam K. Anderson, "Attending to the Present: Mindfulness Meditation Reveals Distinct Neural Modes of Self-Reference, Social Cognitive and Affective Neuroscience, Oxford Academic," OUP Academic, Oxford University Press, August 13, 2007, https://academic.oup.com/scan/article/2/4/313/1676557/Attending-to-the-present-mindfulness-meditation.

8. Bryan D. James, Robert S. Wilson, Lisa L. Barnes, and David A. Bennett, "Late-Life Social Activity and Cognitive Decline in Old Age," Journal of the International Neuropsychological Society," Cambridge University Press, April 8, 2011, https://www.cambridge.org/core/journals/journal-of-the-international-neuropsychological-society/article/late-life-social-activity-and-cognitive-decline-in-old-age/91C0CD4DF1817938EB16E3179567D76E.

9. Daniel Kahneman, Thinking, Fast and Slow (New York: Farrar, Straus and Giroux, 2015).

10. "Understanding the Power of the 125-400 Rule of Listening," Oscar Trimboli, November 28, 2016, https://www.oscartrimboli.com/understanding-power-125-400-rule-listening/.

11. "Listening: Our Most Used Communication Skill," CM150 Listening: Our Most Used Communications Skill, University of Missouri Extension, http://extension.missouri.edu/p/CM150 (accessed October 14, 2017).

12. Bill George, Discover Your True North (Hoboken, NJ: John Wiley & Sons, 2015).

13. Johnny Cash, Hurt, CD, Americans Recording Studios, 2002.

CHAPTER 19: APPLYING EQ SKILLS AT HOME (PARENTING)

1. "Stress in America Findings,"American Psychological Association, 2010, https://www.apa.org/news/press/releases/stress/2010/national-report.pdf.

2. Aimee Picchi, "Young Adults Living with Their Parents Hits a 75-Year High," *CBS News*December 21, 2016, https://www.cbsnews.com/news/percentage-of-young-americans-living-with-their-parents-is-40-percent-a-75-year-high/.

3. "Stress in America: Paying with Our Health," *PsycEXTRA Dataset*, February 2015. doi:10.1037/e513292015-001.

4. Justin Parent, Laura G. Mckee, Jennifer N. Rough, and Rex Forehand, "The Association of Parent Mindfulness with Parenting and Youth Psychopathology Across Three Developmental Stages." *Journal of Abnormal Child Psychology* 44, no. 1 (2015): 191–202. doi:10.1007/s10802-015-9978-x.

5. Thomas Jefferson University, "Trauma-Informed, Mindfulness-Based Intervention Significantly Improves Parenting," *ScienceDaily*, www.sciencedaily.com/releases/2017/07/170727130606.htm.

6. "Teaching Gratitude in a Culture of Entitlement," *Greater Good*, accessed July 23, 2017, https://greatergood.berkeley.edu/article/item/teaching_gratitude_in_a_culture_of_entitlement.

7. Ann Vernon*Cognitive and Rational-Emotive Behavior Therapy with Couples: Theory and Practice* (New York: Springer, 2012).

8. Adam Mansbach, Go the F**k to Sleep (New York: Akashic Books, 2011).

9. Bruce Feiler, *The Secrets of Happy Families: Improve Your Mornings, Tell Your Family History, Fight Smarter, Go Out and Play, and Much More* (New York: HarperCollins, 2013).

10. M. R. Lepper, D. Greene, and R. E. Nisbett, "Undermining Children's Intrinsic Interest with Extrinsic Rewards: A Test of the 'Overjustification Hypothesis,'" *Journal of Personality and Social Psychology*, 28 (1973): 129–137.

11. "What Parents of Successful Kids Have in Common," *Time*, http://time.com/money/4738936/parents-of-successful-kids-tips/ (accessed October 1, 2017).

12. Daniel J. Siegel, *Brainstorm: The Power and Purpose of the Teenage Brain* (New York: Jeremy P. Tarcher/Penguin, 2013).

Chapter 20: Do or Die: It's Called Practice for a Reason

1. Brown, Les, "To Be Successful, You Must Be Willing to Do the Things Today Others Won't Do in Order to Have the Things Tomorrow Others Won't Have," *Twitter*, November 17, 2012, https://twitter.com/lesbrown77/status/269893070298955776?lang=en.

INDEX

Page references followed by *f* indicate an illustrated figure